DANCE AND THE LIVED BODY

DANCE AND THE LIVED BODY

A Descriptive Aesthetics

SONDRA HORTON FRALEIGH

University of Pittsburgh Press

Published by the University of Pittsburgh Press,
Pittsburgh, Pennsylvania 15261

Eurospan, London
Manufactured in the United States of America
10 9 8 7 6 5 4 3

Library of Congress Cataloging-in-Publication Data

Fraleigh, Sondra Horton, 1939–
Dance and the lived body.

Includes index.
1. Dancing—Philosophy. 2. Existentialism.
3. Phenomenology. 4. Modern dance—Philosophy.
5. Aesthetics. I. Title.
GV1588.3.F72 1987 793.3'2 86-19288
ISBN 0-8229-3548-1
ISBN 0-8229-5579-2 (pbk)

Title page photo: Daphne Finnegan in *Blood First* by Donald Kutschall. Photo: Patrick Hayes.

The essay "Poetic Body" from chapter 4 first appeared in *Word and Image* 2, no. 4 (November 1986).

I know nothing, except what everyone knows—
if there when Grace dances, I should dance.

—W. H. AUDEN

CONTENTS

ACKNOWLEDGMENTS

I would like to acknowledge a debt of gratitude to author and theater critic Sarah Watts for many things, above all for teaching me how to translate my enthusiasm for dance and existentialism into words. Other friends have also contributed immeasurably to this book, photographer June Burke, and dancers Susannah Payton-Newman, Danald Kutschall, Annette Macdonald, Pamela Trippel, and Daphne Finnegan. I must express my appreciation to philosophers Richard Zaner, Drew Hyland, Arnold Berleant, and George Stack for their suggestions. Warren and Christina Fraleigh have aided this work with their patience. My thanks to Warren, too, for his valuable suggestions on the development of the text. I am indebted to the Brockport dance faculty for their support, to Diane Hammond for her careful editorial work, and to editor Catherine Marshall for her encouragement of a book bridging dance and philosophy.

This book is dedicated to Warren and Christina, my partners in the dance of life.

PREFACE

I discovered existentialism through dance and phenomenology through existentialism. My interest in aesthetics derives from all three. The present work attempts to develop an aesthetic perspective of dance through existential phenomenology — particularly through the concept of the lived body. This concept is central to existential phenomenology, which is important as a philosophical and literary movement influencing the art, religion, and psychology of the twentieth century.

Because dance is in essence an embodied art, the body is the lived (experiential) ground of the dance aesthetic. Both dancer and audience experience dance through its lived attributes — its kinesthetic and existential character. Dance is the art that intentionally isolates and reveals the aesthetic qualities of the human body-of-action and its vital life.

This book is addressed to students of dance and to the dancer in all of us, for I believe that all our vital thoughts and movements pass through that alert and vibrant spot where dance (and also our experience of freedom) arises. I will examine and describe dance through my consciousness of dance as an art, through the experience of dancing, and through the existentialist and phenomenological literature on the lived body. Keeping in mind an intelligent but varied audience, I avoid (or explain) the technical language of phenomenology, dance, and aesthetics. This approach is in keeping with the descriptive method of phenomenology, which aims for an exact simplicity. In this task, I am reminded of my dance classes with Hanya Holm, who taught me that a simple straightforward walk is the most difficult movement in dancing.

Phenomenology is first of all a method that, as its point of beginning, attempts to view any experience from the inside rather than at a distance. Ensuing theories of the structure, value, or meaning of experienced phenomena are based upon such a view. Consequently phenomenology often takes the form of first-person description. As it takes the perspective of consciousness, the style of phenomenology shifts liberally between the rhetorical and inclusive *we* and the experiential but also inclusive *I*. While Sartre's famous phrase, "I exist my body," is stated in terms of self-evidence, it is descriptive of the body of everyone. I use the phenomenological method (which will be explained further) to describe the experience of dance as it is lived, necessarily, through the body. However, the present work is not purely descriptive, since phenomenology has definitional, analytical, and critical aims, also. Description in phenomenology is primarily a tool that seeks to get at the core of things. The work resulting from this approach is usually termed descriptive. While it utilizes self-evidence, phenomenology is not autobiographical; rather, it is propelled by a universalizing impulse as it seeks to describe what is basic to the phenomena being considered.[1]

Thus my description of dance depends in part upon my own experience but only as this experience is held in common with other dancers. The problem of describing dance leads me to look at not only dance and dancers but also dances of various styles. Ultimately, I am led to aesthetics, since aesthetic value is basic to everything we call dance. Contrary to the spirit of phenomenology, I do employ previous aesthetic and philosophical theory where they apply, as well as theory from mythology, psychology, and Eastern philosophy that elucidate the bodily lived source of myth and its relation to dance.

The rich phenomenological literature on the lived body provides a foundation (as yet unexplored) for a nondualistic view of dance, but I do not make exhaustive use of this foundation. For the most part, I do not engage in a critical analysis of existential phenomenology, since this would sidetrack me. Rather, I use the primary insights of existentialist authors as ladders toward a descriptive aesthetics of dance. Certainly this has required much selection and interpretation on my part.

A brief topology of the whole book may be helpful at this point. In the introduction, the existentialist background that has inspired the literature on the lived body and also motivated this study is explored through my personal experience of dance and existentialism. Relative to this, the introduction delineates the existential context of modern dance, which is further developed later in the text.

Part 1 first summarizes existential phenomenology and the lived-body concept, which arose at the crossing point of existentialism and phenomenology, and explains the nondualistic feature of the lived-body concept in view of its implications for dance. It then introduces the major themes of body and self as lived through dance and the self in relation to others, since dance (as art) is performed with and for others in a communal context. The aesthetic purpose and phenomenal essence of dance is defined as it exists in a relation between the dancer and the audience.

Part 2 explores tension, the root name-essence of dance, and the cosmological, phenomenal, historical, and mythological pairs of opposites that contribute to aesthetic tension in dance. The emergence of expression and meaning in dance is studied in terms of a tension of oppositions, and dance receives further definition as a mythopoetic art, founding the aesthetic truths of the human body.

Because dance is grounded in human movement, part 3 examines the dance image (movement shaped in time and space) as the fundamental aesthetic expression of dance—one that grows out of its lived ground as a creative extension of the imagination. It deals with time, space, and movement as human qualities—or lived qualities—in dance. Movement is the most inclusive; time and space are embodied in movement. But dance is more than movement; dance as art is human movement intentionally created for an aesthetic purpose; therefore dance incorporates time and space as intentionally formulated aesthetic characteristics of human motion.

Part 3 shows that we experience the lived substance of dance through our own kinetic flow of being. The dance unites the dancer and the audience in a lived metaphysic. In the work and play of dance, we come to value the transcendent, which generally goes unnoticed in our everyday movement. In dancing, our acts stand out for themselves; they remind us of the transcendent in all our purposeful work.

Throughout the book, the dancer as the dance is the irreducible point of departure and return. Other concerns stemming from the bodily lived nature of dance enter from this point, including the communal intention of dance, as it is directed toward and brings forth the dancer in all of us.

We understand the dance because of the expressive nature of our own bodies. Through dance, we seek our ideal human likeness in the dancer, the ultimate athlete of our expressive body. (I believe there is a sense in which we may speak of our body in a collective way.) The dancer communicates not through words but through the body — through *our* human body and its lived character. What philosopher Paul Weiss says about athletes applies to dancers, also — but in the sense that dancers represent our expressive vital body through aesthetically conceived movement: "The more we are driven to be at our best, the better do we epitomize all, and the more worthily do we represent the rest. The athlete is matched here by the thinker, the artist, and the religious man. Without loss to their individuality, they too instantiate man in a splendid form, which the rest of us accept as an idealized portrait of ourselves. But the athlete shows us, as they do not, what we ideally are as bodies."[2]

To experience the dance is to experience our own living substance in an aesthetic (affective) transformation. To express the dance is to express the lived body in an aesthetic form. The body, understood in its lived totality, is the source of the dance aesthetic. It is not simply the physical instrument of dance, nor is it an aesthetic object as other objects of art are. The essential reduction and significance of dance lies in this distinction: *I am embodied in my dance, I am not embodied in my painting.* The painting is separated from me; it is, finally, out there in front of me, but my dance cannot exist without me: I exist my dance. Yet it is also true that we are embodied in all of our actions — or more properly that we enact our embodiment in all of our projects. All performing artists are embodied in their art, but the dancer most clearly represents our expressive body-of-action and its aesthetic idealization.

Thus the art of dance draws upon the meanings we attach to our bodily enacted existence as a whole, as these may be made to appear in movement. Its main material, its medium, is human motion — and its opposite. The movement medium of dance is continuous with and also an enactment of our embodiment. Our collective embodiment is most clearly demonstrated in dance. The art of dance draws upon both the personal and the universal body — tending, I believe, toward the latter as it becomes a source for communion, testifying to our bodily lived existence, our mutual grounding in nature, and our shared bodily acculturations. It is also true that individuality has been valued in dance (indeed, the existential context of modern dance has encouraged this) but still within the overarching, for-other, universalizing obligation of all art.

The universal impulse to dance is one of celebration; in its most fundamental state, dance celebrates embodiment. We dance our sentient, embodied existence. Dance stems from an impulse to express and sustain a vital life and to project and share its aesthetic dimensions. Certainly we may dance somber and despairing themes; but underneath thematic intentionality is a basic impulse that is positive and live engendering. In dance we celebrate our living, concrete reality — our embodiment — and within the complexity that embodiment proffers. It is thus that dance may be called *a sign for life.* As dance is experienced through our vital body — the source of both dance and celebration — it signifies vital human embodiment, or *life,* as we typically use this word to describe both a vital force and the history of our experience — an indivisible physical and spiritual whole. Dance points toward our moving and perishable embodied existence, holding it before us, filling and freeing present time that we may dwell whole within it.

This view of dance is decidedly influenced by recent positive existentialist outlooks (or *new existentialism,* as I shall consider it along with Colin Wilson), which focus on human purposefulness rather than on human contingency. This is well represented in the modern existential psychology of theorists like Abraham Maslow, who base their work not only on the study of "illness," as has previous psychology, but also on a study of what promotes "well-being" and creativity.[3]

Existential phenomenology aims for an accurate first view (an original apprehension in the sense of capturing the experienced whole) of a phenomenon. With this aim, I attempt to clear away *what I know* about dance to see it fresh, involving the contradiction that it is what I know that will emerge. However, the very process of clearing away assumptions (throwing away familiar definitions of dance to uncover "that which has been assumed" and "that which has become familiar") should yield another level of knowledge.

Yes, dancers do pause to ask what we are doing when we dance, why we go through the pain, and what "is there" in its pleasures and complexities. Surely there are many answers, because we dance for many different reasons. Some answers may be basic, growing out of the irreducible structure (or the phenomenological structure, as I later call it) of dance as art.

The fullest answers, I believe, come with studied reflection that seeks to know what "is there." These answers do not come easily, perhaps because it is so difficult to distance dance from ourselves. Dance is the embodied art, that which we each perform in our own immediate way through our own flow of being. To be sure, theater dance arts are set apart from this spontaneous flow by an express aesthetic purpose, but they are based upon aesthetic capacities within human motion and are never completely separated from immediated, bodily lived values.

I am attracted to an existential view of dance and dancing through the constitution of the art itself. Havelock Ellis recognizes dance as the art closest to life. He is right in this respect: dance exists through the life of the body. Dance cannot exist outside of the body; it is wholly lived. In this respect, dance is body. Dance stands "at the source of all the arts that express themselves first in the human person."[4] It is foundational to the lived arts, those that exist in performance alone, leaving behind no material product.

It strikes me that all performing artists and athletes at some time or another grapple with the essence of dance as they seek to free the ultimate mover, alive in the moment of their best utterance and action—for the dancer in us serves no necessary purpose beyond a vital execution of aesthetic motion. However, it is through the accomplishment of this basic (intrinsic) purpose that dance may return us to our source in nature and may also link us to ideas and issues beyond its aesthetic manifestation. It is thus that I explore aesthetic value as the only nonderivative value in dance—that upon which all other values depend—and strive to see what is there in the dance aesthetic.

Phenomenology is not new to aesthetics, of course. The applicability of phenomenology to aesthetics is shown by Arnold Berleant and Mikel Dufrenne.[5] We see through their work that aesthetics has the task of accounting for aesthetic phenomena—of rendering our experience of art more understandable. Berleant sees that to do this we must formulate conceptual tools directly from aesthetic experience. He outlines a phenomenological approach to aesthetics that begins with description rather than judgment, that develops its standards from observation, and that avoids prejudging aesthetic phenomena by theory accepted in advance.[6] The role of aesthetic theory is no different from the role of other theories in fields of inquiry. As with historical, physical, and psychological theory, aesthetic theory attempts to account for phenomena by discerning patterns and clarifying interrelationships.

A phenomenological study of an art should define and describe it in terms of the relations that hold within it, accounting for the perceptual element in aesthetic experience suggested in the etymology of the word *aesthetics,* which derives from *aesthesis,* or *aisthesis,* the Greek word for sense perception.

I believe that we gain nothing by claiming that art, or our experience of it, is inexplicable (as I have often heard). For this is to deny art a definitional identity—and to silence attempts to understand what each art in its particular way teaches us about ourselves.

INTRODUCTION

Dance and Existentialism: Personal Notes

Perhaps I should not be surprised that my study with modern dance artists stimulated my interest in existential thought and art, even though connections were seldom drawn by the artists themselves (and it is not my intention to label them existentialists). Even some philosophers who are identified as existentialist deny an affinity with the term, which surfaced in the nineteenth century in Kierkegaard's call for existential inwardness and was later made popular by Sartre in his defense of existential humanism. Common existentialist threads in the literature and art of the twentieth century have been traced, nevertheless.

What interests me now is that I am beginning to identify points of convergence between modern dance (including its postmodern school) and existentialist literature (which also has postmodern manifestations). The similarities are striking. In addition, existential phenomenology's concern for "things in themselves" (reducing anything to its most basic, or phenomenal, manifestation) bears a similarity to "dance as dance," the pure dance aesthetic shown in the work of Merce Cunningham, George Balanchine, Viola Farber, and others, which emphasizes the human body-of-motion as the inmost phenomenal essence of dance.

I can best explore relations between modern dance and existentialism and explain the existential context of modern dance (a singular and basic juncture, which informs the work throughout) by briefly recounting my personal experience of the German and American modern dance mainstreams.

In the German school, I studied with Mary Wigman, Hanya Holm, and Alwin Nikolais, but in reverse chronological order. My first teacher, Joan Woodbury, introduced me to Nikolais and the entire German (now German-American) school. Nikolais was to become the most prominent artist of the late modern period in this school. I studied subsequently with Hanya Holm, who was Nikolais's teacher and the transitional figure, since she had brought German modern dance to America and eventually evolved her own style here in the early modern period. Holm encouraged me to go back to the beginnings of modern dance by studying in Berlin with her teacher, Mary Wigman—which I did in 1965–1966.

That year we celebrated Mary Wigman's seventy-ninth birthday with a student concert at her school. The Wigman school was still operating under her direction; but of course the modern dance aesthetic in Berlin had moved far away from its origins in her work and was already being influenced by American dance (especially Merce Cunningham's). What I gained from Wigman was an understanding of the philosophical foundations of modern dance, which have their source in her choreography and teaching. She often placed the central existential question, Who am I?, at the heart of dance.

Throughout the German school, dance was a means toward self-knowledge—not a disclosure of personality but a construction of it, not self-expression as self-indulgence but a creation of self in expressive action that moves one beyond the confines of self. I began to grasp the idea of "becoming" through dancing, which was later reinforced by my study of existential humanism and its view that human beings create who they are through their actions and choices (expressed most succinctly in Sartre's famous essay: "Existentialism Is a Humanism," included in his book *Existentialism*). These concerns influenced my first articles on dance and existentialism and the view that the body is created in dance.[1]

The dance growing out of the German school was marked from the beginning by what might be called the existential spirit of individuality. Little rebellion was required for new forms to emerge, since individuality was encouraged and respected. For instance, Don Redlich was Holm's student and assistant for several years, yet his own work bore little resemblance to hers—or to early modern dance. His solo *Reacher* (1967), integrating film, movement, and sound, and performed on a huge rope-linked net without typical dance movement, was closer to the avant-garde.[2] Encouragement of individuality did not mean, however, that just anything was OK. Holm was adamantly opposed to vacant, uncommitted dancing. She jostled and prodded her students. Mistakes were not a crime. Apathy was. The individuality that emerged was infused with expressive energy but not to the exclusion of technique or an understanding of abstraction in dance.

From Nikolais I learned the most about abstraction. In composition classes, he dissected movement in terms of its interrelated space, time, and energy. We experimented with the aesthetic possibilities inherent in the elements of human movement. Time was not just beats and rhythmic patterns. It was a dimension of movement that could be projected or diminished, and each student was encouraged to find an individual way of doing this. During that period I was not aware that phenomenologists also concerned themselves with time, space, and movement—more particularly, with describing these phenomena as they are "lived," not as they are measured in objective terms. When I began to study phenomenology and theories of the lived body, Nikolais's works took on new meaning for me.

His works demonstrated the lived nature of the elements of human motion by giving them aesthetic attention through a lived medium. At first he was accused of dehumanizing dance; later he was recognized as one of the first to open modern dance to (radical) abstraction.[3] I qualify this statement with the word *radical* in the belief that some level of abstraction is present in all dance.[4] Certainly abstraction was well understood even in early modern work. Many dancers remember the difficulty of pleasing Louis Horst's requirements of abstraction in his "strange space" studies, for instance. Nikolais's work became especially interesting for me in light of José Ortega y Gasset's existentialist treatise, *The Dehumanization of Art.* Ortega explains the advent, impact, and meaning of abstraction (the move away from realism) in modern art as follows: "All the great periods of art have been careful not to let the work revolve about human contents. The imperative of unmitigated realism that dominated the last century must be put down as a freak in aesthetic evolution. It thus appears that the new inspiration, extravagant though it seems, is merely returning, at least in one point, to the royal road of art. For this road is called 'will to style.' But to stylize means to deform reality, to derealize; style involves dehumanization."[5]

In all of my studies, regardless of the period, I have been aware of abstraction, acknowledged as a process in making dances and, in some cases referring to an aspect of style in opposition to representation. I have been equally aware of the difficulty – perhaps impossibility – of a level of abstraction in dance comparable to other arts. Dance can never be wholly abstract because the dancer is a person, and a person is not an abstraction. I remember a lesson to this point at the Wigman school. Frau Mary (as we called her) stood me in front of her class one day along with another pupil. She let us stand there in silence for what seemed like a very long time. When she spoke, it was to examine with the students how we two people standing before them were extremely different in our appearances and how various qualities of our beings were apparent through simple observation. She was, in a way, reading our bodily presence as it appeared to her. She observed us as individuals. But not resting there, she moved to the universal point – our similarities and shared humanity, our essential corporealness. She taught me that both my individuality (which is unique) and my human condition (which is universal) are inescapably present in my dance – because, I am there. Seen in this way, abstraction in dance takes on a special significance.

I met with similar concerns, and some new ones, studying within two phases of the American modern dance – first with Martha Graham and Louis Horst and second with Merce Cunningham. I took technique classes with Martha Graham long enough to be inspired by her views of the discipline of dance and by her ability to relate dance to the wider world of art and literature. Like Wigman, she was not interested in the pretty romantic line so common in ballet. The right angle and conflicted line often suited her expressive intentions better. She brought dance down to earth and gave the dancer (especially woman) a footing on terra firma. Her dance gave us a new vision of feminine grace, one more true to our age. Strength and grace were not opposed in her technique or choreography – effort, work, and muscle became apparent. Woman achieved grace through strength not through hiding it, as in the ballet. The ideal for Graham's dance was not ethereal and otherworldly. Yet, there was a superhuman, heroic directness and precision in the movement. The intent of her work was decidedly – and demandingly – human, even though her dancers were divine athletes. They may have presented love as a "diversion of angels," but it was their capability as human beings that interested Graham. She thought of the dancer "first . . . as a human being."[6]

Louis Horst, whose interests in art and literature were wide ranging, was Graham's mentor, and had a strong influence on the growth of American modern dance in general. Horst identified himself with existentialism and encouraged his students to read Nietzsche.[7] He taught the basics of musical form as a method of composition for dance. He initiated dance composition as a viable classroom study within the American tradition of modern dance. Rudolph von Laban and Mary Wigman had already founded some compositional principles and the pedagogy surrounding them within the German tradition. Unlike Horst's, Wigman's approaches to teaching composition were not based on musical form, although moods produced by music might enter in. The formal properties that concerned her were space, organic rhythm, and intention. They derived from Laban's movement theories but did not depend on them. She invented studies involving characterization, pantomime, and movement for itself (she called this absolute dance). And she often used improvisation toward a compositional end.

Compositional problems in both the German and American schools were specific and were directed toward the problems of dancing itself. At no time in either school of expressionist modern dance do I ever remember being told to express myself. Although my individuality was encouraged, somehow I knew that did not have to do with me personally; it was the dancer in me that was supposed to manifest itself. Both Wigman and Horst wanted to see original work, something they had not seen before. I could not even copy myself; each work had to be truly new. That was indeed more difficult than mere self-expression.

Finally, I took classes in technique and composition with Merce Cunningham, who gave us movement problems to solve through his famous methods of making dances with chance procedures. I now use these methods in teaching composition when students get stuck and try to force solutions or to get them out of movement ruts. I find (as I think Cunningham intended) that methods which trust chance can release the intuitive, nonlinear sensitivities to let (rather than make) the dance happen. I first saw his work when I was studying with Graham. It made no sense to me at all. Gradually I began to get the point, after some acquaintance with mystical philosophy through Zen and yoga. Eventually I understood that it was not supposed to make any sense beyond being itself. I gained a new appreciation for the moment.

Many years earlier, Wigman called dance "the art of the fulfilled moment."[8] In this spirit, Cunningham was not so distant from the early forms. But his work had an entirely different look and feeling. He became noted as a purist for his finely tuned focus on movement for itself, founding the formalist aesthetic of the late modern period. He had found new aesthetic solutions to perennial concerns for abstraction, form, and expression in dance. His aesthetic was new; the concerns that motivated it are historical and continuing concerns in dance.

In both early and late modern dance, there was a concern for straightforward purposefulness in movement and for clarity in the use of space. Earlier forms often stressed symbolism, however—pointing beyond the movement itself. Wigman stressed the aliveness of space—the pull of, and the difference between, up and down. Through study with Cunningham, I began to detach myself from the logic of those pulls and tensions. Space stood for itself, as a medium for experiment and play, and the body was not always presented frontally. The movement did not have a front and a back. I began to feel in my choreography that the audience was at every angle.

Like the early moderns, Cunningham favored the dynamic body—but for itself alone, since he did not seem interested in the drama that proceeded from symbolism, gesture, or narrative. He revealed the drama of the body itself. Cunningham found his own individual way of dancing by turning away from his background in Graham's heavily symbolic dance and Horst's musical structuring of dance.

For Cunningham and John Cage, dance and music could be composed separately in time spans, then put together. In composition classes, Cunningham taught us how to use "time units" rather than beats and measures as frames of reference. (This way of working with time differed from Nikolais's approach, where we attempted to isolate time as a movement factor and delved into questions of what time was.) Linear time determinations were suspended as we constructed our works in Cunningham's classes. Some control was given up in the conscious choice to use chance, acknowledging happenstance in life. Unlike reasoned logic, and perhaps closer to lived unorder, "anything could follow anything" in the Cage-Cunningham philosophy. Events might overlap, and simultaneity of happenings was also apparent in the use of time. This was similar to what I knew as stream of consciousness in literature. Much of what I was experiencing with Cunningham had been written about and was being talked about, pro and con.

Cunningham also admitted the irrational and the unpredictable as an aesthetic thematic in dance, through incorporating chance methodology in his choreography. His imposition of chance *by design* added an intellectual element to the mystical dimension of his dance, which removed it from the emotional and almost religious attraction that early moderns had toward the mysteries of self, universe, and the cosmos. I am intrigued now by a similar challenge to "reason" that had developed in existentialist themes, in recognition of the nonrational (or, more to the point, the irrational) as it is experienced. Existentialist (anti-Hegelian) philosophy and literature had moved against idealism and rationalism to depict humanity in its full complexity, admitting the irrational, the accidental, and the mysterious in life. People were not abstractions; unpredictability helped define the human existential state.

I am still aware of the intellectual and formalist edge of Cunningham's influence on modern dance. Now when I introduce the problem of chance to my students, they become fascinated with the dialectic that builds up between chance and choice as they work through chance methods. In the first place, they choose whether or not they will involve themselves with the problem (most choose to try it). They soon realize how much choice is involved in constructing a chance method: How many straws will be drawn or dice thrown? How many movement variables will be determined by chance? Will chance determine the timing of entrances and exits, length of phrases, or placement of movement in space? Usually, in the course of structuring the actual movement, it occurs to students that such consciously structured movement is willed (eventually we take this up through Paul Ricoeur). This involves selectivity—hence choices at many levels. While a throw of the dice may determine a move to the right or left, it is impossible to give intentional movement—dance—completely over to chance. These exercises inevitably bring chance and choice to the foreground as dialectical principles, as do those existentialist philosophies that hold that existence is subject to chance (or contingency) but choice (and taking responsibility for one's choices) is the ultimate basis of authentic human freedom.

Throughout my dance studies, I was reading existentialist novels (however sporadically) and the existentialist plays of Sartre and Camus. I was also aware of the connections between existentialist thought and the theater of the absurd in the works of Beckett, Ionesco, Albee, and Pinter;[9] and of Kafka's earlier works expressing a similar human predicament in mythic and symbolic literary images. Through Nikolais, I linked existentialism directly to dance. In composition classes, he introduced ideas stemming from the theater of the absurd, incorporating them in dance studies of the absurd.

But I was only vaguely aware of existentialism as a philosophy and the important thematic threads that identifies works as existentialist until I had the good luck to study existentialism with Arturo Fallico, the author of *Art and Existentialism.* He blends expertise in art, philosophy—existentialism and phenomenology, in particular—and aesthetics. (Perhaps my study with him was not just good luck; he told us that existentialists do not trust in luck—they make their own.) He had studied aesthetics with Benedetto Croce in Italy but then moved away from that source in developing existential aesthetic views. He had experienced firsthand the existentialist revolution in Paris and spoke of his acquaintance with Sartre and Picasso, who had greatly influenced his existential outlook. He considered that Sartre and Heidegger had developed existentialism as a philosophy.

Through Fallico, I learned of the connections among existentialist literature, philosophy, and art, and that existentialism was not limited to our age. Some of Shakespeare's lines bespeak particularly poignant existential views, admitting both the absurdity and emptiness of life:

> Life's but a walking shadow, a poor player
> That struts and frets his hour upon the stage
> And then is heard no more. It is a tale
> Told by an idiot, full of sound and fury,
> Signifying nothing. (*Macbeth*, act 5, scene 5)

Nothingness is the existentialist's point of beginning. For him, life has no predetermined essence; therefore everything is possible. But nothingness was the most difficult concept for me to grasp. I could understand it, however, as a beginning point for modern art and dance. Their rejection of essentialist rules and aesthetic standards governing classical and romantic arts had opened these arts to new possibilities. Through this opening, radical abstraction, chance, absurdity, suffering, doubt, and even intentional ugliness became possible. Life could be traced from underneath as well as from above, through the night of the unconscious psyche, with its rich and somber colors, as well as through the daybreak of lucid consciousness. Nothingness held a particular poignancy for those writers, artists, and philosophers seeking to erase the world—to begin over again. It became a place, a something, a sentient opening.

While existential viewpoints had been present throughout the history of literature and philosophy, they became especially concentrated in contemporary forms. The darker, despairing expressions in art stood as a corrective to a one-sided view of life, and against romantic artifice. As an attitude, existentialism appeared with particular intensity in every modern art and literary form. The term *existentialism*, which became popular after World War II, represented concerns of particular relevance in the twentieth century. Nietzsche had set the stage for these concerns in the nineteenth century, as he foresaw the crumbling of unquestioned values, a time of nothingness and uncertainty, in his madman's prophecy of our fall "away from all suns."[10]

In Fallico's classes, we studied strands of thought contributing to existentialism as a philosophy and to the existential attitude, an attitude emerging from existentialist literature that may be understood in intimate terms. As Paul Tillich puts it, "the existential attitude is one of involvement in contrast to a merely theoretical or detached attitude. 'Existential' in this case can be defined as participating in a situation . . . with the whole of one's existence."[11] Fallico taught that existentialism was born out of man's "ontological insecurity," a "disturbance," and a deep "self-consciousness."[12] (I now interpret this as "uncertainty" in the face of "not knowing," which is how dancer Daniel Nagrin defines the human existential predicament. Nagrin, who claims an affinity for existential views, believes that "not knowing" is the human condition that allows for "differences" and "compassion." The existential view is, thus, positive, not nihilistic.)[13] When I began to study existentialism, I knew I was being given words for what I had known in other ways and had struggled with in dance. I was coming home to a place I had somehow known all along.

One question loomed large for me: Where was dance in the existentialist writings? Commentary was abundant concerning the other arts, but I could find very little comment on the relation of dance to existentialism. Yet I felt many relations could be drawn. In addition, I learned that existential phenomenologists place great emphasis on the problem of the human body in philosophy and that the wholistic, or nondualistic, concept of the lived body had developed out of these concerns. But, even phenomenologists writing on the problem of embodiment did not deal with dance, although, it seems a natural connection to make.

It was then 1968, and Maxine Sheets-Johnstone's book, *The Phenomenology of Dance,* had been published just a few years before. Later, she and I became colleagues and discussed dance and phenomenology often. I appreciated her contribution—making the first general connections between dance and phenomenology—but she, too, did not deal in particular with the major concern phenomenology has with the body. In fact, she wrote that dance appears as "forcetimespace."[14] Now when I question this, I close my eyes and try to picture a dance. Is it forcetimespace that appears? How can forcetimespace appear? Forcetimespace is an abstraction until it is concretely manifested, until it is embodied. No, I do not see forcetimespace; I see the reality of dance in its corporealness—its lived concreteness. I cannot visualize a dance without visualizing a dancer.[15] I can see embodied human motion, but I cannot see forcetimespace.

It became clear to me that the subject of the human body in dance had been overlooked by phenomenologists and that commentators on existentialism in the arts never used dance as an example. In later years, I became aware of a general lack of philosophic and aesthetic discourse on dance. Francis Sparshott blames Hegel's system of the arts, which excludes dance.[16] David Michael Levin believes Western philosophers, grounded in a patriarchal tradition, neglect dance because dance has its origin in the mythological female principle.[17] Hilda Hein writes that performance in general is neglected as an aesthetic category.[18] Arnold Berleant considers that artists and performers could contribute to aesthetics, as a corrective.[19] Dancer-philosopher Erick Hawkins does just that, focusing on the body in dance, especially with his beautiful image, "the body is a clear place."[20] Writing as a philosopher but out of the spirit of dance, Levin eventually contributed a phenomenological view of dance (and the body) in several articles that aid the present work. Sheets-Johnstone began to concern herself more directly with problems of the body in dance in a 1981 article and in her selection of articles for a recent book written mainly from the philosopher's point of view.[21]

Dance and its bodily basis is notably not neglected in the philosophic poetry of Nietzsche. The inside of dancing is there – and it is not complex, either. It comes through Nietzsche's Dionysian passion about being body, doing, risking, and creating – hitting the center, as the archer's arrow does in Zen. Nietzsche expresses the wholistic embodied truth of dance directly. Zarathustra speaks it with compelling urgency in the section of *Thus Spake Zarathustra* called "On the Despisers of the Body."

No wonder Nietzsche (though he was physically frail) is the dancer's philosopher. His ideas influenced early modern dance through Isadora Duncan, who was inspired by his writings, and postmodern dance through Kenneth King, who based a work on Nietzsche's philosophy. Doris Humphrey, the first to create a systematic technique for training the modern dancer, based the theory behind her technique on Nietzsche's imagery of oppositions between Dionysian and Apollonian aesthetic tendencies as set forth in *The Birth of Tragedy*. Fall and recovery, the basis of her technique, was inspired by Nietzsche's aesthetic views. Her image for the zone between fall and recovery is "the arc between two deaths." She defines motion within that arc, both physically and emotionally. Ernestine Stodelle associates Humphrey's movement imagery with Nietzsche's oppositional paradigms, Apollo and Dionysus, this way: "Translate Dionysian licentiousness to the precarious state of off-balance motion, and you will encounter the imminent danger of 'dynamic death.' Translate Apollonian serenity into the security of symmetrical balance, and you will have the locked-in perfection of 'static death.'"[22]

While Nietzsche's work, which provides the early foundation of existentialism, is thus also directly linked with the origins of modern dance, it cannot be claimed that Sartre, who stands foremost for modern existentialism and who defended it against assaults, was so directly influential. Yet we might see that Sartre's philosophy as a whole illuminates the basic existential context of modern dance. Sartre says that we write for our own age. In the same sense, we dance for, and are understood within, our own age; thus we cannot ignore that modern dance has grown and changed through an age colored with not one but several existentialisms. Sartre died in 1980. His philosophical views shifted throughout his lifetime, as he explains in a final interview. But he did adhere to the core of his existentialism, that "man makes himself" despite his "contingency" in an "absurd world."[23] Broadly stated, his philosophy is activist, a call for the human being to vindicate personal freedom, to act (and create) as a free and responsible agent in spite of uncertainties. It is a philosophy that holds freedom and individuality at its foundation.

As a witness to the times of modern dance – from its theatrical beginnings as expressionist modern dance, through late modern formalist dance, through nonexpressionist dance, full circle to neoexpressionist works – I have observed and experienced its similar rootedness in freedom and individuality. *I view freedom and individuality as the existential context of modern dance,* which is in relation to Sartre's fundamental statement of the existential principle, "existence precedes essence." This means that, as human beings, we have no predetermined essence. Rather we are free – and subject to the hazards of such freedom. Sartre's philosophy posits freedom as the inescapable truth of existence. We are, in Sartre's view, "condemned to be free," to become what we will. All of this bears further explanation.

Existential Context of Modern Dance

Modern dance entered the American theater as boldly and as "ungracefully" (some critics thought) as modern existentialism entered the American consciousness, and at roughly the same time. They matured through the same times. And they are both points of view rather than systems.[24] The most plentiful and clearest illustrations of existential aesthetics in dance are found in the modern dance genre but are not limited to it. (For instance, in chapter 3 I look at one of Balanchine's modern ballets in view of its existential values.)

I use the term *modern dance* to include a continuum of dancing marked by highly contrasting styles and methods, beginning with the expressionists in the 1920s and 1930s, and continuing into the present.[25] I believe the aspect most typical of the modern dance forms that demarcate this continuum, providing a definitional tie among them, is *discovery:* to discover by uncovering, revealing, and creating something not seen before; or to discover in the sense of inventing out of one's own bodily being. Modern dance forms develop through courageous individual discoveries, through the will and imagination toward individuated movement creativity. The various periods of modern dance are linked through this open (or free) aspect of method. At the same time, such freedom has resulted in many and widely varied styles.

The existential context of modernism can be explained from the dancer's vantage point. The modern dancer who has experienced the art in two or more of its phases will have experienced radically different styles (or ways of moving) and many reasons (or no reasons) for the movement produced. And she will have experienced various technical and choreographic methods behind the movement styles. Most likely, however, it will have occurred to her that all of the approaches in technical training, and the particular stated or unstated methods of choreography, grew from a common concern – or, I should properly say, a common search. Moreover, it might seem that the end results have not been as important as the search itself.

Modern dancers all seek their own way. Those who have influenced the art have found new ways of making movement aesthetically meaningful and have created distinctive styles of dancing as a result. All forms of modern dance emphasize discovery modalities – finding (or creating) value in dance through a questioning attitude and way of working, rather than assuming without question the already established models. Originality and inventiveness are at the heart of every period of modern dance; hence the invention of ever new ways of moving, of valuing dance, and of accounting for change.

Behind this inventiveness is the assumption that the uniqueness of each person is valuable and that individual creativity is valuable. Thus the existential context of modern dance appears in its emphasis on the importance of the individual and the principle of creativity. The makers of modern dance, its choreographers and dancers (who are often one and the same), assume a radical (or root) freedom at the core of their work, holding that nothing necessarily has to be – therefore, all things are possible.

As a result, unlike ballet dancers, modern dancers have no universal vocabulary of movement to draw upon. They have invented, utilized, and discarded several vocabularies of movement. For the modern dancer, the creative act involves origination of movement – a root invention of movement – which calls upon imagination and experience but also upon technical training. Usually, however, technical training is assumed in the making of a dance, although sometimes it is set aside, or questioned, or consciously discarded. The discovery of movement appropriate to intent is primary. The modern dancer works through her imagination and her movement possibilities until the intended form (the dance image) takes shape. Although known vocabularies of movement may be used when they suit her purposes, movement invention — or discovery — is her essential problem.

In every dance there are choices to be made, but the modern dancer typically faces a freer range of choice than dancers who work within established traditions. If all things are possible in modern dance, that does not mean that all things are desirable, as Erick Hawkins so rightly puts the problem.[26] In whatever manner modern dance has developed its aesthetic norms (and there are many, according to period and style), it has been from a place of radical, open freedom and within the dilemma of free choice. Modern dancers become responsible agents by turning toward that freedom and taking a stand in it. They create not out of nothing but *as though there were nothing* to depend on — and everything to discover. Maybe they only reinvent the wheel, but it is significant that they invent something out of themselves by wrestling with the blurred outlines and thousand hazards of freedom. The security of rule that grounds classical dance forms is painfully, but gratefully, absent.

The courage to be as oneself, or the courage of the individual, a form of courage explained by existentialist theologian Paul Tillich, is central to modern dance.[27] In essence (or seeming lack of it), modern dance is composed of individualized aesthetic norms; consequently there is no ideal image for the modern dancer and no ideal body. Early on, it was called creative dance, because it emphasized creativity as opposed to the imitation of preestablished, normative, or idealized movement forms. Permanency, through reproduction of a given form or a well-established movement model, is not as important to modern dance as creativity. In contrast, the ballet concentrates on achieving idealized movement forms. Or more loosely stated to account for the several schools, styles, and periods, ballet is based on historically idealized and regionally normative embedded movement models. It has an established movement vocabulary, embodying balletic ideals subject to stylistic interpretation.

Modern dance created new and individualized movement models for dance, demonstrating that dance as art might *be* and *mean* in many differing ways. We can briefly consider why this emphasis on creating original dance forms out of one's own resources, time, and being identifies modern dance with existentialism, while arts grounded in imitation and idealized form, such as classical ballet, are linked to classical idealism, an idealism hinted at by the early Greek cosmologists (and the Egyptians) in their notions of an all-embracing universal order and specifically stated by Plato in his doctrine of ideas, which was concerned with the principle of form. This fundamental difference will crop up again in the text.

Huntington Cairns illuminates Plato's development of his doctrine of ideas, explaining that it is rooted in pre-Socratic philosopher Heraclitus's view that the world of the senses, which is in constant flux, cannot yield permanency and knowledge. He sees that Plato's ideas (permanent entities distinct from the senses, sometimes called "ideas in the mind of God") deal with "the principle of all laws, the *logos* or Intelligence itself," and that his doctrine contrasts with "naturalism, pragmatism, positivism, analysis, and existentialism" because it refutes the view "that all is flux and that man is the measure of things."[28]

In Plato's *Timaeus*, the artist works through God as the intelligence within the order of the world, and art becomes an imitation of the ideal order of the world. In this sense, the artist is an imitator, not a founding creative agent. He becomes an artist when he actualizes an order already present in God (ideal form).

Plato's classical philosophy never exalts feeling above reason. In this he is a formalist. Likewise, classical ballet is sited in the sphere of ideal formalism. Its sights are set beyond everyday existence and painful realities. It is generally not disturbed by the twist and torque of the visibly physical, which is seemingly hidden. The body seldom falls; it moves off center only to return to a state of equilibrium. The loves and sorrows of classical ballet are filtered through centuries of an established and still-evolving movement hierarchy. And while creativity certainly operates within the ballet genre to keep it alive, it nevertheless operates in relation to an established hierarchy of movement. Creativity in ballet operates out of a set of principles—physical, psychological, historic, and aesthetic. The rules are sometimes broken, but this reminds us that they are there. Even when the ballet is not representing anything, it still conforms generally to the attenuated aspirational lines and lived-body attitudes embedded in the classical technique. The courage that the classical dancer illustrates is the courage to be as a part—the courage to be a participant in a larger whole, in universals, collectives, and essences—which Tillich delineates as well.[29] This form of courage is easy enough to observe in the corps de ballet but is also apparent in the soloist, who brings the distinctive essence of classical ballet to our attention.

The difference between the classical outlook and the existential point of view can be explained according to the principle of creative agency. The Platonic Greek view does not emphasize creative origination. This is not a negative or dead-end point. It is a positive view, which holds that beauty lies in the imitation of the underlying and preexisting order within and beyond us. In this view, artistry is a matter of drawing upon qualities already given in form. Existentialism, on the other hand, speaks to a fundamental constitution of values (hence an original creation of values, including beauty) through an active struggle with freedom and responsibility stemming from an individually responsive human agency.

Selma Jean Cohen's identification of the qualities that characterize classical ballet (with varying degrees of importance according to the particular style) suggests its close kinship to the Platonic view as opposed to the existential.[30] She describes these qualities as *outwardness* (an extroversion of the person developed from the five positions of the feet, utilizing the principle of *en dehors* (turnout); *verticality* (which is often associated with reason, she says); *skill* (she hesitates to use the word virtuosity); and *clarity* (spatially and in time) accompanied by the self-revealing nature of the classical style (which does not mean that the dancer calls attention to self but that she follows her own movement, calling attention to its kinetic qualities). The classical dancer, Cohen holds, is in conformance to the classical image and embodies the classical qualities with grace (defined as effortless, seamless flow). The turned-out, extroverted, extended, and reaching line of the body (in both classical and modern dance) indicates the line of infinity and exposes the body to full view. The turned-in, introverted, concentric, and drawn-inward line (seldom seen in ballet but typical of modern dance) gathers in the body, moving toward the inside of the body and the self. It is easily associated with the inward poetry of existentialism, from Kierkegaard to Sartre.

Modern dance evolved partly as an impulse to free the body from the tradition and strictures of ballet, an art with roots in the Renaissance revival of classical values and shaped thereafter amidst the baroque splendor of courtly formality. Modern dance eventually incorporated much of ballet's formalism and technique but always within a perspective of individual creative play upon the movement. Thus new variations are continuously arising out of modern dance's incorporation of the vocabulary of classical movement. Likewise, the open (originating) play and urgent agency of modern dance has influenced ballet's modernist styles, notably the ballets of Jerome Robbins, which portray modern existentialist themes in works such as *Age of Anxiety, Events,* and *West Side Story. Moves,* a work performed in silence, and *Eight Lines,* a work of pure motion, reflect Robbins's interest in the rigors of modernism. And his ballet *Les Noces,* on a peasant theme, in its dramatic lyricism and even in its sense of weight and inner strength, is similar to dramatic modern dance, which reached its high point with Graham and Limon.

Rules and formulas, tradition and boundaries, inevitably arise in modern dance, but as soon as a dance achievement can be defined, the next one is in process. Discovery and defiance of definition are interwoven with freedom and individuality in modern dance. Taken together, they may constitute an existential context that links disparate modern styles. Modern dance has thrived as an art of tenuous becomings, discoveries, and conflicting aesthetic standpoints. When Cohen attempts to define the characteristics of modern dance, she recognizes this most difficult task and is forced to find exceptions for the qualifications among its highly diversified manifestations. She states finally that she "would not dare claim that anything about the modern dance is irrevocable."[31]

It seems that for the modern dancer—as for Sartre at the foundation of twentieth century existentialism—lack of definition is the beginning point. The existentialist view that man is a being without given essence, a being-in-the-making, is a philosophy of *becoming.* Once again, Nietzsche's poetic imagery foreshadowed this view:

> What is great in man is that he is a bridge and not an end:
> What can be loved in man is that he is an *overture* and a *going under.*
> I love those who do not know how to live, except by going under, for they are those who cross over.[32]

The overwhelming assumption behind existentialism is that we start from scratch; the human being is without given essence and not determined. It is a philosophy that accounts for change and the precarious stance at the falling edge of the unknowable (the symbol of the abyss). True to this position, the modern dancer has developed off-balance motion and falling, generally not admissible in ballet. Modern dance also emphasizes asymmetry, which is related to off-balance and falling rather than to stability. In fact, Humphrey teaches that by itself symmetry is lifeless.[33] The off-centered, vulnerable posture behind existentialism is also behind much of the creative individualism of modern dance—which is an effort to see life in dynamic transition rather than balanced stasis, to make the individual count, or in Nagrin's terms, to act in spite of "not knowing." He underlined the importance of the existentialist's position as he finished a guest teaching class with my students: "Each person makes a difference," he advised them. "You *can* change the world."

Existential Themes in Modern Dance

The fairy tales of ballet could not express the dancer's concerns in the twentieth century. Graham worked within her belief that "movement never lies."[34] Like the existentialists, modern dancers approach *being* as a quest and a questioning: being is open—not closed and decided. Thus dancers evolved a new approach to dancing and dance movement. Over time, audiences came to see nonballetic movement as dance. New ways of perceiving dance were called upon, casting perception itself in the active mode. Passivity, complacency, and the accumulations of tradition had no place in the spirit of modern dance.

Death is a major theme for modern dancers as well as for philosophical existentialism. It became almost a preoccupation for Wigman. Death is a natural theme for an art that came on the heels of World War I, grew through World War II, and emerged as postmodern within the time of the Vietnam War, becoming a protest art partly because of it. Continuing threats of war have produced such groups as the Performing Artists for Nuclear Disarmament, whose work juxtaposes images of death with birth, exalting the female life-bearing principle—the mother, the earth. The significance of death in shaping life is important throughout existential thought. In the postmodern, existentialist, and mystic stories of Carlos Castaneda, death is depicted as a presence to be reckoned with.[35] It sits nearby and just over the left shoulder; it is a teacher; it informs life; it will not go away or be outwitted. Much earlier, Martin Heidegger declared that death was "not to be outstripped," that "holding death for true" as "just one's own" was the source of authentic being.[36] Anna Sokolow's dance work deals in large part with just such recognition, reflecting the understanding that "death cannot be brushed aside."[37]

Like the existentialist, the modern dancer reveals time and space as they are lived. As other modern arts, modern dance shows time as discontinuous, elongated, condensed, and repetitious. Nagrin's *Peloponnesian War* provides a good example of this. In modern dance, as in cubism, space can be disrupted; Nikolais's works do this with a high level of abstraction. Ed Emshwiller's film of Nikolais's *Totem* further abstracts the body and more drastically than is possible in the dance itself, even dispersing body parts and restructuring the body's given form. Real body space is distorted for aesthetic effect.[38] From Wigman to Nikolais, the spatial contours of the human body are distorted and surrealized. Directly to this point is modern dance surrealist Alice Farley's work, which involves dreamlike exaggerations and distortions of the body.

Existential nothingness (as a background for something) might be sensed in modern dance through its acceptance of, almost a penchant for, beginning at zero. I see existential nothingness as the same openness out of which modern dance has grown. Often a mood of emptiness and a search to fill that void pervades modern dance. The early postmoderns gave in to emptiness in walk-around blank dances, or nondances, seemingly searching to become something. Postmodern dance finally succeeded in becoming something—and something of aesthetic value—by relieving the surface of dance from intentionally dramatic expressive values (although Nikolais and Cunningham had paved the way for this change). Late in the postmodern period, David Gordon's dances walked a lot, but it was a walking that achieved something—delightful, difficult, and precisely timed.

As an individualistic and creative art, modern dance looks upon and expresses the darker and problematic side of life as well as the arcadian, light, humorous, and joyful side. To this point, the pastel palette of romantic ballet and the clean, geometrical, well-balanced lines of classical ballet does not suit its fullest purposing. Like the existentialist, the modern dancer seeks expression relevant to the times, one that can exorcise the painful realities of "spiritual poverty," as William Barrett describes this goal of existentialism.[39] Mircea Eliade writes of the modern existential dilemma in terms of a "desacralized" Western world where God is, to a greater extent than in any other historic period, no longer the centering principle of life.[40] The loss of God was Nietzsche's concern in declaring "the death of God." It is sometimes forgotten that he added, "We have killed him!" And that he then pressed this question: "Who gave us the sponge to wipe away the whole horizon?"[41]

Accompanying major existential themes are those seemingly negative terms we are so familiar with—despair, nausea, fear and trembling. They echo the prominent existential symbol of the broken center or T. S. Eliot's "heap of broken images." Well (we might wonder), why associate this loathsome heap with any kind of dancing? Should dancing not be treasured as the most immediately joyful, the most invigorating, of all the arts? And should it not remain in an idealized domain, protected from such seriousness? Art, however, takes its own course—sometimes apart from our wishes but never apart from a human conscience. Louis Horst recognizes, as he often said, that it is difficult for the modern dance to express joy. The problems of modern life impelled much of modern dance in the beginning, and still do. Urban dehumanization, modern alienation, and the senseless numbing of vital life prompts the conscience of Anna Sokolow's modern dance work and some of Steve Paxton's postmodern work. The aesthetic results are different; the themes are existential.

In contrast (though point by point contrasts do not always hold between modern dance and ballet, especially now), joy comes more naturally to the airborne, classical ballet, which seldom expresses a disturbing level of anxiety, angst, or loneliness—although some modern ballet works of Agnes de Mille, Jerome Robbins, Gerald Arpino, and Robert Joffrey provide exceptions to this. But even modernist ballet uses the classical vocabulary of movement to a great extent. We thus recognize it as within the rarefied, uplifted ballet genre. When the tormenting and the undesirable appear in ballet, it is often through a gauze, at a safe distance, well balanced, or on a luminous cloud. The classical ballet vocabulary is ill suited to express the grip of torment or the exhausted body of futility. The ballet evolved out of spectacle and the European courtly dances; it is, by and large, an aristocratic art, which still binds the female foot in toe slippers, places her on a pedestal, and displays her like a doll. Only with the existential and modernist revolution in art has ballet begun to divest itself of these social anachronisms.

Great joy has nevertheless been expressed in modern dance, and also sublime playfulness. Modern dance shows a full range of values—and without a singular vision or movement vocabulary as an aesthetic guide. Two of my favorite dances to this point are Paul Taylor's exuberant *Esplanade* (1975), performed to the music of Bach, and his *Aureole* (1962), on Handel's music, a modern version of a nineteenth century white ballet—as light, lifted, and breezy as classical ballet. The style of these dances, however, is closer to our human, everyday body-of-action than ballet is. Both dances make much use of quite naturalistic running and walking, crossing over very easily into rhythms and patterns of dancing that exaggerate, extend, and exalt the body. The joy in Taylor's dancing does not generally exude from a mannered body. We know we are not watching a dance within the ballet genre. The joy does not follow its own lines, is not conscious of itself; it is most simply there, in the movement. The effect is one of spontaneity; the movement seems to proceed of its own accord.

Behind the weightiness of existentialism and the early seriousness of modern dance is the positive mainspring for both, human freedom. Spanos states the positive meaning behind existential freedom: "'Existence' refers to man and ultimately means that he is free, that, unlike objects, which merely *are* and thus are at the mercy of their preestablished essence, man alone is capable of choosing his own future, that is, of determining his own essence."[42]

But for the dancer, like the existentialist, a positive embodiment of freedom entails responsibility. Martha Graham says that the dancer's goal is to become free through discipline. Goethe conceives of freedom similarly and states the problem existentially: "He only earns his freedom and existence, who daily conquers them anew."[43] Freedom is, in the words of Dostoevsky's Grand Inquisitor, "a terrible gift."

Sartre explains his famous statement that "man is condemned to be free" this way: "Condemned, because he did not create himself, yet, in other respects is free; because, once thrown into the world, he is responsible for everything he does."[44] Thus freedom is linked to responsibility in his philosophy. Freedom here is not permissiveness, it is not freedom *from* but freedom *for*. Freedom thus recognized becomes the wellspring for responsible creative action. As Sartre says, "Man is nothing else but what he makes of himself. Such is the first principle of existentialism."[45]

PART I

DANCE AND EMBODIMENT

1

DANCE AND THE LIVED BODY

Existential Phenomenology

THE CROSSING POINT

Existential phenomenology fuses a theory of conduct (existentialism) with a theory of knowledge and meaning (phenomenology), resulting in a humanistic philosophy that includes investigation into language, art, psychology, ethics, epistemology, psychiatry, psychoanalysis, religion, law, anthropology, and sociology.[1]

There are obvious connections between existential thought, the body, dance, and art in general, since they are all founded in lived and experiential values. Particular existentialist authors, however, developed views of the human being growing out of theories of the body, which have specific implications for understanding dance (not to mention the other arts, sport, or movement in general). These views of the body arose through the joining of existentialism with phenomenology. To this point, Maurice Merleau-Ponty and Jean-Paul Sartre introduced Edmund Husserl's phenomenological method (as a systematic study of the contents of consciousness) into existential philosophy through their concerns for explaining "bodily being" and their attendant attempts to elucidate "perception." Thus the concept of the lived body was technically developed through their joining of existential concerns with the phenomenological method, although the lived-body concept had antecedents in the works of Friedrich Nietzsche, Husserl, and Henri Bergson. It also became central to Gabriel Marcel's metaphysical outlook and to Paul Ricoeur's philosophical investigations of the bond between voluntary and involuntary movement. Martin Heidegger, who was so influential in the development of existential phenomenology, was not explicitly concerned with the lived body, but he developed compelling movement imagery in his descriptions of experiential values, which have implications for the lived body and for dance, as we shall see.

The lived-body concept attempts to cut beneath the subject-object split, recognizing a dialectical and lived dualism but not a dualism of body-soul or body-mind. A phenomenological (or lived) dualism implicates consciousness and intention and assumes an indivisible unity of body, soul, and mind.

Dualism, which connotes the classic body-soul separation in Western philosophy (principally known as Cartesian dualism), views the body in a negative, mechanistic way and regards the soul as superior. On the other hand, the lived body as a concept is a positive view, because the philosophers who developed the concept view the body as meaningful (Merleau-Ponty, Marcel, and to some extent, Sartre) and innately purposeful (Ricoeur, Hans Jonas, and others). For this reason, and because it was formulated in the joining of phenomenology and existentialism, I associate the lived-body concept with what Colin Wilson identifies as the new (and positive) existentialism.

Wilson proposes that we call phenomenological existentialism "the new existentialism," because it is "less of a mouthful" and because the old existentialism, which he associates with Soren Kierkegaard, Heidegger, and Sartre, was unable to penetrate the fog of negativity that surrounded it.[2] Wilson argues that for Sartre there are no peak experiences, only the negative ideal of doing good for a "lack of anything better to do."[3] However, Wilson believes that the root of existentialism – in Nietzsche – is optimistic.

Jonas is no less concerned than Wilson with a grounding of values in a positive view of being. He is critical of Sartre's argument that "there is no sign in the world" and interprets Sartre's freedom as a negative and desperate freedom, which "as a compassless task, inspires dread rather than exultation."[4] Jonas, unlike Wilson, reduces Nietzsche's philosophy to its nihilistic rather than its optimistic dimension. He sees in it a world diminished to a mere manifestation of power and mastery, since in Nietzsche the transcendent reference (God) has fallen away and man is left with himself, alone.[5] However, Nietzsche finds cause for both alarm and joy in modern man's aloneness, whereas Sartre declares that "even if God did exist, that would change nothing."[6]

In any case, we shall not be able to ignore what Wilson criticizes as the old existentialism, since it provides insights for the new. He sees the problem with the old existentialism as an "error in judgment," which concentrated it in a gloomy outlook and a limited range of values, rendering it contrary to the optimistic impulse behind existentialism as a whole.[7] He is unable to clearly separate the old from the new, since the values are interwoven up to a certain point. Yet he does identify a vision of the new that counterbalances what he considers the shortsighted negative tone of the old. A concern for human existence as *purposeful* is crucial to this vision. Human beings are at their best when motivated by a purpose. But what purpose, Wilson asks. The old existentialism "groped towards an answer but never reached it." He suggests that the purpose must be grasped by a visionary intellect that does not get trapped by a sense of contingency, a sense that life is accidental rather than imbued with purpose and transcendental values.[8]

The new existentialism asks whether there might not be some means of looking into the nature of experiences beyond ordinary consciousness. We might call these *peak* experiences (as existential psychologist Abraham Maslow does), *mystic* if we mean an experienced unification with nature, *sacred* if we mean the experience of a transcendent ground of being; or we might simply understand them as expansions of freedom experienced through a conscious exercise of creative agency. Wilson describes the latter as "the joy we feel as obstacles collapse, as the field of our freedom abruptly increases." New existentialism has the problem of providing "an exit" from debilitating boredom and the devaluation of life.[9]

Accordingly, we might ask what is gained by joining phenomenological method with existential philosophy: Arturo Fallico believes that it connects philosophical efforts with ontological, religious, and aesthetic interests. For existentialism, it means a transition from unsystematic literary expression to technical writing. For phenomenology, it signals a change in application to concrete problems of human existence.[10]

Heidegger, Sartre, and Merleau-Ponty apply and interpret Husserl's phenomenology in view of existential values—qualitative dimensions of existence such as dread, alienation, death, freedom, self-deception, and authenticity. Wilson holds that Heidegger and Sartre limit their perspective by emphasizing man's contingency.[11] He feels that it is Merleau-Ponty who points the way toward a new and purposeful existentialism, remaining more faithful to Husserl's insight into the *intentional* nature of consciousness.[12] Merleau-Ponty's problem is the study of the body (and its nervous system), which he interprets as primordially expressive and meaningful (as I shall take up in terms of dance).

It is enough for us to recognize here that a modern phenomenological approach, broadly considered and applied to disciplines outside of philosophy, still concerns itself—as Husserl did—with getting at the essence (or the heart) of intentional consciousness. It holds that consciousness is directed and has an object—that consciousness is *consciousness of something.* The descriptive method in phenomenology attempts to describe the contents of consciousness, to state that which is before us, which we accept as commonplace and obvious. Fallico states the difficulty in this: "For contrary to what is ordinarily supposed, that which stands simply and plainly exhibited before our very eyes is not easy truly to understand. Layer upon layer of culturally derived preconceptions and predispositions obscure a direct view of life and of the life-world. Philosophy is difficult just because it requires us to be simple; to look at what is there to be seen, see it, and describe it."[13]

Since, as a method, phenomenology aims at insightful description of that which presents itself to consciousness, isolation of "the thing itself," I have even heard insightful poetry defined as good phenomenological description. Technical phenomenologists might disagree. Certainly in the strictest sense, phenomenology is more complicated than the poetic, insightful, and intuitive grasp of things (though this may be difficult enough); in addition, it is systematically analytical, taking an objective stance at some point. It requires one to take a thorough look at the object, or phenomenon of inspection, through *phenomenological reduction* (originating in the philosophy of Husserl). This involves "a narrowing of attention to what is essential in the problem while disregarding or ignoring the superfluous and accidental."[14] In so doing, one suspends not only one's own presuppositions but also previous theory and commonly held beliefs. Along the way it becomes evident that it is ultimately impossible to remove one's own consciousness. When the existentialists applied and further developed Husserl's method, joining existentialism and phenomenology, they emphasized the latter point.[15]

I employ reduction in the present work not in the strict scientific sense that is the aim of some phenomenology but in the spirit of phenomenological reduction, which is concerned with removing commonly held beliefs that obscure our understanding and which may in fact misdirect our attention away from core definitions. For instance, the notion that dance is self-expression is very popular. If we accept this view, we are never led into the substance of dance itself, since many of our actions, from screaming to casual conversation, might qualify as self-expression on the unexamined face of this term. Even if we agree with John Dewey that an expression is not simply a discharge of emotion but requires a medium and a conscious development of that medium,[16] we would still need to identify the particular medium of dance – and to describe how the self is expressed in the dance medium when it functions as art – to justify a view that dance is self-expression. Every art is expressed through a particular medium, and every artist's *self* is a conduit for that medium. Dance is no different in this respect. One of my aims, then, is to reduce the belief that dance is self-expression, so that we may more clearly see the unique substance of dancing and the self that is created, known, and expressed in it.

I seek in general to develop the phenomenological concept of the lived body in terms of dance. I "reduce" the complications that inevitably arise in order to describe the phenomenon of dance. This results, inevitably, in an aesthetic perspective of dance – a view of its basic (irreducible) structure, its experiential values, and its significance as art. In the descriptive phenomenological approach, I nevertheless accept that *I am there* in my attention to phenomena (anything that appears to consciousness). Related to this, I also understand, through Husserl and Merleau-Ponty, that consciousness is intentional; it depends on one's perceptual attention to phenomena. Phenomenology stresses that consciousness is an activity, not a passivity.

While there are diverse points of view within the phenomenological movement,[17] phenomenology in principle seeks to describe the essence of that which appears to consciousness – thus the reduction or stripping away to arrive at what is most basic. Existential phenomenology seeks, in addition, to maintain an attitude of being in the world. Husserl's phenomenology culminates in a transcendent principle. More to the point of this study is that the existentialist development of his philosophy took another direction: "Whereas Husserl saw the task of transcendental phenomenology to be that of describing the lived-world from the viewpoint of a detached observer, existential phenomenology insists that the observer cannot separate himself from the world."[18]

NONDUALISTIC LIVED BODY

Body am I, through and through, and nothing else; and soul is only a word for something about the body. — Friedrich Nietzsche

Existential phenomenology developed nondualistic views of the human body, which provide a foundation for overcoming well-entrenched dualisms in dance. In fact the most distinctive feature of the lived-body concept is its nondualistic thesis, its rejection of classical and Cartesian dualism. "Nothing," Marcel writes, "is less instructive than the Cartesian 'I am.'"[19] It does not allow questions of existence to be raised. Marcel contributes a view of self as the "I am" in quest of itself (exigence). The question Who am I? remained urgent for him, as for Nietzsche before him and existentialists who followed. They answered it with refutations of body-mind and body-soul dualism. Marcel's belief that action is the negation of dualism[20] provides impetus for development of concepts of the body viewed nondualistically as a body-of-action, affirming a bodily lived metaphysic and mystery.

The existentialist attack on the primacy of mind (expressed in René Descartes's "I think; therefore, I exist") brought forward concepts of the body as lived (or experienced) *in action* — or as Richard Zaner says, "theories of the animate organism." Through Zaner we see that Marcel, Sartre, and Merleau-Ponty each developed "a systematic phenomenology of the animate organism."[21] Zaner concludes that these three philosophers were "at war with dualism" and against the "message theory" of sense perception. Each rejects the body as *passive,* or merely receptive, and tries "to establish the body as fundamentally *active.*"[22] As the existential phenomenologists emphatically reject traditional dualism, they reject instrumental definitions of the body. The view that the body cannot be an instrument like other instruments, that it cannot be reduced to *an object,* is the central focus for concepts that evolved into nondualistic lived-body theories. The corrective of body-soul and body-mind dualism that emerges from existential phenomenology as a whole, has implications for dance.

Dance and Dualism

While many works are devoted to the problems of dualism, the problems of dualism in dance have barely been recognized. The dualistic language of mind versus body (with related distinctions of soul and spirit, which usually refer to an inner essence) pervades the literature on dance. Habits of language reinforce a view that the body is simply material substance and mechanical physiological process, moved by something other than itself; and that mind, as pure thought, escapes the material body.

In addition, dance is very often defined as an art that has "movement as its medium," and uses the "body as an instrument." Even Martha Graham defines dance this way but tempers this dualistic definition by associating the body with the self, speaking of "the body" becoming "its ultimate self" through technical training in dance.[23] Dance literature is rife with references to the body as an instrument, without explaining how the body as instrument may (and definitely does) differ from other instruments. Agency (or will) is attributed to the mind as distinct from, and in control of, the body—mind over matter.

For instance, in the opening pages of a recent book, intended as a text for beginners, we read: "through dance technique, you learn how to control your body and make it your instrument."[24] An instrumental view of the body then occupies the first chapter. In the last chapter, when the mind is discussed as a separate issue, we are told that "when beginning a dance class, it is important to be present with both your body and mind,"[25] as though it would be possible to be present with only one or the other. Of course, we get the intended meaning: that learning to dance requires concentration. In the meantime, a dualism is reinforced. The point I hope to develop is that dancing requires a concentration of the whole person as a *minded body*, not a mind in command of something separable, called *body*.

The dualistic thesis in Western philosophy inherited from Descartes (and somewhat from Plato), which supposes that body and soul are distinct or that they differ as instrument and agent, is at the heart of confusion about the body.[26] The body is relegated to a status below the soul, mind, or spirit. The great lesson of death, Plato tells us, is that the soul is superior to the body—thus, granting us our being. In the words of Plato's Athenian, "soul is utterly superior to body. . . . what gives each one of us his being is nothing else but his soul, whereas the body is no more than a shadow which keeps us company."[27] Although Plato advocates dance, he sees it as an art of imitation (as part of poetry, along with music), and the arts of imitation, in spite of their poetic, physical, spiritual, and educational values, hold no exalted place in Plato's philosophy.[28] To the point of dualism, however, Plato does relate body and soul through dance, holding that dance benefits the soul in a therapeutic way, producing mental calm through rocking motion and ritual.[29]

Plato is viewed as a dualist because his doctrine of ideas posits permanent forms (ideas) beyond, and superior to, sense knowledge. Descartes identifies the body wholly with material reality and sees the soul as completely immaterial. Thus we note a difference between ancient and modern dualistic views. Even though soul and body are empirically distinguished throughout the ancient tradition, the "original togetherness" of body and soul is, nevertheless, an empirical fact for Plato and Aristotle.[30] Modern (metaphysical) dualism precludes this unity; because of Descartes, we still accept without question a metaphysical gulf between things mental and things material.

Problems arising from dualism are compounded by confusion about the words *soul, mind,* and *spirit,* which were interrelated in Plato's thought. According to Huntington Cairns, "the word soul, with its accretions of meanings during the centuries, is an unfortunate translation of the Greek word *Psyche.* It is more properly translated, according to the various contexts, as Reason, Mind, Intelligence, Life, and vital principle in things as well as in man; it is the constant that causes change but itself does not change. In fact, Plato's use of many different words for the rational order has caused much confusion. . . . In any event, the soul, because it is intelligence, is tripartite, it is one and also many and the proportion that fuses them."[31]

Part of the problem of dualism also lies in modern language. The English language has only one word for body, while other languages express the body's varying levels of reality with different words. The German *Körper* refers to a physical object; *Leib* indicates the body as it is lived and experienced. German also distinguishes between bodily experience (*Erlebnis*) and the experience of an object (*Erkenntnis*). French makes the same distinction between *vécu* (lived experience) and *expérience* (experience of a detached nature). To overcome the subject-object dichotomy in English, phenomenologists use the terms *lived body* and *lived experience.*[32]

Dance has not escaped the effects of dualism nor its basis in language. British philosopher David Best thinks Susanne Langer is partly at fault, as he considers her work from 1953 and 1957.[33] Yet Langer, whose early work was sometimes labeled dualistic, later (1967) defined mind in terms of the highest articulation of physiological processes.[34] Mind obtains "felt" and "organic" bases, as she turns to physiology, biology, psychology, and art in order to explain it.

Dualism in dance is perpetuated, I believe, by the practice of dance as well as by the language that supports this practice.[35] Habitual use of language that distinguishes body from mind in the teaching and learning of dance reinforces a view that the mind tells the body what to do; then the body responds to the command. It also reinforces an erroneous view that the inspiration (soul or spirit) for dance lies outside the ken of the body. This is not a *thinking body* (to borrow the theme of Mabel Todd's book);[36] nor is it a *feeling mind* (to recall Langer's work).

Another consequence of dualism is that it encourages the all too common view that the training of a dancer is the training of the body, simply understood as physical. The body then is conceived mechanistically, as *a thing* to be whipped, honed, and molded into shape. But in reality the whole self is shaped in the experience of dance, since the body is besouled, bespirited, and beminded. Simply stated, the body is lived through all of these aspects in dance. Soul, spirit, and mind (or varying aspects of the psyche, if you will) are not separate from what we call the physical; rather, they are intrinsically tied up with it. A closer look at dance, which reduces (or sets aside) traditional dualism, should allow us to see this more clearly.

Overcoming Dualism

LIVED DIALECTIC

What the dancer experiences and projects when she succeeds in doing her dance is an expiation of dualism. Yvonne Rainer put this well in the title of her dance, *The Mind Is a Muscle* (later called *Trio A*). When the dancer succeeds, neither body nor mind is held at a distance; they are the same in action. But what happens when she does not succeed? Or when she gets tired? What happens when she becomes painfully aware of her body as matter to be moved, as stuttering and stubborn substance, and sees herself (through her body) as having failed? (This is possible, even for highly accomplished dancers.) A form of dualism arises at this point, but it supposes a fundamental unity underneath. To explain this, Merleau-Ponty's view of a bodily lived dialectic is helpful.[37] Dualism is admitted, but not the traditional dualism that makes an absolute or metaphysical distinction between body and soul.

Merleau-Ponty states that the body-soul problem is clarified when one sees the body as "the bearer of a dialectic." He admits a dualism that *disintegrates* the basic lived unity:

> Our body does not always have meaning, and our thoughts, on the other hand — in timidity for example — do not always find in it the plentitude of their vital expression. In these cases of disintegration, the soul and the body are apparently distinct; and this is the truth of dualism. But the soul, if it possesses no means of expression — one should say rather, no means of actualizing itself — soon ceases to be the soul, as the thought of the aphasic weakens and becomes dissolved; the body which loses its meaning soon ceases to be a living body and falls back into the state of a physico-chemical mass; it arrives at non-meaning only by dying.[38]

Thus he arrives at a fundamental point: the terms *body* and *soul* "can never be distinguished absolutely without ceasing to be."

Merleau-Ponty says he is not speaking of "a duality of substances," as traditional dualistic theories posit. He holds that the notions of soul and body must be related and offers a view of body and soul that interweaves, rather than separates them. He does not propose that the soul is an entity in itself; rather it is the evolving *meaning of the body:* "The body in general is an ensemble of paths already traced, of powers already constituted; the body is the acquired dialectical soil upon which a higher 'formation' is accomplished, and the soul is the meaning which is then established."[39]

The present study is undertaken in the belief that lived-body concepts, which refute traditional dualistic notions, provide a basis for describing the lived wholeness of the self in dance (being the dance) as well as the lived dialectic between self and body, which sometimes arises in the process of dancing.

For instance, a dialectical dualism is apparent in dance as the choreographer forms the dance and as the dancer learns it. This grows of necessity from an objectification of the body in rehearsal and performance through creative experiment with, and critical observation of, the body in motion. A psychic distance from the body is necessitated in the dialectical creative processes of dance. It is significant, though, that such a phenomenal (or lived) duality is formulated upon a basic unity and according to intent, as existential phenomenology has held.

Lived-body theory provides a means toward overcoming dualistic concepts of dance, which regard the body as an instrument, movement as the medium, and mind or soul as the mover or motivational source for dance. Lived-body concepts hold that the body is *lived* as a body-of-action. Human movement is the actualization, the realization, of embodiment. Movement cannot be considered as medium apart from an understanding that movement *is* body, not just something that the body accomplishes instrumentally as it is moved by some distinct, inner, and separable agency. Embodiment is not passive; it is articulate. In other words, I live my body as a body-of-motion, just as I also live my self in motion. Body, movement, self, and agency (implicating human will and freedom) are ultimately not separable entities, which is not to say that lived dualisms (or dialectics) may not appear in consciousness within certain contexts. Thus we might recognize phenomenal (lived) dualisms without accepting metaphysical dualism.

BODY-OBJECT, BODY-SUBJECT

In phenomenology, it is significant that body-object and body-subject both refer to the body. Body-subject does not refer to something (a soul or a mind) that animates or operates the body while transcending it. However, body-subject is a transcendent principle in phenomenology, because it eludes our full knowledge. It refers to the body lived wholistically and prereflectively as the self. It is a temporal concept, describing the time in which consciousness is present centered, or prereflective. The body-subject can be sensed in dance and through the dancer when she is unified in action; that is, when she is not reflecting on her self or her action but living the present-centered moment in her dance as a unity of self and body in action.

Body-object and body-subject are not correlates of body and mind. Body-object describes a conscious, intentional position taken toward the body as an object of attention. It is the position science necessarily takes in studying the body. And it is the reflective position I necessarily take when I become aware of my body as something to be reckoned with in dance. When I focus on my body — when I look at my hand and consider it, for instance — it becomes an object of my attention. When I do, my prereflective (before-noticing) stream of being is interrupted. Thus objectivity — the solid otherness of myself, things, and other people — can and do appear to me; the body so regarded and reflected upon may be termed body-object.

However, there is a complication in speaking about the body as an object. The alive body retains a personal identity. I can objectify my hand by looking at it, but it is nevertheless alive and mine, unlike the table it rests on. I can examine my steps (as I do when I am learning a dance), but I am only objectifying my body (myself) in the particular manner of my steps. For, as Sartre recognized, "the body is lived and not known."[40] I can never fully become the object of my own attention. Body-object does not refer to material body; it refers either to the body when it becomes the object of attention or to an objective attitude toward the body, be it one's own body or that of others. In theory, body-object is a neutral concept. It becomes positive or negative according to intention. Certainly, people may objectify others with an intent to exploit. On the other hand, an objective attitude is necessary to certain processes of science and art, when we stand back to observe and learn.

In contrast to such reflective observation, *body-subject* refers to prereflective consciousness. It refers to all that I am as I live my body spontaneously in the present moment, not noticing it, not looking back upon it, and not anticipating or imagining it in some future state. It refers to my lived and complete wholeness. Body-subject does not refer to some rare entity beyond the body, such as mind or soul. Nor is it an agency that moves the body, since it is synonymous with body.

Yet mind and soul are not denied, either. A full description of the body admits of mind, spirit, and soul as bodily lived attributes, which describe and differentiate bodily lived qualities. Certainly we can understand mind as mental activity arising through a concentration of the body's mental powers, powers with an organic and neurophysical basis. And we also commonly use the words *spirit* and *soul* to describe mythopoetic attributes of the body. These attributes describe lived qualities of the body that are valued in experience. They may be associated with depth of feeling, as when we use them to describe an experience as full of soul or as spiritual. However, our ordinary, unremarkable, prereflective awareness is no less a description of body-subject, the body understood in its prereflective, lived unity.

The body-object can be *known*, in the sense that the body itself can become the object of our attention, but the body-subject can only be *lived*. And it may also be experienced in the unreflected (immediately experienced) present time of dance. Dance allows us to speak, and to listen, out of a prereflective wholistic state. We (the audience) envision and affirm our own resounding presence through our direct lived experience of the dancer's present-centered performance.

Spontaneous Body

FREEDOM AND INTENTION

Existential phenomenology relates freedom, perception, and intention in its nondualistic concepts of body, a relation influencing this study throughout. Phenomenology holds that consciousness is intentional, that we are not merely passive observers subject to the imprint of the surrounding world. Consciousness selects, sorts out, and organizes stimuli according to present purposeful perception—purposeful because it is directed toward, and involved in, its objects. The body, in this view, is a sensitive perceptive actor. It does not *have* a consciousness—rather, it *is* a consciousness. When we understand the body in terms of intentional consciousness, body and consciousness take on new meaning. The body is intentive; it is implicated in, rather than separate from, will and freedom. Freedom as it is realized in action is a major existential theme. For the existentialist, freedom is not an abstraction; it is an experience.

Phenomenology lends to existentialism the essential point that *perception is active*, often no less active than imagination.[41] Existential phenomenology rejects message theories of perception in order to explain a bodily lived purposing (the intentionality of consciousness). It holds that we perceive through the senses in an active way, finally constituting the shape and meaning of our world as we consciously engage ourselves with it.

Accordingly, if I view my life-world as constituted by my bodily action, I am not just a helpless recipient of stimuli; I participate in and control my own destiny. The question Who am I takes on a particular meaning when I understand that I am spinning my own world of feeling, knowledge, and meaning through my own body-of-action.

Much recent thought in existential phenomenology is optimistic. It sees purpose in life and attempts to explain the body's innate purposefulness. Erwin Straus stresses the unique positive values in the human upright posture and its function in the "esthetic attitude" permitted to human life.[42] Jonas's work offers an existentialist interpretation of biological facts in a phenomenology of life, which takes into account both Aristotle (in the belief that organic life prefigures mind) and the moderns (in the belief, inseparable from the first, that mind remains a part of organic life). He contends that the principle of life, which the body exhibits in its organic and minded nature, stands "under the sign of freedom," although the mystery of its origins are closed to us.[43]

For Jonas, freedom is prefigured in life in a most fundamental sense, implying a transcendent possibility. Its first stages may be observed in the depths of our bodies — in metabolism, the basic level of organic existence. Life belongs to nature and is privileged with freedom; nevertheless, life carries the burden of its own precariousness, paradoxically singled out and set over against the physical context of the world from whence it arose. The polarities that allow for distinction and relations are thus introduced: metabolism, at the foundation of life, is both freedom and need. Life holds death as immanent, and being is seen against its ever-present contrary, nonbeing.[44]

The polarities Jonas proposes are positive, because they suspend us between receptivity and action, from whence grows our awareness and exercise of freedom and choice — the voluntary aspect of life — and our ability to commit ourselves to one action rather than another. These polarities, inherent in life, permit (but do not guarantee) a conscious transcendent creativity. They are the condition of relation necessary to it. This study will develop the view that it is bodily lived *oppositions* and *polarities* (rather than substantive dualisms of body and mind) that permit differentiation, tension, and relation in dance (part 2 takes this up thematically).

FREE AND LIMITED BODY

Jonas posits a freedom lived at the very foundation of our biological life. Wilson emphasizes "the experience of freedom," as our vision of life's possibilities increases on an existential and positive plane. Behind these views is Sartre's insight into the "inescapability" of our freedom, as we are "condemned to be free" and must make choices. Thus we may also experience freedom's negative as well as creative dimensions.

But poised in agon with our free and open essence are our limitations.[45] I am limited by being this particular body, which is mine and mine alone, with its intricacies and individuated form and sensitivities. Whether I like it or not, my particular embodiment and my images of its powers and limitations condition my general comportment in life. Zaner calls distinctly individuated embodiment an "inescapable limitation," saying that "'limitedness,' hence a sense of 'otherness,' is essential to embodiment." Not only is my body mine—but I belong to it. I experience myself as implicated by my body. In some sense, I experience helplessness and vulnerability because of this inescapable implicatedness. Hence I experience what Zaner terms "chill."[46]

Tied up with my sense of limitation is Sartre's "gaze of others." My body is made other to me when I take account of its appearance to others. Thus I may become other to myself; my body may become set over against me or seem other to me. Alienation, the sense of separation from others, seems located precisely in this experience. Embodiment is thus the ground for all experienced values, for both intimacy and alienation, freedom and limitation.

CREATED BODY

Still, my body is not determined by my limitations. Rather, I create my body through my choices and my actions, in this I also create myself. My entire lived experience determines my body; my choice to be athletic or sedentary, my habits of walking, talking, eating, and even dreaming, result in what I may call at any moment—for that time—by body. My body is mutable, changeable, living substance. It is continuous with my mind, which is no less subject to temporal change, mutability, growth, and decay, and no less a product of my exercise of choice and free will.

I create myself as I enact my freedoms and push back the boundaries of my limitations; my purposes project me into action, not my contingency. Likewise, I create and define my body as I enact my purposes. I am not moved by superior energies, *I move myself*. My flow of motion grows in part from my given nature, this is admitted; but it is also created through my intentions as I exercise my choices and direct my energies.

I create my reach into time and space; no one does it for me. It is, furthermore, my reach alone—as each person's is. My reach, extended or tenuous, is part of how I am. I become defined in my actions and created through them. These are usually habitual, ingrained actions that I am completely *unaware* of. But actions singled out for themselves, as in dance, are actions I am *aware* of. Hence my feeling of living a pure power (a sheer freedom) in the skill I acquire.

MOVING FREELY

Our will becomes the form of our body.—Paul Ricoeur

The human being is not unconditionally free, if by *free* we mean free from any and all constraint. Constraints of many kinds impose themselves everywhere. We are subject to physical forces, social, cultural, economic, and political factors, and to the conditions of our birth, to name just a few. We are, however, completely free in our powers of self-projection. That is, we are free as we utilize our powers to create, to question, to initiate change, and so on. We are free in the choices we make about others and about our world. I believe we are most free in our arts, as we create self-contained complete worlds, and freely project our being.

It is also true that in this creation we work with the givens of nature. In dance, this is the human body, lived as the self is lived. Therefore we do not create from scratch but from preexisting materials. It is most significant that the null point for creation in art lies in ourselves, in the originating imagination. That is, until we conceive of a work, until some spark of imagination is ignited in view of it, the work has no existence. In the case of dance, this begins with our ability to give image to movement and culminates in the world of movement we create through this ability, which testifies to our freedom.

We dance to assure our bodily lived freedom. We ourselves determine our dance as we conceive of it, and perform it of our own free will. We move only for the sake of moving, and for the sake of dancing. The movement we call dance must fulfill an aesthetic purpose; accordingly, dance is not just any movement. But it is significant that movement is the medium of dance and the intentive human body its immanent source. As we express our embodiment in dancing, we create it aesthetically and experience it more freely. Dance frees us from the constraints of our practical lives and utilitarian movement. In short, we experience a sheer freedom in dance as we move free of any practical outcome.

We dance to enact the bodily lived basis of our freedom in an aesthetic form. We experience freedom when we merge fully with our intentions and fulfill the aesthetic purpose of the dance. These are related forms of freedom, since we fulfill the aesthetic purpose of the dance as we realize our intentions in action. The aesthetic intent of the dance is nothing more than the aesthetic intent of the dancer as he understands and bodies forth the dance. As dancers, we do not move to fulfill any goal beyond the aesthetic requirements of the dance; we understand and experience our freedom as a release from instrumentally intended movement. In dance, we exercise the sheer freedom of going nowhere and doing nothing. We move for the moving; but more, we dance for the dancing.

This description is not capricious; it speaks to the capacity we have to choose and create ourselves as free in our embodiment, to isolate and understand our intentional motion—volition itself. Such is the potential of dancing, when we direct our attention to it as of our free will and its demonstration. In dance I am allowed to experience my will in its purest form because I am not exercising my will toward a practical or useful outcome. Yet I am exercising it to the fullest as I dance. And if my dance is difficult and risky, it will require an inordinate commitment of will.

A curious phenomenon arises in the latter instance. I must exercise my will, but in the final analysis, I seek to move free of effort and willfulness. I seek to move freely, spontaneously, or in total accord with the willing. I seek (as I describe later) to "become the dance." Thus, I may understand that freedom, like grace, is a gift, but one which comes through commitment and effort.

In dance I am permitted to examine and understand effort because I attend directly to my own effort. I literally stare it in the face, since there is nothing compelling me to move; I choose to move. I choose to dance, to exert and pay attention to my effort. I accomplish nothing through the effort but the movement of the dance itself; and thus my will toward accomplishment stands out as freely chosen effort. I do not have to dance; I choose to dance. Thus I exercise my will in a unique manner when I dance. My dance and my effort of will stand out for themselves.

Through Ricoeur we learn that the will is not imperial; it is constantly sinking back into nature, as it is absorbed in "the *structural* involuntary of an acquired gesture."[47] The bond between the voluntary and involuntary is basically outside of the will, or beyond effort, supporting the quality of ease in our experience of freedom: "The hold which I can have on the world and which makes freedom efficacious presupposes this initial continuity between the perceiving Cogito and the movement of personal body: knowledge and movement are more fundamentally and more basically bound together than a concerted voluntary effort can bring about. Here the mental and physical Cogito, thought and movement, bring about an undecipherable unity, beyond effort."[48]

Thus mastery in dance does not rest on willful domination of ourselves in our movement but on discovery of the ideal effort in our embodiment of movement. When we go beyond our intentions or fall short of them in fulfilling a task or a movement, we fall out of the open center, where intention is dissolved in action, being indistinguishable from it. Then there appears, not grace, but the effort to retreat or to move ahead of ourselves in action.

Grace, freedom, and mastery appear as willfulness disappears and as effortless ease is achieved. This does not mean that the movement is vapid or weak. Indeed, ease and weakness are not equatable. Strong movement may be performed with ease. Neither does effortless ease of performance imply light floating movement, only. Heavy movement, weighted, sharp, or energetic movement, may also be performed with effortless ease when such movement is intended and fulfilled with the right fit of effort—that is, effort in perfect proportion to intention.

Effort in dance may be intentionally hidden or intentionally displayed, because the motions of dance are intentionally performed. The dancer learns how to control efforts of movement and their effects, and thus she may be as graceful in the display of effort as in hiding it. Effort that appears awkward is effort out of phase with intent, or conscious of itself because it is not yet dissolved (realized) in action. I am bound to such effort in my consciousness of it. Then I do not move freely.

I realize my freedom when I move as I intend. Then I experience my movement powers as personal powers. I experience such freedom most intensely when I solve challenging movement problems that extend my skill and imagination. When the problems are solved and I can completely give myself to the dance, I live it as of my own nature – albeit, one I acquired through solving the problems of the dance, learning its forms, and creating its feeling. Those dances that become second nature return me to nature – to the spontaneous and graceful arising of my body through nature. Then I move freely.

2

DANCE AND SELF

A crowd is an untruth. — Soren Kierkegaard

Only in the self can the drama of truth occur. — Hayden Carruth

All works of art bear the stamp of individual creation. Neither Martha Graham nor Yvonne Rainer escaped self in their dances. Yet they were both concerned, each in her own way, to transcend self-expression in dance. Rainer's efforts in this regard are well known, but it is too often forgotten that Graham openly rejected what she termed "self-expression dancing." Instead she sought a form of "communication" adequate to her own time.[1] Dance is a form of expression — and communication — that necessarily involves the self. But how? Or under what conditions is self involved when dance is viewed as art? Graham and Rainer both understood this as problematic for dance.

In examining self-body-dance relations throughout this chapter, I reduce the notion that dance is self-expression and expand the terms of spontaneity, freedom, and intention introduced in chapter 1. These concerns arise within my primary purpose of establishing a contextual view of the self as known and lived in dance.

To *express* is to manifest the self toward another or others in some comprehensible medium. All of the arts are aesthetic and created forms of expression. That is, they are shaped through human action into objects that we can perceive as apart from, yet related to, our selves. As they are presented or performed for others, they intend an other, demonstrating a desire to communicate. Dance is not completed *as art* until it enters an intersubjective field. It involves the self in a world of others – a communal and cultural context. I think the best dancers (certainly those who have earned the right to perform for others) come to recognize this as a responsibility for which they prepare assiduously. Performing for others imposes a particular kind of responsibility.

As a performed art, dance is not a display of self, a show, or a showing: it is simply given. In this, the self is given over to the other. Good dancers know that the dancing self dies when it looks back either to visualize or to admire itself. The present tense is lost. Spontaneity is lost, and with it the dance. The dancer is at her best (she becomes her dance) when she is present centered. Good dancers become absorbed in the problems and pleasures of dancing itself. They get caught up in a larger-than-self pursuit and transcend the egotism and narcissism of which dancers are often accused. The art of dance will tolerate neither trait.

Dance is a form of participation in culture and a way of creating culture. Thus the dancer is required to move beyond the confines of self; yet her self is there in her art. She brings that self into her dance by necessity: self is both problematically and joyfully there; it is both sharpened and mollified. In good dancing, self becomes submerged as the dancer's awareness becomes concentrated in the dance; only thus is she able to take the audience into the dance with her. Nor is the dancer's focus on her own personal body; rather it is tuned toward a particular ideation (image or ideal) of embodiment as she strives to worthily represent the aesthetic (qualitative) nuances of our human embodiment through the particular ideas present in the dance.

In dance, a tension between the personal and the universal arises. This tension is seldom recognized in dance aesthetics and is certainly obscured by both expressionist and formalist aesthetic theory. The first concentrates on the subjective or expressive-emotional content of art, and the latter concentrates on its objective-formative character. Neither one alone accounts for subjective-objective relational factors in art – and thereby misses the whole.[2] Indeed it seems to me that dance has as much to do with objective mastery of movement as it has with self-expression. Skill moves one toward freedom, beyond self and toward others, affirming human worth in work that strives for excellence, while self-expression emphasizes the finite personal self. Yet dance is innocently called self-expression. Perhaps there is both a truth and a fiction in this commonly held belief.

Certainly there is an effort of attention in dance, as in all art, that none can make for me. The personal I is inscribed in my dance—but in some larger sense than self-expression. Even a cursory view of some aspects of self-body-dance relations should reveal this.

Let me begin with the elementary assertion that dancing can direct the person toward wholeness, toward an easy connection of self and body. I could even say that this oneness of self and body is an occasion for using the word *dance.* But the many possibilities inherent in varied aesthetic intentions within dance art complicate this simplicity. For instance, the aesthetic surface of a dance may project a schism between self and body. I can perform a dance in which I seem not to be investing myself, not willing my own movement, not present to my own life, but—like a marionette—moved by the will of another. In fact I have performed such a dance, motivated by Heinrich von Kleist's view that perfect grace is not possible in conscious human movement but appears only in the lack of consciousness of the marionette or in the infinite consciousness of God.[3] Aesthetic intentionality in dance opens up problems of relations between self and body.

As a further complication, the shifting of attention in the journey toward accomplishing the dance one intends has feelings within it of sometimes being at one with one's body and sometimes not. Self and body are sometimes felt as identical and at other times felt as distant or doing battle. I nevertheless cannot escape a general awareness in dance that *I am body,* and that I and my body are a fundamental unity, albeit this is usually subliminal and goes unstated. Later we shall consider why.

In dancing I come to know several selves, or I might think of these as phases or differing moments of my one self. There is the self that is the dance easily and affably, and there is the self that also is the dance but meets it with intentional effort or a restrained edge. Then there is the self that strives to become its intentions, the self that is not yet performing the intended dance, not yet the embodiment of the dance. Thus mastery enters the picture—mastery of the dance, which involves self-mastery, the self that has worked to attain its intentions and is no longer aware of striving. This is the dancing self in moments of sublime play, freedom, and accomplishment.

But these moments have an opposite for every dancer, since even the best dancers may fail. In order to grow, the dancer comes to know the self that incorporates failure and uses failure for positive forward momentum rather than being defeated by it. The good dancer maintains a critical faculty without turning it against herself. There is always something more to be mastered or invented in dance. Thus I come to know myself in various ways through the unique situations and processes of dancing. What is expressed of my self in dance will be derived from how I relate to these processes and how I interpret the specific *aesthetic intentions* involved in each dance I perform.

Self Known in Its Works

Few subjects are as elusive to our grasp as self. From the above, we might ascertain that self is not a fixed phenomenon. Like dance, it is flux and flow. It is manifested through change and only stands still for momentary insights. I recognize my self, or I fail to, by indirection. This is as true in dance as it is in other human endeavors. The mystery of self, as we know ourselves through the mystery of embodiment, is that the self is both the known and the knower, the possessed and the possessor. I have a self that is, if you will, the very self that claims to have a self. Thus if I seek my self directly, I am multiplied, duplicated, and diminished in each successive self-mirroring; or as Kierkegaard puts this closed circularity, "The self is a relation which relates itself to its own self. . . . the self is not the relation but (consists in the fact) that the relation relates itself to its own self."[4]

The self is that which says I and that which at the same time exists I. Bodily existence is given in "I am." I *am* body at the same time I claim to *be* a body; or more curiously and dualistically put, as I claim to *have* a body. When I say "I have a body," I distance my self from my body in order to be in possession of it. I hold it apart; I objectify it. This is not the same thing as saying with religious mystics and modern existentialists, "I am body." Gabriel Marcel recognizes the body as the essential mystery of metaphysics, most fundamentally recognized in reference to self as one's own body. His views eventually influenced contemporary existentialists Paul Ricoeur and Richard Zaner, who interpret self in terms of body and in context.[5] Existentialists from Kierkegaard to Ricoeur have sought to interpret self as indirectly known through its works, its symbols, and its myths.

The existentialist study of the human being as an embodied reality focuses a new attention on the subject of self and authentic selfhood.[6] This focus might be criticized as narcissistic self-absorption were it not an attempt at critical self-examination within a perspective that the self is manifested in a communal context—a world of others. The self that needs vindication through constant surveillance of its effects on others, social critic Christopher Lasch's "performing self," is the self immersed in "the banality of pseudo-self-awareness."[7] This is the self that constantly asks How am I doing? How am I impressing others? This performing self is too often seen in our times. It is not the self that asks the existential questions: Who am I? Does my existence matter at all? Do I have the courage to be as I think I should be? And will I risk standing apart from the crowd? Neither is this the disciplined performing self that is realized through the performing arts, the self that strives for freedom through skill. Nor is it the self that is freely projected into creative endeavors and affirmed as free through them.

The self known in dance is indeed a performing self and is at its best as it moves toward such freedom. The self known in dance moves beyond the limits of our mental cogito. We dance to become acquainted with that which cannot be known by any other means—to find out what can be known through the body as a mental, physical, spiritual whole. Thus we acquire a kind of knowledge we might designate as *experiential*. Indeed, we commonly speak of skill in dance as a form of knowledge and also speak of kinesthetic intelligence as an aspect of skillful dancing. But dance involves more than just knowing how to do a movement. It also involves knowing how to express the aesthetic intent of the movement and how to create aesthetic movement imagery. All of these forms of *knowing how* are forms of bodily lived (experiential) knowledge. As such, they are avenues for self-knowledge.

In fact we commonly speak of dance in terms of knowledge. I might say, for instance, that I know how to do a particular dance or that I do not; or that I am able to make dances out of my knowledge of dance and through my imaginative use of such knowledge. Taking the audience's point of view, I might say that I know a particular work because I am familiar with it or because I have an intimate understanding and experience of it. Well, what do I mean when I say these things? I do not speak simply of an intellectual knowledge accruing from a mental process. I speak of a kind of knowledge that at some point engages what we generally refer to as thought yet ultimately lies outside of it. The thinking that dancing strives to release in both the dancer and the audience is the thinking of the whole-body consciousness. We move beyond (or release) this thinking as we merge with the dance, not as we strive toward it. Martha Graham says that "dance is knowledge."[8] It is, however, knowledge of a particular kind—one not rendered through mental processes but experienced more directly through the body as a feeling, thinking, mysterious whole.

As I come to know my self in my works, they are signed with my being. I cannot know myself in a void; rather, I come to know who I am through the actions I take. In my works, I come to know my possibilities by projecting myself into a future of what I might do—and by following through. To know our selves in our work is to realize our possibilities in action. Ricoeur states how this occurs: "The 'myself' figures in the project as that which will do and that which can do. I project my own self into the action to be done. . . . In projecting myself thus, I objectify myself in a way, as I objectify myself in a signature which I will be able to recognize, identify as mine, as my sign."[9]

Through work the possible is made actual. Ricoeur holds that to project is to open up possibilities by charting the actual. The self that is projected into the work of dance (which is also play and creation) is well attuned to the self of the possible. When I dance, I project myself into the future of my possibilities in Ricoeur's sense, that "what I shall be is not *already* given but depends on what I shall do. My possible being depends on my possible doing."[10] A primary value in dance appears through the actualization of one's possible self, the self freely projected in its works and realized through them.

SELF CREATED IN DANCE

Still further, the dancer's project is qualified through her intention. Thus another value appears in terms of the aesthetic. For the dancer realizes the self that moves with an aesthetic intent; she experiences freedom through consciously willing the dance: deciding, moving, and consenting in the dance for itself.[11] Dance (I will continue to say) is movement detached from instrumental usefulness; it has a primary aesthetic intent. By contrast, movement in sports is goal oriented with a testing intent.[12] The primary intent is not the aesthetic, although the aesthetic may appear — as it may appear in any movement, including those generally unnoticed movements that constitute our daily rituals. In dance the aesthetic is the consciously intended and desired end. Dance has no intrinsic purpose beyond the aesthetic (as I shall take up in detail in the next chapter). When dance is used for other purposes — as in ballet competitions for instance — extrinsic values are imposed. Thus dance provides a unique aesthetic context for self-knowledge and self-expression in terms of human movement.

Movement becomes dance (art) when it fulfills an aesthetic purpose, being valued for its own qualities and not for what it accomplishes. If dance is aesthetically constituted, then the self expressed in dance is also aesthetically constituted. This impersonalizes it, while the self engaged in ordinary expressive discourse and bodily action is personalized. Although dance contains the personal self, it is larger than this self. Dance moves the self beyond a personal identity because it is conditioned by the aesthetic.

Relative to this, dance is also conditioned by the given expressiveness of the human body. This fact may be best explained through Mary Wigman's work, which provides a good point of departure because it is identified with expressionism and, consequently, with self-expression, the latter obscuring its deeper truth. Wigman's work is even more deliberately within the condition of expression than Isadora Duncan's and Rudolph von Laban's. She liberated the body's expressiveness in dance, as she discarded centuries of balletic manners to explore the body's expressive nature — to listen to it and to reveal its primal energies, its pastoral moods, its sharp edges, its tenderness, and its violence. One of Wigman's goals (unlike Duncan's) was to free the body in dance from the dictatorship of music, and she carried Laban's efforts more successfully from movement theory to aesthetic realization than he himself did. Wigman opened a self-searching approach to dancing, which influenced succeeding forms of theater dance, dance education, and even dance therapy. Yet the expressive element, even as Wigman dealt with it, had little to do with personal self-expression. Her dances were not about her person. They were an extension of the expressive condition of the human body.

Maurice Merleau-Ponty explains the expressive condition of the body this way: "All perception, all action which presupposes it, and in short every human use of the body is already *primordial expression.*" Further, "the spirit of the world is ours as soon as we know how to *move ourselves* and *look*. These simple acts already enclose the secret of expressive action."[13] Certainly, the expressive conditon of the body may be dealt with in different ways in dance, but as a condition of the body, expression is always present. Wigman saw dance as "one of the original vehicles of human expression."[14] Her themes were not personal; they were universal. Many of her titles evoke the mysteries of nature, life, and death: *Storm Song, Dance for the Earth, Death Call,* and *The Witches Dance.* Individuality, however, was important to her work, which grew out of introspection and a belief in communicating "the personal experience of the creator."[15] Wigman spoke of the personal in art, but within a larger view of the creative and the human.

She concerned her art with the tension between individuality and universality, a tension illuminated by Leo Tolstoy.[16] Her initiation of modernism in dance theater afforded a new awareness of the expressive body, the body belonging to a more inclusive world of nature and a wider world of others.[17] Similarly, Doris Humphrey, another innovator in early modern dance, dealt with the dynamics that move the self beyond the personal in relation to larger enveloping spheres of meaning. The individual's relation to the group is one of her major themes; her *New Dance* (1935–36) provides the most explicit example of this.

In view of the aesthetic and the expressive conditions of dance, a broad summary statement of the self created in dance can be formulated, one that explains the self in relation to the dance — the self overlooked in most aesthetic discourse. In dance, the self is created in two oppositional but reconcilable ways. As a dancer, I am both universalized (like dancers in every culture and time) and personalized (I am my own unrepeatable body; I am my own dance). Taking this thought one step further, I recognize that when I reconcile these two aspects of dancing, the larger one wins. I move beyond the confines of persona (meaning mask or that which *appears* as evidently personal about me) to union with the larger aesthetic purpose of the dance and in communion with others. The magic here is that self is surpassed toward the dance and toward others. This is the aesthetically constituted, universalized (impersonalized) self.

The self the dancer comes to know and express emerges from a synthesis of the personal and the universal. This is the self known in and through the dance. In the dance, the dancer's individuality is transcended and affirmed as it is overcome in favor of the dancer she becomes. Her individuality is present *in tension* with the universalizing impulse of the dance as it unites her self with other selves in understanding through the dance. Thus her individuality is engaged in surpassing self and is affirmed not as it sets her apart from others but as it becomes a binding element. The dancer transcends the limits of self in shedding her everyday persona, so characteristically and habitually assumed. She achieves this by consciously embodying the characteristic aesthetic qualities of each dance she performs.

THE I THAT DANCES I

"I," you say, and are proud of the word. But greater is that in which you do not wish to have faith—your body and its great reason: that does not say "I," but does "I."—Friedrich Nietzsche

As the self embodies the dance, something changes in the I that dances I. The self that dances I is not the same self that thinks I, not the same self that ordinarily speaks and gestures I. Something changes in my perception of myself and of my body as myself in the I that dances I.

Self-perception in dance grows out of the wholeness of the deeply and subtly minded body-of-action. When I dance, I call upon resources not ordinarily called for in everyday life. Dance movement is not functional movement used to accomplish a purposeful task. While functional task movement may appear in a dance, it is divorced from its original intention and changes by virtue of being placed in a dance context. Dance is movement set apart from life; that is, movement seen for itself, most particularly its aesthetic qualities. Thus when I dance my attention must be lifted out of my useful body-of-tasks, my body-of-habituated-movement. Bodily awareness—my awareness of myself (and my-body-as-myself)—changes.

When I dance I assume a new body. I reach into a sacred and mysterious ground. Gabriel Marcel believes that the modern age in pursuit of technical progress and comfort has lost a sense of the mysterious. If I accept that I am just like everybody else, I am excluded from the mystery of my own body. In dance, however, this mystery is tapped. The art of dance exists mysteriously and ineluctably through the body and the dancing self.

The dancer dances the mystery of the body not as uniquely apart from others but as universally a part of them. In this she is her own unrepeatable self but moves beyond personal limitations in union with the binding (communicable) substance of the dance. In this it is not she who is presented but the dance itself. It is her obligation to present the dance, not her self – to become one with the dance and the other for whom it is intended.

In art we attempt to unravel the mysteries of self indirectly – through work, play, and creation. The self is not revealed by design but *because* design is created. Self appears in its works; it remains impervious to direct assault; it recedes when confronted as something set apart. The self is revealed in context of intention and action.

Self is manifested in the I of the present-centered, temporal subject of *I am*. To say "I exist," Marcel states, is to "put myself forward," to actively exclaim myself to "*produce* myself."[18] This is existence experienced as an "exclamatory consciousness of self," expressing the sacred, astonishment, and wonder.[19] *Self is known* through action in the I of the realized possible self of *I can*. *Self is experienced* as materially or concretely limited within this skin and none other in the object of *I-it*. This is the distinctive I that relates to a tangible world of objects and others. *Self transcends objectivity* altogether in its most intangible context, the I of mystical union in Martin Buber's *I-thou* (the I that might also be associated with the peak experiences Abraham Maslow writes of).

The I that dances I is the I that affirms all of these selves. The I that dances I affirms concrete existence as well as the metaphysical mystery of embodied consciousness. Dance may be essentially an aesthetic expression of this mystery and, as such, its acknowledgement. It is thus that I understand dancer Pamela Trippel's definition of dance as "shadowboxing with God."[20] Since we cannot live in a perpetual mystery, we invented dancing to give the shadows visible form, if only in the fleeting present and of that particular mystery dance can manifest.

The Dancer Is the Dance

MORE THAN SELF

Dance is a creative and aesthetic extension of our embodiment. The body and the dance are inseparable. The body is the dance, as the dancer is

Pamela Trippel in *Dance Da Da* (1979). Photo: June Burke.

the dance; the body is concretely there in the dance. The body is not the instrument of dance; it is the subject of dance. The body cannot be an instrument, because it is not an object as other instruments are. Even when it is objectified in dance, it retains its subjectivity.

The body is not something I possess to dance with. I do not order my body to bend here and whirl there. I do not think "move," then do move. No! I am the dance; its thinking is its doing and its doing is its thinking. I am the bending and I am the whirling. My dance is my body as my body is myself.

Calvin Schrag also rejects an instrumental view of the body: "The body is not itself an instrument. The body is myself in my lived concreteness. It is *who I am* and indicates the *manner in which I am.* The lived body refers to my personal manner of existing, and the meanings attached to this manner of existing, in a world in which I experience presence."[21] Although I am embodied in my dance, it is not *who I am* that is projected in my dance. Something changes. My dance presence is not the same as my personal life presence. I do not express the personal manner in which I am nor my self; *I express the dance.*

The dancer does not project herself. If she is good, she projects the dance. Yet the dancer has herself to deal with in the dance; it is she who dances. She dances her dance as an aesthetic projection for others, a projection that includes them since they are reflected in the human material of her dance. As her dance includes others, it moves beyond the personal; yet it is inextricably bound up in her individuality. We rightly speak of the art of Balanchine, Astaire, or Isadora, but it is not a strictly personal identity that we attach. It is an aesthetic or a stylistic identity. We identify Balanchine's work as abstract, Astaire's as charming, and Isadora's as free. Dance works are individualized works with distinct aesthetic characteristics. The human material of dance remains the same, but artists continually find new ways to state or stylize it. Dance works express not so much the self as the seemingly endless ways in which our bodily lived existence can be aesthetically (or affectively) moved. So the dancer is more than who she is as she becomes the dance; she fulfills its aesthetic essence, instantiating others in it as she dances for them.

WELL-DOING, UNLIMITED SELF

When I am my dance, I am not limited to being myself. When I am my dance, it is my self unlimited that is expressed. And I cannot *be* my dance until I can *do* my dance. Then the dancer that I am appears.

The dancer does not show the audience what she cannot do. If she is good, she performs with ability. If there are movements that she just cannot do, and there certainly will be for every dancer, they will not be in her dance. What cannot be done, technically speaking, will not be done. Of course she can attempt to do something and fail. This is always possible. When she succeeds in uniting with her intentions in the dance, she expresses infinite possibility.

This is why the best dancers seem to have no limits; they seem to be able to do anything, however contrary to fact this may be. The good dancer does not project her limitations; rather she projects her mastery of the dance she is performing, engendering a sense of limitlessness in an infinite (unrestricted) present. This may be described as an expansive experience of present time, which the dancer's mastery of the dance may engender in her (as she fulfills the purpose of the dance) and in the audience (as they meld with it).

The self the dancer projects is chosen: a selected, aesthetically constituted, and practiced self. The audience does not want to see what the dancer can only attempt to do. They want to see what she has mastered. Graham saw dancers as God's acrobats in her work *Acrobats of God* (1960). Dance exists in correct doing. The dancer seeks aesthetic doing. Whatever is being expressed through her movement seeks its right form and most perfect execution. What she is doing is often less important than how she does it. Or maybe the *what* is completely qualified by the *how,* because what we see is qualitative action.

When I dance, I want to get it right. Like all dancers, I do not want to make mistakes. Good dancing is simply right doing, right in rhythm, sense, shape, and image—an image I feel and live, for I am concretely in it and all there can be of it. If dance can project human infinitude in the right moment, it need not be complex or extremely difficult to be valued as art. Even the simplest movement has infinity in it when it is lived by the audience and the dancer together as the right movement, in the right moment, in the right image.

Am I saying that a dance can be right? This implies that a dance can also be wrong. Can art, and dance as art, be right and wrong? There is no moral imperative here. Yet, curiously, these words apply. When I make a dance, I search for the right movement. When I perform, I want to get it right. I think all dancers do. Right in this case is an aesthetic imperative. The quest is the aesthetic responsiveness of the lived body to the requirements of the particular dance being done. A dance can be right—and accompanied by feelings of unbounded presence, projecting that image to the audience. It can also be wrong—and accompanied by feelings of boundedness or self-limitation in relation to the requirements of the dance. I can be wrong, which makes the dance wrong. Then I fail to become the dance, and what appears before me is my self, not the dance. The dance terminates in self-consciousness when I experience an acute awareness of self-limitation.

In dance the body can be concretely lived as the right movement and the infinite moment. It can also be lived as failure. If failure was not possible, dance would not be potentially valuable. In a well-done dance, the self is lived beyond personal finitude and limitations. The body is experienced as all of self and more than self. Perhaps this is why dance is used to mediate between mortals and gods in ritual practice. Among the African Asante, the chief must also be the best dancer.[22] The value of bodily well doing is embedded in the dance aesthetic, the affective in dancing. And it crosses all forms: sacred, folk, social, entertainment, and art. That which moves us in dance must be well done. The dance, in fact, is not aesthetically constituted until it is well done. Its aesthetic being is in its doing.

The Dance Object: I-It

THE BODY-OBJECT KNOWN IN DANCE

Dance can be right or wrong in its aesthetic formulation and in its performance, because it is objectively constituted. This means simply that it is an object that can be appraised; it appears before us as a phenomenon with discernible structures and qualitative characteristics. In dance, human movement is objectified, shaped, or defined. Once it is defined, it is there with all of its inherent performance challenges. Every dance presents different problems to the performer. The aesthetic solution is what the performer seeks. Right doing is aesthetic doing in dance.

When my dance has been objectified – that is, given a repeatable movement structure – it stands on its own as a concrete object that can be perceived by others. My body also becomes concrete in the dance object and in my perception of myself, as my dance is known by me and performed for others. And if my dance becomes qualified as an art object, it must stand out for others. No, I cannot decide by looking in a mirror whether what I make has value as art. I must risk myself toward others. I can judge, and I must judge, my own work; the artist's judgments are actually the basis for the work. But part of the work's reason for being is not realized until it becomes an aesthetic object for others, until it is finally subjectively realized in them, lived through their own experience and body aesthetic. Something in dance causes me to risk myself toward the world, to test my reality – indeed, to create myself beyond my body as ordinarily lived. My dancing is most real when it is realized in an other. The other intensifies and tests my experience of myself.

Consider the first project of a beginning dance student. He practices in his basement, in his bedroom, anywhere but in front of others, until he finally has it right. He is both attracted and repelled by the prospect of dancing his dance for others. At this stage, he doesn't perform for a theater audience, and maybe he never will; but he will experience one of the conditions of dance as art as he *objectifies his body* in movement and expresses it for others.

The condition of dancing before others, and consequently one of the values of objectifying in dance, imposes the problem of expression. To express or to give form to something to be received by an other, whether in words or in movement, is to manifest one's body toward the other. The knower (the other) and the known (the dancer) become dynamically interrelated in a communicative process through the object (the dance), which mediates what can be known (the substance of the dance). If I dance only for myself, I am not brought into a dynamic intersubjective relation with the other. I am simply bound up in my own subjectivity. I am not required to meet the objective world where concrete things are presented, known, and qualified as art.

THE DANCER AS BODY-OBJECT

Because dance is presented (or performed) for others, it objectifies the body. The dance produced is an art object. Like other objects of art, it has an observable form. Thus the dancer, inseparable from the dance, is also objectively known as the dance is perceived by the other, the audience.

In the object seen as visible movement — the dance flowing through time and shaping space — we see the dancer. As material form moving through space, she is not separable from the *thing* we perceive as the dance. She is the concrete form before us, even though we see her passing through time, which makes dance seem transparent and illusive. In the time of the dance, the dancer's body becomes the objective dance — an object, an it — but at the same time an I, because the lived dimension is always present. Although we may see the dancer as a solid moving object, the body can never be completely objectified in the manner of nonhuman material (as in the plastic arts and architecture).

The body is living, dynamic material, and each body aesthetic is dynamically individual, impervious to complete objectification. The dance dynamic is created through the lived dynamics of the body moving through time and space and inevitably passing away. While a dance usually has an objective, repeatable structure (it can be performed by several people), it is subject to individual interpretation and dependent upon the individual body aesthetic of the particular dancer. Once more the self appears. All of this contributes to the difficulty of capturing the dance object and the dancer as an object. The lived dynamic continually surpasses the object, the concrete continually eludes us. Yet we see that the dance and its lived dynamic exist through a concrete presence, the dancer.

THE SELF OBJECTIFIED

As shown above, the audience may observe the dance as a dynamic object. But what about the dancer? Objectification of dance and consequently the body is also required of the dancer in learning, knowing, and presenting the dance. Part of the dancer's power lies in her ability to objectify, to visualize herself as she may appear to others, to make herself into the dance she visualizes. The dancer objectifies her body, and her self—but in a curious and unique sense that I can describe best in terms of self evidence. The dance is distanced from me as an object when I visualize it or seek to convert it into my own movement. The object dissolves when I achieve my intentions in motion. My awareness changes as I become the dance, reminding me that the significance of my dance—its signifying power—depends on the inescapable lived moment of its execution in which I experience my body as subject (myself) and object (the dance), simultaneously.

The self is objectified in dance within the condition of its lived ground. Dance is created form, because it is created as an object with discernible form.[23] Preceding objectification, however, is the subjective condition of its lived ground, the human body—the first, the given, and the assumed (the hidden) condition of human movement. Dances are created through the objectification of movement subjectively lived through the body as the self is lived. Consequently the dancer's body and her self are created in the dance object—created as the dance.

Objectification (or creation) of the body in dance occurs in a positive way when the body is understood as the self. Objectifying human movement—giving it presentational, objective form in a dance—is not a process that can be divorced from the self. For instance, the dancer is restricted by self-limits, the limits of being *this* body with *these* abilities and not others. And she is bounded by the limits of her will and daring. These are experienced as bodily limits and, at the same time, as self-limits in performing the dance. They are tested and eventually known as they are dealt with in performance. Shortly, we shall see that these known limits can become challenges, limits to be overcome in extending self-boundaries and self-knowledge.

I am created in my dance, because I am objectively constituted in the structure of the dance. At the same time, I am extended beyond my personal identity. A larger identity appears as I meet the dance. The self that appears before me is the self of my possibilities. The dancer realizes the self—or comes to know herself—in terms of her capacity to create the self of her fullest possibilities.

Here Arturo Fallico's description of the "possible-self," which is revealed in art objects, takes on special meaning.[24] For nowhere is the self and its possible modes of expression (from representational to abstract) more concretely incorporated in the art object than in dance. The dancer's accomplishments and failures as she attempts to meet her possibilities will certainly be realized in terms of what she attempts in dance. But they will be experienced intimately as her own successes or failures. The paradox is that, although she is not personified as herself in her dance, she lives her successes and failures in dance as inescapably as she lives herself.

Dance may bring the dancer into harmony with that which is already invested as good (or assumed to be good) in dance—the creative, the aesthetic, and the lived values of dance. Thus the possible self may be realized as creative, aesthetic, and vital. On the other hand, dance also opens the dancer to the existential problem of nothingness. The dancer faces the existentially open problem of creating value, as all artists do at some point. What is given in her own nature will become extended or changed in training, patterned by her choices, and influenced by her exercise of will and imagination. She may become aesthetically valuable if she succeeds in her performance or aesthetically disvaluable if she fails.

THE BODY-OBJECT: I-IT

For the dancer, the I that dances I is in the performance. All of the performing arts are qualified in a unique manner by this I. They communicate through the artist, but they transform the artist's personal qualities through an aesthetic projection. I am aesthetically constituted as an object in my dance—an it. Even though I am I, I become an it, objectifying myself and the dance as I strive toward this it.

Martin Buber's metaphor "I-It" describes the initial objective positioning of the dancer to the dance.[25] She positions the dance apart from herself in order to learn it. In giving form to the dance as something, an it, the dancer experiences the dance as an objective, sometimes as an obstacle to overcome. Becoming the dance (we shall soon see) is her goal. When she reaches her goal, the dance object dissolves; it is embodied, or the body is "in sympathy with the object" (recalling Marcel).

At first, the dance is necessarily an it. The dancer knows it as an it, as a unique configuration of challenges. Every dance presents unique expressive and technical difficulties precisely because it is an original. More specifically, in virtuoso dance or dance that challenges the dancer's physical performance limits, the dancer strives to move beyond her physical limits. Each limit overcome presents a new limit. The body's material as the material of the dance can change as it becomes more flexible, or stronger, or more articulate in precise expressive quality. But it is material; it is finite. The dancer repeatedly encounters this material it as her limit. As she grows in artistry, she expands her limits. And as the body that is it changes, so does the body that is I.

When the dancer exceeds her past limitations, she embodies the value of achievement as she successfully performs more difficult movement. This is a creation of self, because something new appears that was not there before—a new skill—and she has done it herself. No one can do her dance for her. If her dance is appreciably difficult, it can be valued as an achievement by the audience. This achievement is one of the primary values of virtuoso dancing, which is not a matter of simple mechanics—because, in dance, the subject is embodied in the art. The dancer signifies *human* achievement in moving beyond the ordinary. In an ethereal dance, she might even present the illusion of transcending the material reality of her body, as she embodies extremely difficult movement with apparently superhuman ease.

Bodily lived limits are tested and expanded in dances that stress overcoming the obstacles of space and time by means of such skills as soaring, stretching, jumping, leaping, running, twisting, speed, speed in turning, abrupt and complete stopping, or effortless balancing in risky positions, to name a few. The dancer experiences these motions as she embodies their sensations. Sensations of bodily being are tested and extended as she aesthetically objectifies them (shapes and forms them) in dance.

As the visual artist represents and extends our vision, so the dancer represents and extends our body's vitality. Her art draws upon lived sense ability and projects an aesthetically vital bodily being. Thus the attainment of aesthetic value increases bodily being for both the dancer and the audience. As body and self are objectified in dance, bodily limitations are tested, aesthetically formulated, and expanded. When the object of attention dissolves in consciousness — as the dance is realized — the affective (aesthetic) qualities of human motion are realized; the limited self is surpassed; vital existence and our own vital body (appreciated for itself) are brought to our attention.

Being the Dance: I-Thou

In contrast to the objective positioning in the I-it relation, Buber's I-thou relation is his image for mystical union. The I-thou image best describes for me the preobjective experience of dancing when "I exist my dance" as "I exist my body."[26] Then there is no separation, no thought for the dance, because the thought would turn it into an object. When I become my dance, it becomes consonant with my consciousness. The difference between the dance and myself disappears.

Phenomenology contends that consciousness always has an object. But I have described a pure consciousness, which is nothing unless I can equate it with a state of being, possibly pure subjectivity; not as a metaphysic that escapes the body but as lived by the body because it has become the *body*'s consciousness. As the dance is fully realized, it ceases to be an object of consciousness; it dissolves in perfected action. To understand the dancer as the dance is to understand a point of unification, which is a state of being when the dance is lived not as an object but as a pure consciousness. When the dance has become so thoroughly me that I no longer think about it, it becomes my consciousness. I become centered in my action. I do not look back on it or anticipate it. I am spontaneously present in it.

This merely describes the dance as a point in time when the full body consciousness is present centered. The dance is not an object to me, neither are its time or space. My movement is not an object to me—the dance is not my object, because I am living its moving. The being of the dance is there in its moving. My being is in my moving. I am also not aware of others, lest they become my object. While dance as art is intended for others, the body as subjectively lived in dance is an experience that precedes any awareness of purpose. The lived qualities of the dance are the dance's expressive values. They are only potentially artful values for others. The first requisite of dancing is the unification of the self with the intended movement. Before my dance can be valued by others, I must become one with my intentions in action. At this point, intentions are not objects; they cease to exist—they have disappeared in the dance; or I might say, they have become the dance.

The I-thou relation describes simple wholeness, the dissolution of objectivity. It is difficult to conceive as relation, because there is no *thing*—it has disappeared. I do not live myself toward the dance when I am unified in it because I am not aware of it as a thing. I am its unfolding, with no thought about it. Buber's I-thou image of unification provides an image for understanding the preobjective or subjective experience of dancing, the mystical innocence of the dancer as the dance, the point at which the dance is lived as the self, the point in lived time when the dance has become so completely incorporated by the dancer that it is her body as naturally as her walking is. This point is present in the prereflective lived-body experience of dancing, but it is lost precisely when it is recognized, which transfers the dance and the dancer immediately into an object.

Dancing is a spiritual endeavor in the sense that it is a quest for self-unification. The dancer seeks to become one with her acts, which are none other than her own. She seeks to unite body-subject and body-object, uniting the body she is with the body imaged in the dance. Her self is projected toward the dance, to become the dance. She wants to become that which she images in movement. She struggles for spontaneity in the struggle for correct execution. She seeks aesthetic solutions to the problems of the dance. She wants to be completely present to the dancing, spontaneously centered in it—not behind it or ahead of it. If her concentration is broken, without recriminations, she starts over again. As her ability increases, her concentration increases. She cannot win the dance if she blames herself for mistakes. She does not want to concentrate on herself; she wants to concentrate on the dance. Eventually she wants to be concentrated in it. Her concentration becomes the process of its own erasure, allowing her the possibility of becoming perfectly centered in her dance, or of being unified in a vibrant presentness. As she attains her purposes in dance, the vibrant life of her dance appears. In mystical thought and art, present centeredness is valued as participation in the essence of God.

Marcel and Buber posit a mystical loss of the objective otherness of self, persons, things, actions, and experiences. This may be described as becoming the dance or as dissolving the object. It may also be understood as a bodily lived consonance with intention, with nature, or with other people.

Marcel writes of the preobjective unity of self and other in a way that recalls the transpersonal I-thou of Buber: "As outcome of a conversation with B. I am obliged to admit that it is absurd to speak of the 'thou' and thus to consider as a substantive what at bottom is the very negation of all substantiality. In reality, once I have singled it out, I objectivise a particular aspect of the experience of intimacy. From the core of the *us* I subtract the element that is not-me and call it *thou*."[27]

Buber's I-thou expresses a relation, not admitting of a thou that can be singled out. His is a poetic symbol of preobjective transcendent oneness – a singular presence, yet nevertheless a self-surpassing relation that we "can stand in" with other beings, with nature, and with God. He sees this relation as "the eternal source of art."[28]

3

DANCE ITSELF

Of Our Own Making

I have said that dance is an aesthetic expression of the body and that the body is aesthetically constituted in dance. This involves a concern for an aesthetic constitution of the self. I have also held that what can be known and subsequently valued about the body and the self through dance is known and valued aesthetically. Such statements require further explanations of the aesthetic and, more particularly, the aesthetic in dance, which involves the ever-present subjective dimension of embodiment – the body-subject, which is impossible to know as the body-object is known. Our subjectivity is lived rather than known. This is why I describe the body in dance as objectively known and subjectively lived.

We have considered the difficulty of viewing dances (and dancers) as objects. Nevertheless, I have held that, as works of art with specifiable characteristics, dances may be objectively known; we can perceive and describe them as things. However, when we look for a material structure and substance in dance, it eludes us. Finally, we may see that dance possesses such material identity as may be sensed only in and through human movement: that *dance itself is entirely of our own making, moving, and perceiving.* Here I am concerned with a definition of dance that accounts for this, as I reduce dance to its essential terms as art – as I isolate the dance aesthetic.

Primary to a definition of dance is its aesthetic intent, its purpose. So far, I have held that the aesthetic is the affective. Now a fuller definition can be given. While various aspects of the aesthetic in dance unfold throughout this volume, what follows next (since it is impossible to say everything at once, although this is the temptation) positions the aesthetic as *intrinsic and subjective*. This leads to a consideration of the capacity of the dance itself to elicit our aesthetic response, requiring us to describe aesthetic qualities or values as properties of particular works—and thus to view the *objective* status of the aesthetic, also.

Aesthetic values can be differentiated from ethical values according to the kind of value, or the determined good. Ethics deals with questions of moral value, or what is right or good action from a moral point of view. *Good* has no moral connotation in the aesthetic realm but is, rather, a qualitative measure of perception, valuation, and evaluation. Its realm of effectiveness is the qualitatively affective.

The aesthetic exists intrinsically within the subjective field. It becomes a value when it is termed *aesthetic value*, a quality of subjectivity toward which we take a positive attitude. Such subjective qualities are nothing more than the qualities of our own experience—lived qualities, which are finally affirmed as lived values, or the good in experience. This tells us that aesthetic values are founded in subjectivity, that they have their source in *felt life*—or I could say *sentient life*. I can further delineate sentient life as consisting of affective qualities, feelings that are qualitatively distinct in sensation. We feel good, bad, indifferent, excited, attracted to something, repelled by it, and so on. These are distinct qualities of feeling in sentient life. As affective qualities, they are not only *in* sentience, they *influence* it. An entire range of lived values appears here. Still further, sentience exists within the larger realm of the subjective field, which contains other aspects of the self, such as intellect, judgment, and intuition. Stated less abstractly, the subjective field implies a totality of consciousness, which is lived by each individual as *the self*. It is the condition for realization of aesthetic values in the intersubjective field, which includes *the other*—the topic of the next chapter. I should establish first that it is only in subjective life that perception and aesthetic valuing of any object is at all possible.

On another level, the aesthetic can be defined as those qualities in objects that influence feeling. For instance, in classical art and dance, harmony and proportion are the desirable qualities. An ultimate concern in aesthetic discourse is aesthetic perception itself—or how human beings are constituted so that the aesthetic as qualities in objects can be perceived and felt as the aesthetic in our experience, *those qualities that move us in subjective life.* Correspondence of object and subject appears then as an aesthetic problem.

I am proposing that *the aesthetic,* defined as the affective, is a quality of being moved, in the sense that when I say "I am moved" I mean "I feel something," and in fact my sense of feeling has been increased. Moreover, when I say I feel something, I am implying an awareness of my sentient self. However, the aesthetically affective does not necessarily move us into action; being moved in feeling is the end result of the aesthetically affective.

I am also proposing (at least it is implied throughout this work) that the aesthetic is intrinsically active as a quality of our experience—but in relation to inherent properties in objects. This view of the relatedness of intrinsic values (qualities of experience) and inherent values (qualities in objects) that have the capacity to elicit an aesthetic response is consistent with value theorist Paul Taylor's definitions of intrinsic and inherent values.[1] He classifies *inherent* value as one form of extrinsic value—which is, by definition, dependent value. Conversely, *intrinsic* value is independent and experiential value. It is finally "the good" in experience. Thus the object depends on the subject for its value. This is not to say that objects do not contain distinct properties. It does assert, however, that the process of valuing is founded experientially in subjectivity.

Aesthetic values are qualitatively distinct properties that inhere in objects of attention, including objects of art. They indicate an object's unique potential to elicit an aesthetic response. For instance, Trisha Brown's dance works *Lateral Pass* (1985) and *Set and Reset* (1983) display amorphous aesthetic qualities of flight, light, ease, and fluidity. Uncanny evaporations of movement and the obliqueness of her dancing contribute to the unique effect of the whole. Her works linger tenuously just outside the realm of completion, continuously in motion, seldom resolved in solid shapes or caught in time. These are properties we can identify and describe (in various ways) as belonging to or inherent in much of Brown's work as it came to fruition in the 1980s. These qualities are part of the aesthetic constitution of the dances.

It is through such qualities that Brown's dances open the viewer to the ongoing flow of his own bodily lived aesthetic as they are valued in his experience (intrinsically). Works of other artists may also be aesthetically affective in the same relational way, but with an entirely different emphasis. Natsu Nakajima's works, for instance, allow us to experience our primal emotional selves in highly distilled gestures which we can relate to ourselves. Her dance *Niwa* (The Garden, North American premier 1985), is a journey of passages from infancy to old age. In contrast to Brown's work, it engages the audience with particular intensity through tightly drawn, restrained qualities of movement given dramatic shape and ecstatic emphasis.

Aesthetic values, then, are properties inherent in works of art (or other objects) that influence the aesthetic in experience. Thus the aesthetic is both objective and subjective, with the subjective in the independent position of intrinsic (both first and final) valuing. A dance has intrinsic value when it is *experienced* as good; its inherent values are its constitutive properties, its qualities of movement, rhythm, compositional design, dramatic character, and so on. These qualities are finally realized as aesthetic values, or as aesthetic, only as we relate to them and value them intrinsically in experience.

The aesthetic is also a stasis, or an end in itself, as all intrinsic values are. Intrinsic values are primary by definition and are ends in themselves because they do not depend on other values. Accordingly, I propose that art is a circular process of our own making, which begins and ends in heightened sensibility and involves an intelligent level of creativity toward this end. The very word *art* is equated with a vital level of value realization. The still point of aesthetic realization is this vital level of sensibility, the point at which the object of art is freely valued in subjectivity. I can extend this thought to describe the aesthetic stasis in dance, its aesthetic end, or the particular matrix that centers value formation in dance. I consider this first as *vital movement sensibility* and finally as *the vital body.*

Dance is by necessity grounded in vital movement sensibility, that of the choreographer, the dancer, and the audience. It is grounded in movement that is aesthetically created and valued. In a technically narrow sense, we realize in dance the esthetic in the kinesthetic. We realize beauty or other desirable qualities through movement sensibility, or the kinesthetic sense—our ability to sense energy, temporality, and spatial locatedness through bodily movement. Whatever else it may involve, dance must involve the kinesthetic at vital and intelligent levels. Dance is necessarily experienced and valued kinesthetically — through the movement sense, through the lived body and the sentient self.

When dance is valued as art, it engages us in the vital qualities of its medium — the vital qualities of the lived body. On a primal level, dance expresses and is experienced through the vital body — through movement, not words. Thus it does not necessarily express (or represent) literal emotions or feelings, although it can. It is, however, necessarily rooted in human feeling and founded in kinesthetic sensitivity and intelligence.

Intrinsic value in dance (as in all art) is contained within the experience of dance itself. The dancer and the audience both experience (and may be moved by) the dance, but in different ways. In both cases, however, the experience is valued for itself when the aesthetic is realized. Dance does not end in any action outside of itself but rather is realized as itself. Dance as art is not intended to motivate action but to be valued for itself as an aesthetic expression of the body that opens us to human feeling through our sentient body-of-action and the power of creative agency.

What we recognize as art does not in its intrinsic and first function (aesthetic function) motivate action; its first function is to evoke our receptivity and aesthetic response. Art has an aesthetic end. Any other end for which art might be the means (such as its instrumental use in education, therapy, or politics) is extrinsic. Extrinsic purposes are secondary; they depend on the first (and intrinsic) purposes of aesthetic realization. James Joyce succinctly isolates the aesthetic as the end of art, as its purpose: "Art . . . is the human disposition of sensible or intelligible matter for an aesthetic end."[2]

The dancer, the audience, and the critic come to know the dance as an art object, something to be performed, to be perceived, to be valued or disvalued, and to be judged. The choreographer, whose role I examine shortly, precedes all of this. The choreographer is the first to give image to the dance, which originates in his imagination and through his ability to shape (create) movement according to his intentions. When he creates movement imagery and its qualitative properties, he creates that which may be valued. But still, this value is not complete (as art) until it is made visible by the dancer and valued by another.

I speak of the audience as the other in a general sense, but valuing dance is of course an individual matter. The individual other is required for the full realization of dance as art. The question of wide recognition or critical acclaim is not addressed here. Rather, I am describing a very basic subjective-objective-subjective circular process of valuing, one that begins and ends in the subjective position, with the dance itself (made visible and concrete by the dancer) as the objective presence in between. The dance itself presences as an object through the dancer's movement and our own efforts of attention. It becomes a free essence as it is completed beyond such effort, and evokes our receptivity as we merge with it.

While the critic participates in this valuing process as a member of the audience, he objectifies the dance on another level by describing and judging it for publication. But dance, more than any other art, remains impervious to complete objectification. It is created anew in each action of the dancer and in the perceptual enactment of the other. It can never be completely objectively positioned for the choreographer, the dancer, the audience, or the critic. Their human likeness is in the living material of dance, and they themselves are in the perceptual completion of its valuing. It is of their own making; without them, the dance disappears. The dance begins and ends in lived time and immediate perception. It leaves nothing concrete—as object—behind. It might be critiqued, filmed, or notated; but these are records of the dance—not the dance itself.

Irreducible Structure of Dance

Yet the dance as a dynamic object is there; it is something that has been created and that can be recreated in performance. George Beiswanger writes of the dance as concretely experienced: "That a dance enters experience and is unmistakably *here* with its *there* is all the excuse we have, and all the reason we need, in order to affirm the actuality and inevitability of its *there*. The dance as it unfolds is so strong a fact that, like the hills and the stars, it could always have been and might always be (though we know that its present occasion is for the time being only)."[3]

A dance can be perceived as concretely *there* through its material substance, a substance that has been identified as human movement (and stillness) in time and space, necessarily lived through the self and existing through the body and its lived ground. Furthermore, dance movement presented as art is created to fulfill an aesthetic purpose. I am assuming that, as art it is presented, it is expressed for-other. Within all these conditions, we recognize dance as art. Therefore, *movement* of the human body, *aesthetic expression* of the body, and artistic *creativity* are the defining conditions in the phenomenological structure of dance art — its irreducible phenomena.

I have been considering the dance (and the dancer) as a dynamic and temporal object realized (made real) and valued within the subjective field. This field is a totality of consciousness that is intrinsic (independently valuable) and experiential (lived). Further, it is a field that contains the art object and surpasses it (because art has its origin and completion in feeling and imagination). This is merely to establish that the dance phenomenon appears (as an object or material presence) necessarily within the subjective field. I have also established that dances are constituted as objects with common grounds, or phenomenological features, by which they are recognized as dances.

From the foregoing, a summary phenomenological definition of dance art (also its irreducible structure) appears: *Dance is human movement created and expressed for an aesthetic purpose.* We see in this definition that human movement is the material condition (ground) and unique aesthetic matter of dance. Dance is unique as art through its material condition, which (I continue to stress) is lived through the body and valued through the body.

Since the body is also the center of, and the condition for, the subjective field, dance constantly transcends its material structure. Other arts also transcend their material as they are valued in the subjective field, but the material of dance is constant with (or lived within) the subjective field. In a word, human movement is grounded in the lived body. The body is the condition for both dance and the subjective field. It is (at once) the material and the transcendent lived ground of dance. The body in the dance is consonant with the dance; thus it can easily be lost or hidden in consciousness, as the dance takes on a life of its own.

Classical and Existential Models

The dance begins with the choreographer. It is he who originally envisions the aesthetic values of the dance — values made up of movement lived through the body, unavoidably implicating the sentient self. The choreographer creates through his own movement or that of the dancer and through his own power to imagine (give image to) dance movement. Often the choreographer and the dancer are one and the same, or the choreographer may constitute the dance as he makes the dance for someone else. The dancer always gives the choreographer's composition visible form and interprets it.

Like the dancer, the choreographer faces the problem of creation from a base of known values or givens and, at the same time, as an open project in the struggle to bring forth aesthetic values in movement. Finally, he hopes to create a dance that did not exist before. So his possibilities, like the dancer's, are also involved, but from another position. His problem is fundamentally constitutive. He creates dance imagery through the tension between his imagination and the phenomenal givens in dance.

Behind these given conditions is an even wider implication of values. As dance exhibits phenomenal presence through the creative, it invokes free agency, intention, and initiative. As dance exists through the human body, it derives from the body's aesthetic form and psychic life. As dance exists within the condition of human movement, it involves lived (not simply measured) human time and human space. As dance exists within its aesthetic imperative, it involves aesthetic intention and thus, problems of purpose. In addition, dance is not simply an aesthetic expression; when it is performed for-other, it involves cultural values.

The choreographer may also work with traditional, or stylistic, value givens. Within particular periods and aesthetic schools of dance, some aesthetic models (standards, rules, or even ideals) may be value given (assumed and practiced as the aesthetic good). Let us simply bear in mind for now that values invested as good in particular aesthetic models exist in tension with oppositions. (I explore these later as I consider oppositional tension in the evolution of dance.)

Having seen that dance is a value-invested art in its phenomenal structure and in the aesthetic models for particular forms, we can see that the choreographer's process is not completely open. Openness is always there, however, in the creative element as it introduces free agency. So dance engages the choreographer in both its given and its open essence. He can emphasize either invested values (value givens) or creative agency in making a dance. These contrasting possibilities can be made clear using two of George Balanchine's works as examples.

Balanchine, in some of his pieces, emphasizes the givens in classical models, but within a modern aesthetic. In at least one case, his modern classicism affords an example of achievement according to a model of classical harmony, a widely accepted and culturally invested aesthetic good in Western art, intrinsically valued through satisfaction of the harmonious in bodily lived experience. We might even see through Balanchine's modern classicism that harmony has a basis in the nature of the body.

In *Le Tombeau de Couperin* (1975) to Ravel's music, the perfectly balanced Left Quadrille and Right Quadrille unfold as though moved by nature, according to a physical law of equipoise. There is no ostentatious display of technique, no spectacular movement, no struggle to fill a void, or even to fulfill a meaning. Instead there is a simple unfolding of felt mathematics, of both sides of the body, of the male and female complement in partner dancing. There is a givenness of ballet movement vocabulary and also an easy invention. Expression is given in the simple presence of the dancing body, not imposed on it.

Creating substance is not the problem here. The substance of the dance is shaped according to classical characteristics, as they are known within the tradition of ballet and given in the substance of the body. The classical style is already known through the model of harmony and (for dance) related qualities of flow, ease, geometrically clean linearity, symmetry in movement phrasing, and balance in the rhythm of the whole. The dance is choreographically stated through a stylistic (and culturally transmitted) familiarity and (I shall point out) a kinesthetically innate valuing of the harmonious.

I believe we apprehend harmony through feelings that are kinesthetically concordant. Such feelings are possible through the anthropomorphic given of body symmetry. We live body symmetry through a constant balancing of one side of the body with the other in our motions, through applying body symmetry to walking, running, jumping, and leaping, and through even alternations of inhalation and exhalation in breathing. We also resolve motion or find its center to achieve poised balances. Concordant feelings exist through the resolution of tensions within the body kinesthetic and may be compared to the development of tonal magnetism in music—the building and resolution of musical tension. These are felt conditions, providing a basis for intrinsic valuing (in experience) of harmonious dancing.

When a choreographer creates from a classical base, he works through a whole world of known and interrelated aesthetic values. These are incorporated (or value given) in classicism. When he seeks an aesthetic realization through the classical model of harmony, he seeks to know and to produce the aesthetic as the felt (or bodily lived) good in harmonious movement images, stressing a value-laden base of givens. The classical aesthetic model of harmony unites us with philosophical views that accept given form and value at their root. It engenders aesthetic values inherent in cosmological, metaphysical, and essentialist views. Dances created out of classical aesthetic models stand in contrast to dances that grow out of the existential struggle to bring forth form, to discover new form, to tap the roots of imagination where nothing is taken for granted.

When a choreographer creates from a radically open base, rejecting forms given in established models, invention is central to the choreographic problem. Creativity is thus approached as a value-divested and existentially open process. Here the creation of values from a base of nothingness becomes primary. We can observe this (to the degree that this is possible within the ballet genre) in another work by Balanchine. His *Duo Concertant* (1972) to Stravinsky's music for violin and piano is not based on an assumed harmonious formalism. Fraught with ambivalence, it evokes an existential urgency and creative agency. The relationship of the partners in this duet is dissonant and traced with sorrow. Their moving together and apart in highly individualistic dancing is unpredictable and unresolved. The uncertainty of the next moment, and the interrupted kinetic flow of the dance, lend visible form to the tonal dualism and perplexing qualities in Stravinsky's music.

To try to explain this dance by standards of classical harmony, as in the previous example, would be to ignore the intention of the work. Its expressive source is not the theatrically ebullient classical; it is modern, nonallusive, terse, and austere. And although the work uses some classical ballet movement, the geometrically clean lines of the body are often distorted. The questions we might ask about such a piece would be about expression, or originality of expression, evidenced (in part) through movement contradictions (twists and other contrary motions, which have the effect of canceling each other). The critical standards that apply in evaluating this work involve questions of movement invention, originality, and expressive nuance — not harmony, ease, and balanced proportion. It would be inappropriate to apply standards of traditional classicism in vocabulary, style, or performance.

Inmost Dance: Immanent Body

In *Duo Concertant* an erratic and strange beauty prevails. As in *Le Tombeau de Couperin*, its sensible qualities are also understood through the body. But the strange and erratic in dance is not generally characterized as pleasant, while the harmonious is defined through its agreeable qualities. In art, however, the unpleasant may be valued as well as the pleasant (they are both in the affective realm and influence feeling), both are *valued as felt*, positive or negative. Both have their source in the body aesthetic, which is founded in our bodily lived existence as a whole.

Dance can be experienced simply as a harmonizing of psychophysical energy. Or it can be more complex, involving intense levels of difficulty, explosive force, bleakness, or cool detachment. It may be expressively directed or seemingly withdrawn and withheld. In any case, it involves every possible feeling (as potential), because it is of the body, which is lived (inescapably) as a body of feeling. Some of these feelings we can name, and some we cannot, since we associate feelings with language only when we name them. The body lives sentience on a preverbal level. Dance exists first on this primordial level, not on an intellectual plane (even though it requires skill and intelligence). Its inmost substance cannot be reasoned, only experienced. Dance is perceived through the body and on an experiential and kinesthetic level, which precedes words.

DANCE IS BODY

Finally, dance is lived not only through the body but also *as body* by the performer and the perceiver. This can be explained through further reduction of the structure of dance in terms of its unique condition as art. Dance reduced to its unique condition (as we have seen) is movement of the human body with an aesthetic intent and end result. Further, human movement and human body are experienced as synonymous; they are not separable. Movement exists only within the condition of the lived body, in which intentions are fulfilled or unfulfilled. Body is not other than intention and its terminus in action: it is fulfilled intention in action. Paul Ricoeur stresses the importance of this perspective: "Cartesian dualism cannot be overcome as long as we assign thought (project, idea, motive, image, etc.) to subjectivity and movement to objectivity. . . . We have to rediscover a single universe of discourse in which thought and movement would be homogeneous.[4]

The body is immanent in dance; it is the inmost condition of dance. Because of this, it is often hidden in consciousness, since we focus on what the body displays in dance rather than the body itself. This happens because we generally attend to the explicit rather than the immanent. Photographs of dance reverse this disposition; they stop the movement, thus revealing the central fact of human motion—that it is body. A photograph that arrests the moving body suspends its display of motion, drawing attention to the immanent condition of motion, the body itself—never separated from its motion, always seen and understood within this condition.

A choreographer may intentionally *reveal* or *deny* definitional conditions of dance, including its immanent definitional condition (now identified as the body or, more precisely, the lived body—with all this implies). Alwin Nikolais's abstract modern aesthetic, in which the body is often subjugated to costumes, props, and dazzling displays of light and sound, comes immediately to mind as an intriguing example of denial. Yet the body is affirmed in his dances by its presence. He has often said he would use machines in place of dancers if he wanted to, but he chooses to use dancers. The human body does not dominate in his scheme of theatricality, but it is affirmed as important. The more the body is hidden in his dances, the more it is revealed in imagination; we know it is there, even when we cannot see it. And when it is presented to view, it most often coexists with other theatrical elements as part of the whole.

For a striking contrast to Nikolais's technological abstraction (and sometimes his concealment) of the body in his aesthetic, let us return to Balanchine's work. David Levin sees that Balanchine concentrates his work in "an aesthetic of immanence" because he *reveals the body.*[5] Balanchine's modern formalism (through a blend of tradition and modernism) refers us to the body itself. Theatrical trappings are minimized. It is the body and its own drama that is expressed, not ornate theatricality or symbolic gestures that point consciousness away from the body. Balanchine offers a clear view of the body as the *within* of dance.

With another aesthetic result, and a concentration on movement itself, Merce Cunningham's modernism also emphasizes the dancing body, allowing its significance to emerge, rather than attaching meanings to it. Levin writes that the modernist aesthetic "challenges the work of art to reveal, to make present (I do not say: to represent) its defining condition as art. It requires moreover that the work accomplish this in a self-referential, or reflexive, manner—solely in terms of the abstract, sensuous properties residing in, and constitutive of, the structures itself. . . . Modernist art, to speak paradoxically, reveals . . . itself! Less paradoxically, it exists solely for the revelation of its ownmost (and latent, or immanent) defining conditions."[6]

In existential phenomenology, the lived body is considered the center of the universe. Gabriel Marcel holds that the very objectivity of the world appears (and disappears) in consonance with the body. "*My body is in sympathy with things.* . . . I am really attached to and really adhere to all that exists—to the universe which is my universe and whose center is my body."[7] Something only becomes an object for me, then, as it is separated from my own existence. It is consonant with my existence (and not an object) when it is consonant with my body. *As body,* dance can therefore be experienced as cosmologically and biologically elaborative. Or when I am in sympathy with the dance, my body is vitalized, my sense of being—or being present as the center of my world—is increased. Affirmation of bodily being is a potential value for both the dancer and the audience, because they share the dance—*as body.*

DANCE FAVORS VITALITY

Dance has its value basis (previously described as an aesthetic stasis) in movement sensibility. Dance is assumed to be valuable (valued in essence as good) in a positive attitude, a bias in favor of lived sensibility, or in favor of the vital body. Dance is at root an affirmation of the vital body because as art it has an aesthetic (affective) purpose and end result. To become art, dance must be affective: some measure of aesthetic vitality in its defining condition must be present. Dance also affirms vitality because intrinsic valuing (the subjective and experiential) prejudices value formation and recognition in favor of positive feeling. Intrinsic value is by definition the final good founded in positive feeling. When dance is intrinsically valued, it fulfills positive feeling.

This is a way of explaining that dance is most basically an aesthetic affirmation of the body and of life. The aesthetic underlies life as well as art, since it is itself founded in feeling as this extends into aisthesis, or sense perception. The lived body is a body of feeling, an interrelated system of life; and when it lives toward the world, it seeks an expressive body aesthetic, it manifests and does not withhold its life. Underlying its aesthetic surface, dance is an aesthetic projection of life. This phenomenal significance can be pointed out in the constancy of the lived ground of dance.

Because dance is an aesthetic (affectively vital) expression of the lived body, it is life engendering. The expressive body lives toward the world and others. Although it may be introspective, it does not withdraw. To express is to manifest one's self toward the world and others. Expression portends reception. Withdrawal of expression is a denial of the other; it does not acknowledge the other. While withdrawal might be aesthetically affective, and it is often necessary to withdraw from others in certain situations, withdrawal of expressiveness in general is not the natural order of growth. Expressiveness is required for physical and emotional growth in lived terms. Vitality depends on some effort of attention toward the world beyond the self, on some measure of expressiveness.

When we value dance as an expression of the vital body, we value the lived source of dance; we illuminate and intensify its inmost defining condition. Then the vital life of the body appears as the valued substance of dance. It is substantively named and is held as valuable. Even short of this realization, some measure of vital life (especially the kinesthetically vital) will, of necessity, be present in all dance, because dance itself is grounded in, and favors, the vital body.

4

DANCE AND THE OTHER

Viable in its own exclusive and quiet reality there is a communion between the noticed dancer and the unnoticed spectator. — James Michael Friedman

Passing Between

COMMUNAL CONTEXT

The affective in dance grows out of its lived ground, a ground that is present in all forms of dance, regardless of whether the dance is performed for others or not. The aesthetically affective arises (in any dance) when the lived ground, the full body consciousness, is vitalized. It is thus that I may actualize the aesthetic when I take pleasure in my dance for myself, but I am not engaged in dance as art until my dance is expressed for others and its aesthetic values are realized between us.

It is significant that in art, aesthetic values have a cultural context; they exist within a framework of reciprocity — of community. Thus they attain a reference beyond their source in aisthesis (sense perception) and nature, even as these sources are attested.

The basic sensible matter in dance, I have said, is human movement, and its personal and basic validation as art is grounded in a subjective process. I have also said that, as art, dance is more than movement: it is movement intentionally created and performed for others for an aesthetic purpose and end result. The dance aesthetic is internal to it, both intrinsic (felt) and inherent (objectively present as qualities or capacities) in the lived and sensible movement material of dance. Out of this I concluded that the dance (the object itself) becomes effective as art within the sentient self and in relation to another (in a communal context). All the themes of this study grow out of this basic definition of dance as art and from its implication of the lived body.

Questions of how the body (and the self) become aesthetically constituted in dance have already arisen. I have shown in what manner the self is aesthetically constituted in the dance and considered the temporal and material perishability of the dance. Now I can ask if the other, who is required in the completion of dance as art, is somehow constituted in the dance—and in what manner this may be possible.

This problem is posed only within a definition of dance as art, since, as a performed art, dance is a form of expression: it exists for, and is intended to be received by, another. Dance is performed within the expressive condition of being-for-other. This condition calls for a specific consideration of the communal context of dance; or, using the language phenomenology uses to describe one's consciousness of others, the intersubjective field. This is the field of consciousness wherein the world is recognized in its communal and social dimensions—not that which establishes my world as mine but rather that which appropriates our world as ours.

The communal context is established through an intersubjective field of consciousness that discloses my body as lived in relation to others, the field of awareness wherein I experience myself as seen, touched, understood, misunderstood, loved, or despised. The intersubjective field is the field of communal interaction—my consciousness of my own body-of-action, of others' body-of-action, and my awareness of what passes between us. When I am alone, or when I feel alone, I am not "with" others; my understanding of aloneness or isolation is made possible only in context of my coexistence with others.

Calvin Schrag describes intersubjectivity as "being with the other," and sets forth its two existential qualifications—the possibilities of alienation and community.[1] If, as Schrag explains, all the movements of the lived body express either alienation or the drive toward communion, it is certainly the desire to move in fulfillment of communal value that motivates dance. Estrangement from others is not the natural disposition of any art, least of all dance, which is projected by the dancer and realized in the other by means of a bodily lived aesthetic, which they both possess. Dance as art constitutes the dancer as self-for-other, because dance is expressed for other and thus holds communion as a potential value within its structure. The intersubjective field of dance is qualified by communion, not alienation, even though a dance may intentionally distance or alienate an audience to achieve a particular aesthetic end.

The dancer dances for others in context of community. As theater art, dance is basically, and conditionally, a form of communal expression. As an aesthetic mode of expression, dance seeks to reach an other, although the manner of this reaching may vary according to intent, a variable that creates complexity, aesthetic differentiation, and interest in just how the dance is expressed.

The body itself is an expressive medium; as such, it is always (except perhaps in sleep) an inside moving out. Furthermore, its interior is continuous with its exterior; the former is not a cause, and the latter the display of a cause. The body is a thinking, feeling, acting, expressive whole. We are always expressing something; at the same time, we are constantly influenced by the otherness of objects and other people as we interact with them. To express is to exist for the other, to manifest oneself toward another or others and at the same time to draw others into the orbit of this manifestation. Conscious expression involves communal action and interaction, as do even those less conscious, subliminal, yet subtly expressive, transfers between ourselves and others.

Interactions with others, according to Schrag, can be described in terms of either alienation or community. No existentialist has described the experience of alienation more vividly than Jean-Paul Sartre while, at the same time, analyzing its bodily lived dimensions. The term *body-for-other* is Sartre's. He describes the other as a constant factor in his experience of his own body and subsequent appraisal of himself in relation to others. For Sartre, others are absolute facts that condition our perception of ourselves and indeed create the condition whereby we move outside of ourselves. Thus he could write: "my body is not given merely as that which is purely and simply lived; rather this 'lived experience' becomes—in and through the contingent, absolute fact of the Other's existence—extended outside in a dimension of flight which escapes me. My body's depth of being is for me this perpetual 'outside' of my most intimate 'inside.'"[2]

Sartre explains three ontological dimensions of the body as it is experienced for itself and for others: (1) my body as known by me, (2) the body of the other as known by me, and (3) my apprehension of my body as known by the other.[3] Sartre builds an intricate dialectic on relations with others in view of being-for-others and the body-for-other. His ontology provides insights into separable moments of awareness of the body as "for-itself," "for-others," and "known-by-the-other." In particular, he describes "the gaze of the other," or the power the other has to objectify me as he possesses my body in his "look" (or with his "glance"). The existentialist theme of alienation (more relevant now in its contemporary aspects of cynicism and mistrust) was central to Sartre's outlook, especially his bleak view of "being with others." He sees an unbridgeable gulf between ourselves and others, as we become painfully aware of our essential separation (alienation) from them. Unable to see ourselves as others do, we are powerless against their glance.

Sartre holds that "conflict is the original meaning of being-for-others,"[4] or (as he states more dramatically) "Hell is other people."[5] Indeed the highly subjective philosophy and poetry of existential despair, from Kierkegaard to Sartre and Brecht, stresses our fall from grace in chilling recognition of finite individuality and limited human consciousness. As a whole, existentialist thought examines our loneliest moments—and also our courage to face them. Sartre's dark vision focuses microscopically on the first.

Conversely, Gabriel Marcel and Maurice Merleau-Ponty see the other as a source for communion. Marcel's work in particular provides a corrective to Sartre's negativism.[6] Marcel describes the body as a ground for communion. When I realize that my body is not something I *possess*, an object to be manipulated, but rather that mystery that I *am*, the path is opened for me to also regard the bodily lived existence of others as I regard my own. Then authentic community and creative intersubjectivity become possible. Marcel conceives of an intersubjectivity in which the other is not objectified but is ultimately acknowledged as a subject, allowing the possibility for communion. Merleau-Ponty regards the body "as a primal form of expression" and "a form of speech," through gestures that "signify" or "intend" a world.[7] These insights into the expressive condition of the body and *its disposition toward communion* allow us to view dance in the intersubjective field.

When Mary Wigman describes the relationship between the dancer and the audience as "the fire which dances between the two poles,"[8] she describes a conscious field of relation, a passage between the dancer and the other, which is kinetic and alive. Dance passes directly between the dancer and the audience, actualizing a bodily lived aesthetic between them as it is expressed and experienced intersubjectively. Dance closes the distance between self and other. As the dancer dances for others, she instantiates others in her dance and dances the body-of-everyone.

DESIRE FOR COMMUNION

I have defined the aesthetic stasis in dance as *vital movement sensibility*. This includes the bodily lived sensibility of both the dancer and the audience. It is the basis for the realization of the dance between them. The dance does not communicate with words, and it may or may not represent or symbolize something that can be adequately expressed in words. It is rooted in the kinesthetic, or the feeling of being a body-of-action. Some valued quality of this feeling passes between the dancer and the audience and is affirmed by the audience in its experience when dance is valued as art. Other more inclusive or symbolic significance may be determined from this base. The kinesthetic experience of dance is first and foundational. Reasoned significance, or judgments about a work, are relative to the bodily lived substance of it. The dance, when it is valued as an aesthetic expression, opens the other, the audience, to its own sentient body of action, disclosing and renewing its bodily lived aesthetic. The dance itself, made visible by the dancer, passes between the dancer and the audience and binds them together.

Because the material of dance is lived within this intersubjective field as the self escapes its boundaries toward the other, the dancer and the audience both transcend self-limitations in the dance, the dancer in the performance of the dance and the audience in the perceptual enactment of the dance. *A good dance moves the dancer and the audience toward each other*—they find a common ground when the dance is successful. The dancer and the audience come together for just this purpose. They seek a common ground of understanding and display a desire for communion, a communion that is tacitly undertaken and lived instantly through the body. The dancer and the audience commune through the lived ground of their bodily being. In one sense, they share bodily lived limitations, those of being body; likewise, they share transcendent possibilities because of the self-transcendent nature of the body.

The dance dissolves as an object for us when we achieve consonance with it. I have shown in what manner this is true for the dancer, but it is just as true (in another manner) for the audience. The dance of someone else may become a part of me not distinctly set apart but dissolved in my own consciousness in the I-thou sense of Buber and Marcel. I dance the dance with the dancer, enact it, dissolve it, and take it into myself. In this sense, I also embody the dance. The dance may cease to be other for me when I enact it in my own experience. Then the dancer's dance also becomes my dance.

Eros, the preserver of life, plays no small part in the pleasure we take in experiencing the dance as ourselves. Dance derives from the pleasure we take in being body, analogous to the erotic pleasure released in what Freud called the life instinct — a life wish against which he postulated a death wish, which ordinarily enters less obtrusively into conscious.[9] Magnetic, life-impelling *eros* also enters thematically into dance — certainly, in Martha Graham's works and in European choreographer Maurice Bejart's monumental work *Eros Thanatos* (Love and Death, 1983). But even as *eros* may be directly called forth in a particular dance, or stylistically emphasized, it also enters, unassumed, in the binding communal essence of all dance.

The Dance Stands Out

AESTHETIC PERCEPTION

Accordingly, when dance is valued as art, it is completed through the audience's perceptual engagement with it; it is not passively received. If a dance is perceived as aesthetic and finally judged to be so, it is because it has been affectively experienced. It has elicited our perceptual participation and feeling in favor of it. For feeling is not a matter of simply receiving a message — as existential phenomenology shows and as Marcel puts it most succinctly: "To feel is not to receive, but to participate in an immediate way."[10]

The results of Merleau-Ponty's scientific and philosophic inquiry into the nature of perception supports Marcel's view that perception is active. Merleau-Ponty's work as a whole is a thorough critique of the message theory of perception, the theory that human beings are passive recipients of impressions from the outside world, which are grasped as sense data and simply registered neurophysiologically. Marcel and Merleau-Ponty, and studies that grew out of their work, show that human perception is selective, active, and intentional. This insight has implications for aesthetic perception, since aesthetic perception is no less active than ordinary sense perception. Indeed aesthetic perception grows out of the action of sensing, but it takes on a particular kind of value, which accrues from a subjective process set into motion when we are struck by the outstanding qualities of some object.

Aesthetic perception is, first, a capacity — the capacity all healthy people possess — to relate aesthetic sensations (those felt and judged to be so in subjectivity) to aesthetic qualities in objects. Aesthetic sensations are affective (vitally felt) sensations that are valued as aesthetic by the person experiencing the object. In short, we all have the perceptual capacity to interpret objects as aesthetically valuable through our experience of them. In reflecting upon an experience, we might pronounce the object that elicited it to be aesthetically valuable. As we qualify it culturally, we might also judge that it belongs with that genre of objects we accept as art in its cultural context.

The category of aesthetic value is larger than art, however, and also larger than culture. Art (which is only one source for aesthetic experience) is bound by the aesthetic and belongs to human culture, while the aesthetic field of potentially valuable objects is all pervasive. It encompasses nature, art, and culture, and is apparent in all human action.

It is significant that the aesthetic is founded in perception — the body as lived — and specifically realized through affective bodily lived experience (as I stated in chapter 3). When a quality of feeling in the body is related to an objective source, the body aesthetic is enlivened — or affectively realized. Arnold Berleant states the subject-object relation this way: "The object is the center of attention in the aesthetic field, and it acts as the main stimulus of experience. It is the painting that captures our attention, the dramatic action that holds us, the music that envelops and absorbs us. Still the perceiver must at the same time relate himself to the object. Through his active involvement he must vitalize the object by setting off its aesthetic potential."[11]

The aesthetic experience is described in detail by Roman Ingarten.[12] His description might almost be taken as a description of the perceptual enactment (or inner performance) of an aesthetic experience, initiated and confirmed by means of some object of attention. He describes the aesthetic experience as "a composite process having various phases and a characteristic development." As a process, it differs from the process of sense perception accomplished through an investigative or practical attitude, in which our attention is focused on some functional or practical use of the object in our perceptual field. Ingarten sees that while the aesthetic experience may begin in simple sense perception, it passes from perception of the real object to phases in which we become occupied with something that enriches our life and confers upon it a new sense.

He suggests that we are first struck by a particular quality, which evokes a preliminary emotion in us, a "state of excitement," which compels all the following phases of the aesthetic experience. This initial emotion absorbs us, and we return to it as the object (in our experience of it) begins to separate from its background. In other words, it finally stands out as valuable for itself apart from any practical or instrumental use we might make of it. When our experience of a dance is such, the dance itself assumes a convincing character—even as we have separated it out, giving it value through our engagement with it and embodiment of it.

Ingarten describes the aesthetic experience as a process characterized by a "searching disquietude," a dynamic changeability. In contrast, the final phase is a kind of resolution—a quiet reception of aesthetic qualities and an acknowledgment of their values. These finally are intentional feelings, although they involve what he calls a "passive beginning"—the moment when the object of our attention makes an impact upon us. I would call this beginning receptive rather than passive, since we first open ourselves to an object in order for it to finally capture or hold us there. Ingarten concludes that judgments concerning works of art are based upon the final phase of acknowledgment but are not synonymous with it. Reasoned judgments carry a further intellectual dimension, which is not part of the aesthetic experience.

There is yet another moment, which may or may not appear in the aesthetic experience, that he calls "a moment of conviction." It is not specifically aesthetic but may grow out of it, as a belief that what is represented in the aesthetic object (when it does represent something outside of itself) has a real existence in the world. Beyond this, he sees that every aesthetic experience has a conviction moment concerning the whole aesthetic object; that is, a moment when we are convinced of its reality as a unique aesthetic whole. In this moment, a work of art often surprises and astonishes us with its gestalt coherence and independence from the surrounding world.

This internal integrity of the art object, and its separation from time and space as we ordinarily live them, is what Arturo Fallico identifies as the object's "free essence."[13] Lived time incurs the ever-changing temporal horizon, but the time of a finished work is sealed convincingly within it. We can return to it. The dance that has a convincing identity, the dance that stands out for us, has an internal integrity. It melds time and space in movement of the body that will not fade into the unrepeatable temporal horizon. Even though the material of dance is fleeting and does not stop for our inspection like a painting does, when it is convincing, it is remembered. And if we want to return to the dance in memory or in actuality, it is objectively there as a finished work that can be returned to. In this, it is like some life experiences that stand out in our memory.

THE OTHER IN THE DANCE

When I identify the dancer, the dance, and the other (for whom the dance is intended) as separate elements in the aesthetic field, I disrupt the aesthetic transaction in its entirety. Realization of aesthetic value in dance is a process involving all three. A total description of dance requires a placement of the aesthetic within the intersubjective field to understand the sum over the parts. The sum can only be described in the bodily lived field of consciousness between human beings. As audience and other to the dance, we experience it from our own perspective and through the dancer. The dance takes on its life between us. If it is a convincing presence, we acknowledge that the dance stands out for us. In these terms, we know the dance; we understand it. Our knowledge involves a lived field of transaction. It is not necessarily reasoned: art does not by necessity involve our thinking mind nearly so much as our whole-body consciousness.

In dance, the dancer and the other who perceives the dance become dynamically interrelated in a desire to reach a common lived ground through the dance, the object they seek to resolve between them. The dance (object) dissolves as it becomes consonant with subjectivity. The initial substance of the dance is given life by the dancer but is not meaningful as art until it is grasped as meaningful by the other. Its significance is assigned by the other as he experiences it (subjectively) within himself.

As perceiver, the other is in the dance in two ways. First, the dance already holds his lived nature in its material, the dance is of his body. Beyond this, he vitalizes or sets off the aesthetic in the dance as he generates and realizes its values in his own experience. As he actively constitutes the dance by relating to it and valuing it, he himself is caught up in it. Thus he perceptually enacts the dance and becomes consonant with it. He dissolves its material objective nature as he makes it a part of his vital body.

As I view a dance, I know that I am not physically present in it – but when the dance finds its life in me and I find my life in it, I coincide with it. Marcel believes in just such possibilities: "Perhaps we must admit that to experience a sensation is really to become in some manner the thing sensed, and that a sort of temporary coalescence is established between things situated on different planes of reality, and in consequence belonging to distinct worlds?"[14]

We know that which is before us through ourselves. We can take no other position. We are in the art we perceive to the extent that we have given ourselves over to it. We have already considered why dance among all the arts may be the most difficult to objectively position away from ourselves. Now another reason for this appears. The dance comes closer to us as we consider it not simply as body but also as meaningful only through our perceptual enactment. We are in the dance before us, as body, and the dance moves through our own body aesthetic as we allow it to.

ALLOWING THE DANCE TO BE

When we lend ourselves to a work of art, we assume an aesthetic attitude toward it. This attitude is traditionally termed disinterested, because it is not concerned with a practical or instrumental use of the work. This is a confusing and deceptive designation for an attitude of being *given over to* – or perceptually interested in – a work. There is in this attitude a sweet ambivalence between activity and contemplative receptivity. Aesthetic value is realized through an active perceptual attention but characterized by a release of ourselves, which allows the aesthetic experience to develop within. This may be described as an *active receptivity,* one that is necessary to an assimilation and an understanding of the dance.

In their zeal to correct the fallacy of passivity in message theories of perception, the existentialists overlook the importance of receptivity in perception. They interchange *receptivity* and *passivity* falsely. Thus they also overlook the perceptual complement of activity and receptivity, which is basic to the creation of art and requisite to the aesthetic experience.

Nowhere does this complement unfold on so many planes of meaning than in the Chinese book of changes, the *I Ching.* The first part of book 1 begins with the mythological principles of heaven and earth, or the creative (the active element), and the receptive (the well from which creative activity springs). These are also called the male and the female, the foundations of all that exists. These are not antagonists but complements, which exert attractions, engaging an interplay of forces and bringing about change. The interpenetrating light and shadow – yang and yin – symbolize these two primal powers and are not necessarily applied literally to one sex or another. They are also called the firm and the yielding as they apply to the "two alternating primal states of being."[15]

While we learn through the existentialists that consciousness is intentional and perception is active, we miss the deeper truth of art if we disregard the role of the receptive unconscious in creation and perception, if we disallow the shadowed, receptive side of being, where art escapes the intellect and teaches the mind the freedom of yielding and peace – the mythical female ethic. Regarding the receptive element of the unconscious, the *I Ching* says, "What takes place in the depths of one's being, in the unconscious, can neither be called forth nor prevented by the conscious mind."[16] The freedom that the *I Ching* images in book 1 is achieved beyond the strife of overcoming and through a balancing of active and receptive aspects of being (unlike the Western will to power). In book 2, this is described more concretely, and on an intersubjective plane, as fellowship or communion. When people free themselves from obstacles and succeed in understanding one another, a warm attachment springs from the heart: "their words are strong and sweet like the fragrance of orchids."[17]

While dances are not composed of words, they are nevertheless a source for such communion. As a dance stands out for us, we become participants in it. We allow the dance to be through our active reception of it, as we commune with the dancer.

Body-for-Other

A universal other is assumed in the dance, an other who is no one in particular and anyone who has the capacity to experience himself through the dance. It is assumed, since the dance is performed for him, that the dance might speak to him or that he might recognize himself in it. It is also assumed (since the dancer is entrusted with the dance, and the audience exhibits a trust in his ability to perform it) that the dancer and the audience can meet upon a mutually valued ground, that they can extend themselves toward each other when the dance enlivens something between them.

The universal (and bodily lived) capacity to express, to extend our boundaries through expression, to move out of ourselves and be received by others, is the human capacity upon which dancing is founded. If to express is to manifest oneself toward another (or if not overtly toward, simply for another), then dance is a form of expression. And since the dancer expresses his dance, not his self, dance is not personalized but universalized expression. This does not mean that a dance must be universally appreciated, but that dance extends beyond the limits of the purely personal.

Because of this, the dancer seldom has reason to project his expression directly toward the audience. They are "many as one" in his mind; they are all others in general, specifically all those attending to the dance, and respected in that moment as the other for whom he dances. Therefore he dances not so much in a self-expressive mode as in a mode of being-for-other. His dance is not persuasively directed but simply given with trust in the receptivity of others and belief that the dance holds potential value for them. Good dancing is not personally directed toward another: the dance is lost when the focus shifts from the work to the personality of the performer or to his desire to be appreciated for himself rather than through the dance. As the dancer expresses the dance-for-other, he indicates a desire to instantiate something between himself and others through the expressive material of his art, the expressiveness of human movement. Indeed, we have already considered the body as a primordial form of expression. In its presence, in its nature, and in its movements it is always expressing something. Dance draws inescapably upon such unstudied expression, but is expressive (for-other) on intentional, carefully studied levels also. This kind of intention should not imply lack of spontaneity in becoming the dance one has studied. Nor should dance-for-other imply forwardness. After all, an entire dance may be effectively done with the dancer's back to the audience (just as objects and events in life are often turned away from us). More to the point of intentional expression are the several related meanings of the verb *to express* and the particular way in which dance expresses.

First, are the ideas of expression as *pressing out*, like extracting juice from a fruit, or *opening up*, as a bud opens when it flowers. Related to these is expression as *revelation*, a bringing forth of something hidden or a moving of an interior toward an exterior, such as occurs in nature and in human life. On a social plane, there is a range of expression, from seemingly unintentional body attitudes and gestures (read as expressions of who we are, how we feel at the moment, and what we think of ourselves) to consciously directed verbal discourse, full of intentional verbal and unintentional nonverbal expressive nuance.

In dance, we are concerned with an embodied and aesthetic form of expression which is qualified as art. Here, Jacques Seranno's analysis of the polar phases of bodily lived expression is instructive. Expression passes through the three poles of *description* (bodily-lived presence), *message* (sign), and *creation* (work).[18] At the initial pole, "expression is also the message that I address to the world and through which I *describe myself* and *beckon*. I expressly and intentionally mark my presence, that I am there and who I am. Thus we move from description to sign: language, style, word, problems of communication, etc." At the terminal pole, "expression fulfills and completes me. It was the effect; it is the cause. It goes out from me, but I am brought forth from it. . . . It is thus that we arrive at the idea of a work as the expression of a person, of an artist. . . . it is a dialogue between the creation and its recreated creator."

Just what manner of expression is dance, then? Does it press an inside out, open a hidden interior, describe someone's characteristic being? Does it intentionally mark a presence through a message or a sign? Does it accomplish fulfilling work that, as a creation, returns something of value? The latter two (the intermediate and terminal poles) probably come closest to the way that dance expresses. Dance includes the body as the "organ of description" (the initial pole of expression), but it does not usually describe the dancer's characteristic (personal) being. Rather, the characteristics she embodies in the dance are described (expressed), and only residues of her personal characteristics. (Yet all she is in her bodily lived presence will undoubtedly enter in.) A tension between the dancer's personal presence and her performance presence makes her dance interesting to us. We are not interested in a simple display of the dancer's character, but neither are we interested in thoroughly depersonalized dancing which machines might accomplish more perfectly.

At the intermediate and the terminal poles, dance becomes intentionally expressive. At the intermediate pole, the dancer "expressly and intentionally" marks her presence, but only through the dance. She sheds her persona (mask) and marks (or signs) an aesthetic presence larger than herself. At the terminal pole, dance becomes a silent dialogue between the created dance and the recreated dancer, as she includes the other. The dance is the content that passes between them. It is the creation, the accomplished work—expressed, received, and returned. What the dancer gains back from a work inevitably contains what the audience feels or sees in it. This indirect dialogue, by means of the dance, returns something of value to the dancer, who expresses it, and to the other, who experiences and assigns its worth.

A dance can only be of value when the dancer clearly manifests her intentions in her movement; then she becomes what she signifies, what she marks for us—be that the truth of our common humanity or the play and work of life seen in movement itself. There is trust in this expression—thus always the risk of failure.

Poetic Body

And so, as from the loadstone, a mighty chain hangs down, of choric dancers, masters of the chorus, undermasters, obliquely fastened to the rings which are suspended from the Muse. . . . *Ion,* you are one of these, and are possessed by Homer. . . . your spirit dances. —Plato

What the dancer marks for others as she succeeds in her dance can be described ultimately in its poetic character. Plato well recognized dance as poetic in essence. His view of the poetic (choric) nature of dance is stated in *Laws*, books 2 and 7, and in his short dialogue *Ion*, where he also granted dance an integral place in the cosmological order of the arts.[19]

To conceive of dance as poetic, whether in Plato's cosmic terms or in Heidegger's phenomenal terms (as we see in the next chapter), is to suppose that the body is capable of speaking without words. And in fact we do translate our innately expressive human embodiment into an aesthetic form through dance. Or I could say that in dance we express our poetic body. While dance speaks (or expresses) through the body, it is not a language of words. Dance takes us to the bodily lived source for language. It is preverbal expression, playing beneath words and at the same time moving beyond them. The communicative purpose in dance resides at this preverbal level. While we may find words for the total sense or meaning of a dance, the first level of communication lies in the speech of the body itself. (Or, as John Cage and Merce Cunningham attest in their works and words: "We are simple minded enough to believe that if we had something to say we would use words.") Merleau-Ponty notes that

> It has always been observed that speech or gesture transfigure the body, but no more was said on the subject than that they develop or disclose another power, that of thought or soul. The fact was overlooked that, in order to express it, the body must in the last analysis become the thought or intention that it signifies for us. It is the body which points out, and which speaks. . . . This disclosure of an immanent or incipient significance in the living body extends to the whole sensible world, and our gaze, prompted by the experience of our own body, will discover in all other "objects" the miracle of expression.[20]

Language has a foundation in lived-body experience. The body formulates that which it expresses, taking on the shape of its thought and feeling. Dance therefore captures the first glimmer of language. Dance dwells beneath the word, the word that finally describes experienced thoughts and feelings. Language comes after dance (even though we do move our language forth in action when we speak). Dance exists in movement alone, not in language; and therefore does not parallel it. We can find no direct counterpart for dance in words. The body subtends the word and surrounds the thought. Yet the dancing body is highly intelligent and expresses intentional motion, not vague wanderings, groping toward dance.

The body is not simply an object but a nexus of sensibility, sensitive to and adhering to the expressive world. It is coextensive with the poetry of the world, its sounds, colors, textures, and especially its movements. It is the body that, in Merleau-Ponty's words, "provides words with their primordial significance through the way in which it receives them."[21] My body reacts in opposite ways to the words *warm* and *cold*, as it reacts also to warm and cold qualities in another person. In the same way, my body sees and feels warmth in the color red because it is sensitive to color. This sensation is brought to use by experience; it is not anonymous, isolated, or singular. Our world of sensation is continuous with being and therefore with language. The body as experienced is the immediate source of language and thus is our poetic contact with it.

The body's attitudes and actions are always expressing something. It is difficult to call these attitudes and actions language, since they usually are unconsciously performed and involuntarily uttered. Or they become habit and character as they become second nature, as they bespeak us. Unconsciously performed body attitudes, actions, and gestures are not dance. Although the body is always expressing something, it is not always dancing (even though dance therapists may look upon the characteristic movement of a person as that person's dance).

Dance as art is consciously structured movement for an aesthetic purpose. Dance projects the poetry of the body and is not cast into a void but intends a recipient. Such projection does not necessarily imply exaggeration, although projection is sometimes used to mean this. Danced action may be projected quietly, or strongly, or with directness, or with indirection, or in any number of ways.

Moreover, the expressive values that are projected in a dance may be aesthetically qualified in many ways. While we cannot translate such expression into words (since words and movements are situated on different levels of meaning), we may describe such expression as it becomes meaningful to us. In dance, we attend to the aesthetic values of intentionally formulated movement expression. At times this may come surprisingly close to language, or to narrative. We may feel the word ruminating within the movement. At other times the expression may take the form of a disjointed utterance. The body may speak with inevitability—connecting time, sustaining flow, drawing one movement logically into the next. The body can also shift in starts and stops, as unpredictably as life does. Dance often contains sculpted silence; it can also paint whole landscapes and abstracts of movement.

As impetus toward speech proper, dance founds meaning; thus it is closer to the immediacy, rhythm, and origination of poetry than it is to linear language. Dance is structured as a poetry of movement, not as a language of movement, although dance differs from poetry because it speaks through movement images instead of word images.

Neither is dance essentially gestural, like mime. Choreographers like Anna Sokolow and Pina Bausch use gesture extensively but seldom realistically—and not as a bridge to language. They abstract, derealize, and distill the poetic essence of gesture in dance. Certainly gestures have bodily lived bases, just as dance does. As the body proceeds toward the word, gestures arise and substitute for the word. Gestures are absolutes with restricted meanings. A gesture of the head one way means yes, another way means no. On this there is no equivocation within a given culture. Gestures have word correlates.

Dance produces its own meanings. It has no word correlates. It is of another order, finding its expression through the poetry of the body and patterns of qualitatively lived movement. We might be successful in naming the moods and the meanings we derive from the dance. We name whatever it draws to mind, what it evokes or symbolizes—or what it exemplifies if it is a highly abstract work. We may also name the dance through its power to reflect the substance of life. That is, we may see that it signifies our embodiment, our life as a whole. All dance carries this signifying power in its constitution, since it is never divorced from its lived ground.

Giving a name to a dance (a general title which stands for the dance) is part of the creative task of the choreographer. The name identifies the dance and gives the audience and the critic a clue to its meaning from the choreographer's point of view. Others may find names that better describe the dance for them. As we name a dance, we *symbolize* it with words; we do not translate it into words. Words are symbols and signifiers. They stand for things or events and give us a way to think and communicate about them verbally. Words name dances. But dance founds the meaning that words name. Accordingly, as David Levin says, dancing "is another way of naming akin to the poet's way, and not at all inferior."[22]

A dance, then, is not expressed in words but in bodily lived motion, whose meanings may be captured with words only in a figurative sense.

Since dance passes between the dancer and the audience in an intersubjective field, it is subject to many differing and equally valid interpretations. But a dance does not necessarily call for interpretation in words; it exists as a site for a wordless (yet poetic) communion. The power for communion resides in the human body, which exhibits an expressive condition in its motion and in its stillness. We are drawn to dance because it transports us beyond the literal word and into the body's poetry. When I join the dancer in her dance, it is through my poetic experience of bodily being. I join her in an unspoken celebration of the poetry of our embodiment as it is danced and silently affirmed between us.

PART II

A TENSION OF OPPOSITES

Shelly Zeibel and Ken Lipitz in *Mythic Journey* by Sondra Fraleigh (1980). Photo: June Burke.

5

DANCE TENSION

Every movement is veiled in immobility. — Pierre Teilhard de Chardin

In part 2, we are still moving away from those futile existentialist views that fail to see meaning in life because they emphasize life's contingency rather than its cohesion, and fail to see the impossibility of erasing (even in our thoughts, let alone our actions) the compelling connectedness of self, body, earth, and world — a universe (a single verse), rendering both unity and diversity possible. Disconnection is possible only if connection is assumed. Likewise, irrationality stands in relation to rationality, non-being to being, negative to positive, and contingent properties must be contingent upon something. In short, all oppositions stand in relation.

While despairing and off-centered existentialist art deals with disruptions of continuities, it nevertheless has to assume an interrelated wholeness in order to shatter it. Through existential phenomenology, which views the body in wholistic, positive terms, we can visualize our selves as our bodies and as part of the world's body. We are the world's axis, and it turns with us. Gabriel Marcel sees us as the incarnate center of the universe.[1] Pierre Teilhard de Chardin also conceives our integration with the universe, describing the cosmos as both pluralistic and unified, diverse yet whole: "The history of consciousness and its place in the world remains incomprehensible to anyone who has not seen first of all that the cosmos in which man finds himself caught up constitutes, by reason of the unimpeachable wholeness of its whole, a *system*, a *totum*, and a *quantum:* a system by its plurality, a totum by its unity, a quantum by its energy; all three within a boundless contour."[2]

Here, and in the following three chapters, I concentrate on how expression and meaning emerge in dance through various kinds of oppositions within a tensional whole. Since our body of dance is our body of tension, I view the human body in its living solitary wholeness as a microcosm of creative tensions—cosmic and phenomenal, historic, aesthetic, and mythic.

If I inquire first into the most general philosophical reaches, I encounter views—both cosmological and existential, ancient and modern—of a tension between oppositions in the genesis of movement, dance, and art. I explore these views in this chapter, as I continue to pursue the unique aesthetic substance of dance and the sense in which it attains meaning.

Cosmic Motion and Dance Tension

Early Greek cosmology posits a simple view of the unity of the cosmos through oscillation of oppositions. Aesthetics historians Katherine Gilbert and Helmut Kuhn believe that "even the famous doctrine of art as the imitation of nature lies in germ in these early cosmologies."[3] Dance, in this view, would have come into being like everything else in the cosmos, through an oscillation of opposites within a coherence. Movement, or the ambience of all things, was believed to have come into being as a result of endless alternation. Motion had its very source in the compensation of opposites: wet and dry, day and night, ascent and descent, forward and backward, fast and slow, rough and smooth. The sphere was the form chosen by the cosmologists to represent the universe as a whole, a form created through circular movement set up by oscillation, whereby the beginning and end of the world could meet. The compensation of elements created a whole and became the inevitable rhythm of all things.[4]

At the ritual foundations of Western dance and in the religions of the East, dance was viewed in its power to embody cosmological theory and to link human essence to origins. What could not be explained by other means could be either demonstrated in dance or imagined as a dance that could spin the world into being. Shiva, the Indian creator, is the clearest example of a god who dances the origin of the cosmological order, creating an image of "that Energy which science must postulate behind all phenomena."[5] Shiva's dance, engaging an oppositional interplay of creation and destruction, is understood as the source of all cosmic motion, action, and tension. He dances to release the innumerable souls of mankind from the snare of illusion. The theater of his dance and the center of the universe is within the human heart. He awakens nature with his pulsing dance. He dances the world into being through creation and fiery destruction, and his dance keeps it alive.[6]

Lincoln Kirstein writes that in Egypt, at the foundation of Western spectacle, the most ingenious of Egyptian dances, the Astronomic Dance of Stars, was based upon a conception of cosmic order: "Ranged around a fixed altar which represented the sun, priests clad in scintillating clothes made signs for the Zodiac with their hands, while turning rhythmically from east to west, following the course of the planets. After each circle the dancers froze into immobility to represent the constancy of their earth. By combining mimicry and plastic movement the priests made legible the harmonies of the astral system and the laws of the universe."[7] Plato knew of the Astronomic Dance in a relatively late period of Egyptian antiquity and thought its ingenuity divine; Kirstein concludes that Egyptian dances may have influenced early Greek artists.[8]

In the Astronomical Dance, the human body was valued as a microcosm since it could represent the movement of "heavenly bodies." Dance forms of other cultures also value the body as a microcosm. In Chinese T'ai Chi Chuan (learned in its first phases as a dance and applied in later phases as an art of self defense), movements with smooth and equalizing transfers of weight are performed within an imagined sphere, analogous to the sphere of the Greek cosmologists. In this, as in Greek cosmological theory, the universe is experienced as complete through alternating motion within a sphere.

In common discourse, we still speak of "a sphere of action," perhaps out of these deep symbol systems of early cultures. The sphere is not without significance for dance even today. Rudolph von Laban situates his systematic study of movement on planes of action within what he calls the kinesphere, "an imagined sphere around the individual which locomotes, rotates, extends and contracts congruent with the individual."[9] Similarly, Doris Humphrey conceives the three dimensionality of stage space in terms of height, width, and depth, with all lines converging at the center (although stage space is usually outlined as a box not a sphere).

Humphrey considers the dancer's location along lines of power and weakness within the total space, while Laban is concerned with the dancer's actual articulation of particular movement in spherical space.[10] As founding modern dance traditions, the techniques of Humphrey and José Limon emphasize roundness and molding in the spiraling of the body through the sphere. By contrast, ballet techniques emphasize finding (and often freezing) clear linear planes within the sphere. (Consider the classic arabesque and other poses with attenuated limbs balanced and stilled before the eye.) Classical ballet cuts the cosmic sphere geometrically, whereas traditional modern dance fills it with curves, spirals, and free-flowing breath lines.

The sphere as microcosm maintains significance in Greek thought. Coming after Greek cosmological theory, the Pythagorean doctrine of the music of the spheres was set forth because of music's susceptibility to numerical proportion. Dance, being less abstract because of its expression through the human form, nevertheless assumes a related microcosmic stance in rhythmic human motion, also susceptible to mathematics. Plato proposes a microcosmic view of dance through the body's relatedness to the universe.[11] He stresses the importance of dance in a full education and sees motion as the genesis of human art. He even indicates what kind of motion is best: regular and uniform motion in one compass about a center (like a well-turned cartwheel). In his theory, centering motion is the movement of wisdom, although to be at rest is better than to be in motion. Even now, the formal technical training for classical ballet and, to a great extent, modern dance is based upon finding and controlling the felt center of the motion and upon replicating geometry in clearly defined shapes and mathematically derived rhythms.

Since Plato emphasizes ideal form, formalist concerns modify his view of mimetic motion. The wise and beneficent are for Plato a meeting of like with like. Circular motion, which is self-relational, belongs to this order.[12] He holds that we have the means of learning how to mimic star motion—that we might observe the revolutions in the heavens and profit by them in the revolutions of our own thoughts, which are related to them. By learning the stars' natural courses, we might reproduce their unerring revolutions and order the troubled motions in ourselves. He sees rhythm as a gift bestowed in human nature for the same intent.[13]

Dance became prized in Greece as a means to harmonize body and mind by relating rhythmic motion to the universe's orderly motion. As such, it was a means for educating not only citizens but athletes and soldiers. However, Greek dance could reflect expressive intensity, also – mainly through the worship of Dionysus. The *Dithyrambos*, a ritual spring song of the birth and rebirth of Dionysus, became the source for Western theater. Kirstein tells us that at first this song was accompanied by a flute and by "expressive mimetic gesture." The rite was termed *dromenon* (sacred thing done). Further, these sacred things were not merely done; they were "repeatedly done, prophetically done, enacted, represented, in commemoration or in anticipation." From this grew the artificed drama. "The collective presented utterance had become a collective representation."[14]

Today we are familiar with drama and dance as creative arts with ritual foundations. Both have their phenomenal source in exciting movements and relaxations of the body and its psychic life – in tension, the phenomenal name-essence of dance. *Tension* stems from the Old High German *danson* (to stretch) and Sanskrit *tan* (tension).[15] Tension is a striving between forces and also a cause of extension, which is both a stretching and a release. (We also note that *tension* is the root of *intension*, which phenomenologists define in terms of consciousness and human will.) Expression in both dance and drama, according to Kirstein, arises from a physical and psychological tension: "Tension, the root, name-essence of dance, finds its relief in an expression arising from exciting movement. Its relaxation is both physical and psychological. This violent dance, this essential *doing* is the source of drama."[16]

We see then that tension attained a reified definition in Greek cosmological thought and through the image of Shiva's dance: substantiality was attributed to it. And we understand through Kirstein that tension belongs to dance expression at the root, as part of its essential doing. These perspectives support a view that tension underlies the phenomenal (experienced) interplay of oppositions in the striving toward creativity, and that this struggle releases (or founds) expression and meaning through an extension (ex-tension) of the imagination in actual works of art. Below, I develop this thought through Martin Heidegger, since he gives the most thorough account of phenomenal tension in art in the literature of existential phenomenology.

Phenomenal Tensions in Dance

The world grounds itself on the earth, and earth juts through world. But the relation between world and earth does not wither away into the empty unity of opposites unconcerned with one another. . . . The opposition of world and earth is a striving. —Martin Heidegger

All art may be defined at the phenomenal (experiential) level according to the strife inherent in creative processes. Beyond this, each art will somehow manifest its own distinctive character out of such strife according to its unique matter, medium, or source.

Here I look at phenomenal tensions experienced in the creation of art works, and view the work's completed essence as a resolution of such tension. Through Heidegger, I reduce art to the struggle toward form and meaning and consider what I might say about dance that is unique in this regard. We will eventually see how Heidegger's view enables us to consider oppositions at work in dance from the perspective of the dancing body, which is the source of expression and meaning in dance.

Heidegger's view of the oppositional tension *at work* in art bears some similarities to cosmological views—and some important differences. He considers the origin of the work of art through the idea of opposition, but carries it beyond a measured view of oscillation, compensation, and alternation.[17] His oppositions strive against each other. He envisions them in the poetic images of "world and earth," and portrays them as oppositions of a lived (or experiential) character. The earth is *closed,* sealed off from our understanding. The world is *open,* within the range of our vision and will. These opposing images not only contact each other where they meet (their cut, middle, or center), they pervade each other through grounding and jutting. They can move through their differences like shapes pressing onto and into one another, engulfing and being engulfed (but within their distinctly different characters), finally opening (or "clearing") a place he calls "the open center."

In addition, earth and world are mythic (as images) and psychological ("belligerent by nature"). As they take on color or density through their qualities of concealment and openness, they may be seen as dark and light. Yet he avoids the dichotomy earth-heaven, which is so commonly demonstrated in myth as dark-light and female-male.[18] Still Heidegger is well aware of the mythological, equal-polar opposites of earth-heaven, crossing them with mortality-divinity to describe those aspects that "gather" in all things as a "round dance" of "the worlding of the world."[19] Dance and world are transcendentally bound together in this synthetic mythic symbol, as Levin well recognized in his article on Heidegger's metaphorical use of dance.[20] In "The Origin of The Work of Art," Heidegger envisions "world" in a more vulnerable phase as it strives with "earth" toward a founding. Here his oppositions are dialectical, metaphorical (as all mythic symbols are), primal (of origins), existential, and phenomenological (of an experienced being-in-the-world).

Indeed not all oppositions are of the same kind. C. K. Ogden's linguistic analysis of oppositions shows, however, that all have a directional factor bearing a relation to the human body and are founded in sensation, an observation of special importance in a consideration of dance, its tensional character, and its bodily lived basis.[21]

In his oppositions of world and earth, Heidegger is not concerned with meeting of like with like, with explantions of formal unity, or with imitation as founding or originating principles of art. He is concerned with the emergence of expression through turbulent and lived tensions (as is Kirstein), and what he calls "the riddle of Art," its oppositional "isness," its founding truth. Heidegger turns our attention toward art as a "striving between oppositions" within a final "coherence" or "repose" in the completed nature of the art work. He describes both the struggle toward completion and the terminus (art itself) as truth founding.

THE OPEN OF SAYING

Heidegger defines art as "an origin: a distinctive way in which truth comes into being, that is, becomes historical."[22] *Historical* here means preserved; that is, art works preserve historic truths not subject to scientific correctness. Rather, they are of another kind of truth, a truth grounded by the art work itself, which if it is a work of art is a genuine beginning. Through Heidegger's view, we may understand why originality is so prized in art; that through art we seek to penetrate the core of being to release the "genuine beginning."

The word *origin* in German is *ursprung,* meaning primal leap. Of this origin, which is a genuine beginning, Heidegger says, "A genuine beginning, as a leap, is always a head start, in which everything to come is already leaped over, even if as something disguised, the beginning already contains the end latent within itself." However, a genuine beginning, since it is capable of releasing more from itself, is not caught in the neophyte primitive. On the contrary, it "always contains the undisclosed abundance of the unfamiliar and extraordinary, which means that it also contains strife with the familiar and ordinary."[23]

To the view that art is an origin preserving historic truth he adds the view that this truth is an original poetic founding. All art partakes of the spirit of poetry, which is a founding of truth in a triple sense: "founding as bestowing, founding as grounding, and founding as beginning."[24] Poetry is thought of here in its truth-bestowing nature—its power to unite being with language by saying what seems unsayable. The idea that all arts partake of poetry's founding spirit is not new to philosophy. In *The Symposium,* Plato has Diotima speak to Socrates about poetry, as she is teaching him about love and creation: "By its original meaning poetry means simply creation, and creation, as you know, can take various forms. Any action which is the cause of a thing emerging from non-existence into existence might be called poetry, and all the processes in all the crafts are kinds of poetry, and all those who are engaged in them poets."[25]

Then how is it that truth, understood as a genuine poetic founding (a leap that bridges the ordinary and the extraordinary), sets itself into a work? Heidegger says this is accomplished through the creation of the work, which is "a drawing-up . . . as of water from a spring." Poetic founding thus seems to come from Nothing, but actually comes from "the withheld vocation of the historical being of man itself."[26] This is so because a peoples' endowment—their history—is drawn up from the closed ground (their earth, which is concealed from them) "and expressly set upon this ground."[27]

Thus the image of drawing up is used for creation, the image of setting forth is used for expression. "Founding" is, he says, "a poetic projection" setting forth the truth of being. The truth "striving" in the "work-being" of the work is that which is expressed; it is that message or sign that mediates for us in a poetic way—that unites our being with language—which each art does in its own way. All arts are poetic as they name, say, or project truth, or as they happen in the open of saying and naming.

Nonlinguistic poetic arts, which include dance, "are an ever special poetizing within the clearing of what is."[28] While they do not say anything in words, the open of saying and naming pervades and guides them.

Truth, Heidegger tells us, is both a "clearing" and a "concealing" of being, set into a work through composition or creation. It happens as a "setting-into-work" through "projective saying," which is what poetry is: "Projective saying is poetry: the saying of world and earth, the saying of the arena of their conflict and thus of the place of all nearness and remoteness of the gods. Poetry is the saying of the unconcealedness of what is. . . . Projective saying is saying which, in preparing the sayable, simultaneously brings the unsayable as such into a world. In such saying, the concepts of an historical peoples nature, i.e., of its belonging to world history, are formed for that folk, before it."[29] Here we understand that art is poetic as projective saying and that it becomes historical truth in this context.

Heidegger allows us to see what is "at work" in art, as art comes into its work being through a striving between world and earth. Its striving is its poetic truth, a truth that comes into being as a bringing forth of the concealment of the earth and a sealing into the art work (the preserved object) of the openness of the world. The self-composure of the work, its composed or created nature, is its repose.

Arturo Fallico recognizes this self-containment of art—its being "a possible world" in its completeness—as its "free essence."[30] Art is striving in its work nature and is at repose as a completed work. To envision this movement toward completion in yet other closely related terms with Jacques Seranno, we see that art moves through the three poles of expression we considered in the last chapter, and that its repose is its created character at the completed terminal pole.[31] As mediating expression that passes between the artist and the other in lived present time, art is active and full of movement; as completed expression, it is in repose, historical. And as Fallico points out, it is free from the passage of present time: it remains complete as it is; we move on. Since the work "sets up a world" and opens it to us (Heidegger), we can enter into the work as we grasp it in the fullness of its expression at the terminal pole (Seranno). Its truth, that which is truly at work in it, is "in the open" (Heidegger); it has been "expressed" (Seranno); and becomes thereby "a free essence" (Fallico).

SAYING AS MOVING

Although dance is not composed of words, it bears its own capacity to express, to say, to set forth into the open the unique truth of its own being. Its truth we might also think of as its meaning, since it becomes meaningful only in light of what it is—what it is "in truth."

Let me continue to extract from Heidegger: even art that is not composed of words happens in the open of saying. Such art can "subtend the word"—as dance does—to unite our beings with language by striving "beneath language" as the bodily lived basis for the formation of language. I believe the truths that dance expresses are of this nature. They have their origin in the human body—in its lived, wholistic character and in the human capacity for poeticizing movement. Such truths as dance can express lie in the "saying of moving," a special kind of poetry that unites our being with language because our being is the lived source (origin) of language. Meaning is assigned as we give word to that which is not literate in essence—meaning arises as we associate dance with a kind of knowledge that lies outside the dance and that we ordinarily claim as knowledge because it can be said in language.

Each dance finally means what we say it means to us. The truth of a dance is not scientifically verifiable. It is of another order; it lies in the meaning it founds for us as we grasp the truth of it. Of course, I am speaking here of works that have first founded the truth of their own being as works of art: works whose elements truly speak their purpose. Dance speaks, then, through artistry that finds the right fit of movement and purpose. Martha Graham's dramatic works, for instance, speak their psychic truth through sharp angular movement. Their grip and bite is not simply in plot or theme but in the actual dancing.

Nelson Goodman also considers the issue of truth and meaning in art as a matter of "rightness of fit."[32] The audience's discovery of such rightness is not simply a function of the emotions. The fullness of the aesthetic experience comes into focus as meaning arises through cognitive use of emotions. Satisfaction, then, arises as we are moved and also as we understand that which moves us. Goodman states that cognitive use of the emotions involves discrimination, which allows us to see relations as we grasp the work, integrating it with other experiences and our world as a whole. He emphasizes, as do the existentialists, that aesthetic perception engages our full powers — a functioning of feeling with knowledge, not a distanced passivity.[33] Certainly we relate to the explosive dynamics of Graham most immediately through the pulse and sweep of the motion. However, her works take on a fuller meaning when we understand that they reveal familiar inner landscapes through archetypal figures. Likewise, Merce Cunningham's works reveal truths beyond their cleanly etched motion, as they engage us in mystical world views and meditation on the accidental moment.

It is in truth-founding movement, or movement that speaks its purpose, that dance moves us toward meaning. Works that are true in this sense fulfill their own aesthetic imperatives. The dance is right and becomes meaningful when the movement is true to its purpose. At this point, movement and purpose are indistinguishable. The purpose of the dance is spoken (set forth) only as it is bodied forth in movement.

As dance establishes a community of understanding, it preserves communal and historic truths in the bodily lived truth of human movement. In its movement character, for instance, nineteenth-century dance bespeaks the truth of an age of artifice and romance, while twentieth-century dance prefers the movement of everyday work and play, purity of medium, the starker moods and currents of its own time, reflecting the shrinking globe in its multifarious forms and aesthetic fusions. Modern dance, in particular, is open to cross-cultural assimilation of movement, as evidenced by the works of such artists as José Limon, Katherine Dunham, Alvin Ailey, Mel Wong, Kei Takei, Ohad Naharin, and Molissa Fenley. Many distinctions between modern dance and ballet have also blurred. The truth of a smaller world with increased speed of communication and cultural access is attested to.

What dance expresses — *what it says* — belongs to the human body and its own truth. This truth is founded in our realization of our vital body, aesthetically constituted in the dance work. Dance celebrates our lived body and its poetic truths, the vibrant body — which is yours, mine, and ours in the dance.

As founding these truths, each unique dance is an original, an *ursprung*, a primal leap, containing an end in its beginning. A leap leaps over, and it must land. It is an observable truth. As primal, a leap is naive, familiar, and innocent; in dance, it is designed and genuinely gifted as body-for-other. When a leap is a figure in a dance, it is removed from functional usefulness. But it retains its primal familiarity, even as something of the unfamiliar is also disclosed in it. Unlike walking, which we take for granted, a leap is seldom necessary in the usual course of a day. If it rains, I may need to leap over puddles; or if I go hiking, I may need to leap over streams. But in dance, I am allowed to leap simply for the sake of leaping—to quicken my own giant steps into space and to thrill to those of others. In fact, through dance we are allowed to see how many amazing ways of leaping there are. Dancing brings the endless variety within the leap to our attention—leaps low and long, high, with turns, with outstretched legs or bent knees, leaning on the air, small and in fast succession, and so on. Dancing brings into the open what was concealed (untried or unrealised) in our possibilities of leaping.

The leap holds the poetized body in its arc; it speaks a faith with earth and air. In dancing, we pay attention to our leaping, we celebrate and sustain our body's power to leave the surface and return with grace. We make our every leap speak its particular character within each dance, just as we do our every turn and step.

EVERY MOVEMENT COUNTS

In dance every movement counts. This is assumed in strictly composed dances, but it is also true of dances where movement is left open to improvisation and equally true when dance movement is subjected to accident through method. Dancing makes movement count; it brings to our attention that human movement can be beautiful or poetically meaningful. Dancing makes movement matter, makes it work in dance "works." Dancing makes movement work as it makes it matter, as it brings movement to our attention and into the open, unifying creative tensions—what Heidegger calls the strife between "world and earth"—in the dance work. The unity of world and earth is won in the strife of the work, thereby coming into the open as *"figure, shape, Gestalt."*[34]

In dance, leaping and turning are actually single figures of movement, having specific shapes in time and space. The dance work as a whole is the gestalt that emerges from the integration of single figures. These make up larger images, or fuller movement pictures, contributing to the gestalt. Each figure (however the choreographer and dancer may designate singular movements, units, or phrases as they interpret them within the whole) makes a difference to the whole. The dance work attains its identity through its individual movement elements, which can be discerned and described in specific terms of time, space, and qualitative feeling. However, the work stands out as meaningful only in its entire unfolding. No single movement means anything by itself; yet every movement contributes to the expressive tension and meaning of the whole.

Clearly, then, dance is not simply movement. Dance makes some movement count more, composing it in full gestalts—complete art works that set up a world we can enter. As such, dances are wrested from the imagination. Dance movement stems from our image-making ability, particularly in terms of our tensional body lived in stillness and action, in agon and repose, and suspended between concealment and openness, to use Heidegger's earth-world tensional image. Accordingly, the body's solidity and personal nature closes it in, imposing limits as the solid earth has limits. All things of earth, to which the body (as solid earth) is bonded, have limits. Opposed to this limit is the open of the world, described by Heidegger as that unseen place of our being wherein the path of life is shaped through decision.[35]

More to this point, what Heidegger calls "world" and "the open" is explained by existentialist inquiry in terms of "freedom." If the essence of being is indeterminacy, as Sartre and Heidegger hold, then our choices stem from our open, or free, essence. Our being-in-the-world in the existential view is not predetermined; it is open. The choices we make make a difference. Within this indeterminate *open* (world) the *closed* (earth) of the body may yield itself to the open. In dance, the body's concealment (that which it holds but which goes ignored, unnoticed, or untapped) may be "lighted." Or, in more general existentialist terms, its freedom may be realized (made real in action).

Twyla Tharp's dance, for instance, sheds light on our tensional body-of-action, allowing us to see and experience the dancing body in new terms. The choices she makes make a difference to dance. Tossing, flinging, flopping, and twisting continuously, her incomparable, zany streams of motion—low brow, relaxed, and deceptively difficult—open a heretofore closed ground as they give us a new vision of our poetic body in its serious play. Her way of moving pushes limits and develops new skills and freedoms, as all innovative artistry does.

It is in the open of making choices (or deciding to take one action rather than another) that we enact our intentions in bodily motion, that our body actually strives, acquires skills (of all kinds), and finally experiences *freedom* through them, lending meaning to the word. Paul Ricoeur makes this clear in his study of "freedom and nature," or "the voluntary and the involuntary."[36] Through Ricoeur, we understand the emergence of body spontaneity in the bodily lived tensional dialogue between *voluntary movement* ("motor intention itself" or "directed tension") and *the involuntary* (based in the unconscious, the emotions, and habituation).[37] Ricoeur demonstates that the will is not impervious to nature. In the spontaneity of acquired and skilled motion, nature is recovered. As we achieve our intentions—as we move them forth—that which originally required effort of will becomes second nature to us; in skill, our freedom is realized.[38] That which was hidden in our understanding or beyond our willing is opened to us and becomes possible.

Mastery depends on skill, on testing limits, on opening closed grounds. The body lives the ecstatic repose of completion, composure, and mastery as the tension between its limits and envisioned freedom finally yields a freedom won. This is true of the bodily lived freedom we feel in mastering any movement, task, sport, or art. Dance, however, is the art that brings into view mastery of movement, making it count for itself.

From Ricoeur's and Heidegger's concern with decision, as well as from Sartre's concern for freedom and choice (and his view of authentic being in assuming responsibility for one's choices) I take my clue for stating the place of freedom and choice (the open of the world) in the tensional working of a dance work. Through the choreographer's decisions, movement is made to count in dance; and through the decisiveness and spontaneity, which only skill can lend to performance, the dancer makes movement beautiful. But all of this does not come ready-made; dances are created through a freely undertaken imaginative process. The picture is only complete when the strivings of those precarious decisions toward the fully realized, aesthetic "saying" of movement are at repose in the work's completion. It is then that the work becomes a free essence, affirming the unseen openness of our bodily being.

STYLE AND EXPRESSION

Dance sets up a world of movement wrested with decision out of free imagination. A dance is shaped to make movement count through decisions on just which movement performed in just what manner will count; that is, which kind of movement in what manner of performance will be true to the work as a whole. Its meaning, or its poetic truth, depends on these decisions; which is to say that the meaning of a dance lies in the poetic truth of its particular movement-being—its *style* of movement.[39] Style and expressiveness are poetic qualities formulated as the movement-being of a dance takes shape. They are linked inextricably to each other, since they both implicate the many ways in which movement may be set forth (said).

Let us not, however, form the wrong impression. Expression and style are not simply manners of moving. Expression is not said on top of movement, as something imposed; expression is both the saying and the moving. Style is not just the manner of the expression; it is the result of both movement matter and movement manner—not imposed on movement but founded in it. Style results from the choices the choreographer makes in creating the movement and structuring the dance. It refers to the work as belonging to a group, type, period, or other category. Thus we identify works as being lyrical, formal, dramatic, pedestrian, and so on. Style also results from the choices the dancer makes in performing the work. These we identify as stylistic characteristics or individual signature. Generally, we refer to style in the broadest and first sense. In both cases, movement choices involve shaping and expressing an indistinguishable *what* and *how*, since the matter of movement and the manner of setting forth movement both lie in the act of moving.[40]

In setting up a world, dance draws upon an even wider world of experienced movement, which is colored with existential qualities that inhere in movement and lie beneath the word that names them. Dance draws from experienced movement, mastered movement, and the imagination. Setting up the world of a dance work poses the problem of how to say the seemingly unsayable, how to speak truly with or through the movement so that the movement may speak—and may open a closed ground.

THE CLEARING: MORE THAN MOVEMENT

Dance sets forth the earth as it brings into the open that which has been concealed in the earth of embodied consciousness. The particular way in which dance sets forth the earth has to do with the dance's unique reach into the creative imagination (mysteriously closed and open, opaque and clear) and the way it draws it into the light by way of dance movement. The movement figure or image emerges as shaped movement in time-space. It then says in dance what once seemed unsayable and opens a closed ground. Our body-of-dance emerges from the imagination, as we embue what was hidden in our imagination's body-of-motion with an aesthetic form. Thus each dance sets up and expresses a unique world of poetized (imaginative and meaningful) movement, which founds its truth. We might also think of this unique (or original) world of movement as a clearing.

Setting up the world and setting forth the earth are what Heidegger calls the "two essential features in the work-being of the work." While these features differ, they are yet never separated in the work, and their striving is not a discord or dispute. In the striving of world and earth "the opponents raise each other into the self-assertion of their natures." Both world and earth are carried beyond themselves into an open place in the midst of being as a whole. It is in this that the art work becomes an open center, a clearing.[41] But lest we rest on the thought that this clearing is the bedrock of our search, he sets the striving once again in motion by cautioning that

> the world is not simply the Open that corresponds to clearing, and the earth is not simply the Closed that corresponds to concealment. Rather, the world is the clearing of the paths of the essential guiding directions with which all decision complies. Every decision, however, bases itself on something not mastered, something concealed, confusing; else it would never be a decision. The earth is not simply the Closed but rather that which rises up as self-closing. World and earth are always intrinsically and essentially in conflict, belligerent by nature. Only as such do they enter into the conflict of clearing and concealing.[42]

Within a concern for the immanent defining condition of dance, the lived body, we might now see how dance may be understood in its work being as a unique art. Dancing is at root, like other arts, a saying of world and earth through a bodily lived existence. It is an aesthetic expression. But unlike other arts, it is a poetry of movement, which reaches into the imagination and projects the earth and world of the body, setting forth in movement images the striving held immanent between its concealed and open nature. As such, dance is movement veiled in immobility. But as it stands in the open of saying and clears a place between the dancer and the audience, it is more than movement, it is a poetic art that opens us to our own bodily lived truths and to the words that name them. We call the latter the meaning of the dance—the truth it founds for us.

6

POINT COUNTERPOINT

For is and is-not come together;
Hard and easy are complementary;
Long and short are relative;
High and low are comparative;
Pitch and sound make harmony;
Before and after are a sequence.
—Lao Tsu

Definition-Redefinition

Let us begin to consider that dance evolves by means of aesthetic-historic oppositions, and that it does so in relation to defining constants, which are points of departure and return. The purpose of this chapter is twofold, then, and concerned with tensional factors of definition. In view of this, let us first reject the notion that dance can be redefined, as it is often claimed. Rather, we might see that there are constant points of reference in our understanding of what dance is; sometimes these points are even stated, as we name the aesthetic essence of a particular dance and qualify its movement (since we have just said that dance is more than movement). Its rhythms may appeal to us, or we may take satisfaction in its shape in space. We could also praise a dynamic quality of the movement, its clarity and precision, or the movement's express purposefulness as being beautiful or somehow aesthetically meaningful to us.

Paul Taylor's *Esplanade*, first performed in 1975, fulfills all of the above qualities even though it uses very little typical dance movement. It is graceful because it unfolds with surety of purpose; we are convinced that the movement is as it should be and do not wish for it to be otherwise. The intent of the movement is clear and exquisitely fulfilled in the decisive exuberance of the piece. The movement is dynamic and direct, free and bubbling, bringing out the emotional values of Bach's concerti in *E Major* and *D Minor* (Largo and Allegro), to which it is set—not in an obvious facsimile but in an unforced partnership, the dance falling into the music at unpredictable and thrilling points. Taylor's work is a daring extension of our everyday walking, neither an imitation nor a familiar presentation of it. It grows from danced walking into energetic running, finally extending into sporting and joyful broad jumps, as the women are caught in midair cradle lifts by their partners. There is a childlike ease and innocent freedom in *Esplanade*, which we can live through the work. Surely the most undanced part of it is the understated Largo, in which the entire ensemble groups together with a slow lumbering crawl on hands and knees, recalling the unpremeditated grace of four-footed creatures rather than dancers.

We implicitly accept that this work is a dance (and not some other kind of work) because it bears a family resemblance (as Ludwig Wittgenstein would say) to other known dance works and to that general category of activity we commonly call dance. In this acceptance there are, I believe, some constant values, which we hold as points of reference. Let me state at the outset that dance constants are elastic. Nevertheless, history demonstrates that these constants are there as points, which provide the very possibility for counterpoints.

Michael Kirby observes that once an activity is delimited, such as dance, a talent for such activity can be perceived within those limits. Because of this, he says that "a person may have little talent for dancing in the traditional sense but become a great dancer by changing the definition and limits of dance."[1] This thought leaves us with a view that dance has no identity through definitional constants; that it is not bound by any historical consistency; that it is an entirely open matter.

Kirby's is a radically subjectivist view, conforming to subjectivist philosophies which assert that values have no objective basis: beauty, for instance, exists only in the mind or the eye of the beholder. Value is constituted, accordingly, within situational definitions and personalized limits. Risieri Frondizi outlines the development of subjectivist philosophies, contrasting them to objectivist philosophies and exploring the mistakes in both extremes.[2] He outlines the development of axiological subjectivism in America, seeing it as an outgrowth of atheistic existentialism in continental Europe and also as a refutation of idealism (or axiological objectivism). Subjectivist axiology—that is, the radically personal and situational theory of value—is mistaken as it loses sight of the objective otherness of the world and as it reduces historical consciousness.

If dance (that is, all those things considered to constitute our recognition of it) could be absolutely reconstituted to suit every individual aptitude, it would have to lack any basis in biology, psychology, history, or culture. Then it would truly be, in the most limited sense, a self-expression. It would be so idiosyncratic that it would lack mediating power, which is the aspect of dance that binds the other to it. That which includes the other cannot be wholly personal; it must somehow contain the other as it speaks of him. To say that dance ought not to be understood in reference to any limits is as shortsighted as to say that it is totally bound by them. The real process of creating, performing, and evaluating dances exists somewhere between the two extremes. Arguments that new ways of dancing change its definition cannot be defended. Moreover, such arguments invariably lead us to the wrong conclusion: that dance cannot be defined.

Yet dances are differentiated and identified as individuated expressions; this we have considered. But it is also true that they are created and viewed in a historical continuum. Through Heidegger we have seen that art conveys a people's historical endowment. It preserves their truth. As individual artistic statements, dances are unique expressions—but in relation to history. They exist in relation to historical values and traditions whether they repudiate them or not. We know individuation only in relation to something. Individuation implies uniqueness. Uniqueness means one of a kind. Then there must be a general character constituting kind for anything to exist as unique in reference to it. A phenomenological definition should deal with just this point. In addition, a definition that accounts for historical consciousness would also include specific qualities considered valuable in recognized dance genres—such historically recurring constants as grace, strength, agility, and skill. These are value-given qualities in all dance but are indeed open to interpretation, culturally and stylistically.

If Kirby's statement is interpreted in context of limits determined only by embedded tradition, it makes sense.

I hold that underneath the historical evolution of new dance forms there are value givens in that which we recognize as dance according to *kind*, even though they are open to interpretation and aesthetic emphasis. These contribute to our understanding of everything we call dance.

RELATIVITY WITH OBJECTIVITY

Readers acquainted with value theory or the biases of subjectivist and objectivist aesthetic theories will recognize that I take a particular kind of relativist view concerning the realization of aesthetic value, a view often identified in value theory as *objective relativism*. This standpoint seeks to overcome the extremes of both objective and subjective axiology and is compatible with existential phenomenology, in this respect. I place the element of *relation* at the foundation of value realization. While recognizing that there are properties in objects that influence our perception of them, I recognize that these properties are valued as aesthetic in subjective experience. This we have explored in considering aesthetic value in chapter 3. Dance is not without foundational values, but these values are realized in terms of relation. In chapter 4, we saw that the perceiver stands in an active-receptive (as opposed to a passive-receptive) relation to the dance, and that the dancer, the dance, and the other for whom the dance is performed are inseparable aspects of the aesthetic field.

As a matter of the communal function of dance, we considered that dance values are realized intersubjectively. They are not realized, however, in a historical vacuum; there is a historical consciousness in any relationship. Dance is historically biased by already accepted forms and specific qualitative value givens. Dance favors grace over clumsiness, for instance, and is biased in favor of the vital expressive body. It does not favor the vapid, aimless, or inarticulate body.

CONSTANCY AND CREATIVITY

A dance, then, is understood in relation to valued constants and qualitative value givens (such as the strong, skillful, graceful body). Value givens might be seen as specific valued qualities of purposefully formulated dance expression. A movement may be expressed with grace, with skill, and within a range of strength. These are some of the qualities we value as given in dance. The art of dance progresses as a whole, moving with value givens or against them, to create new elements in the aesthetic field. It is significant, however, that constants can be identified. A tension between such givens and the free imagination of the artist motivates creativity. Freedom is attested when our understanding of an art is increased, but this freedom has a reference. If tradition is rejected, as the renewal of art dictates, it must first be experienced and understood. One cannot reject that which one does not know. Dance artists who have expanded the limits of dance, those who have given us new interpretations of its essential structure or qualitative value givens, have done so in reference to them.

Dance is not so open a concept that it is subject to redefinition; redefinition works in terms of definition. Work that produces fresh value brings us into a new relation to constants; it does not destroy them. *Redefinition assumes the existence of defining essence.*

What is usually termed redefinition might be viewed with less confusion as an expanded definition. Something new might be added when redefinition is attempted or even exclaimed; but this does not destroy valued properties in our understanding of dance. If clumsiness or unskilled movement is shown in a dance, we do not suddenly decide that dance is a clumsy and unskilled art. Essentials exist in our recognition of dance. For the most part, they go unstated *because* they provide the given, constant reference points. They are basic points of departure. They provide something to rub against, or redefinition could not be attempted. Further, that something remains—but may be seen in a new light when creative effort within the kind of activity that we recognize as dance is successful. *Kind* does not shift; rather, new styles of dancing continue to emerge through creative tension, as both phenomenal and aesthetically qualified dance givens are challenged and explored.

And it is with good reason, in terms of the vital aesthetic body as well as the healthy physical body, that we assume fundamental beginning points or constants in dance. The reasons why dance is prejudiced in favor of the vital, graceful, strong, expressive, and skillful body might well be related to the biological law of complexification, or the disposition of the organism to grow, which involves increasing levels of psychophysical complexity.[3]

It might even be argued according to theories of value importance that these beginning points, or constants, are valued in dance because they are value ascendent (other valued qualities in dance and culture depend on them), rather than descendent.[4] Weakness and clumsiness, for instance, may be aesthetically portrayed in dance, but as constants they do not define dance. They exhibit a descending order of importance. They also act in counterpoint to their opposites. Strong is only strong in relation to something weaker. And we have an understanding of what grace is partly through our view of clumsiness. Unskilled movement is also a good case in point. Because it may be possible to value unskilled or pedestrian movement in dance, it does not follow that dance is, in essence, unskilled pedestrian movement. It does imply that dance exists along a continuum of skill. *Skill* is the constant, because it implies degrees of accomplishment; lack of skill does not.

GRACE AND CHANGE

Constants that contribute to a definition of dance undergo change, however. This can be shown through a brief look at grace, a value-given quality in dance. Our concept of grace undergoes historical change as dance, the art that exemplifies grace, changes.

At the same time, grace may possess some constants, such as centeredness in action, movement from a gravitational center, and absence of self-consciousness, which Heinrich von Kleist portrays as its essential qualities.[5] While Kleist's view accounts for grace in spatial terms and as a matter of consciousness, Henri Bergson describes its dynamic and temporal qualities. He sees ease of motion as the important aspect of grace, describing it as a matter of "mastering the flow of time." The graceful dancer makes us believe that we can control time and, with it, the future.[6]

I hold that such ease (in the mastery of time flow) lies in the achievement of spontaneity and fulfillment of intention when movement attains surety of purpose. I describe this as moving freely, dissolving the object, and becoming the dance. At these points, there is just the right investiture of energy—no more or less than the intended movement requires. Graceful ease is a matter of the right fit of motion and intention; it may be apparent at both high and low energy levels, in both strong and soft movement, and in curvilinear as well as sharp angular movement.

Modern dance has required us to revise stereotypical visions of grace inherited from ballet. It shows us, for instance, that grace and gravity are not antagonists. Through modern dance, the dancer is allowed to acknowledge and work with gravity, not against it. In admitting the reality of gravity, the dancer can work with it and come to know it in experience, not only in dreaded dead weight but in weight that is alive and mobile. Grace is not just any light and floating motion; it is the weightless light that floats free of actions we perform in harmony with nature or those that become second nature, having passed through effort to finally release us from it. These are integral, not defiant, actions, which bring us into harmony with our surroundings and others. They are cognizant of weight, thus they can relinquish effort and will as well as exert it. Such actions are not defiant of, detached from, or unaware of gravity but exist in relation to it.

For instance, one of the movements cultivated in modern dance but seldom in ballet, and still informing the modern aesthetic (particularly through the influence of Doris Humphrey and José Limon), is the weighted pendular drop of the upper body (or a part of the body such as the head, arm, or leg) followed by a rebound, which lifts the motion to a floating suspension at its height. In early modern dance, such motion was variously called fall and recovery, pendular swing, or *der swung* (in Germany). This movement encompasses both the body's weighted earth and its floating heaven. It grew out of the polar mythical body, as it affirmed an aesthetic tension between up and down, weight and weightlessness, gravity and release, falling and suspending. Most significant, the fall and the suspended floating release of the lifted recovery exist in relation to each other; in fact, they are not possible as movements without each other. If I lift my arm and hold it there, it is not really suspended, it is held. Soon it feels more and more of its weight, and wants to drop. If I drop the arm, letting it fall with relaxed weight, it will pass through the weighted bottom of the fall and follow through naturally into a floating lift. When it reaches the natural end of the lift, it will have an ecstatic moment of suspension, seeming weightless at the top, but only as a result of having continued through with the original drop, and only if I do not hold it there, but let it drop again.

Martha Graham's grace (in contrast to the aerial grace of ballet) also gave the earth its gravitational due. She revived an ancient choric grace concerned with magnetic relationships among dancers in space, a space acoustically alive with psychic energy. Her grace was displayed through right angles as well as curves, through organically inward and expressively direct effort-full movement, originally criticized as ungraceful. Her dances were not graceful in the soft ethereal sense, which characterizes the best of romantic ballet, nor in an ornamented, effete sense, which was the degenerate side of the pedestaled ballerina, now anachronistically graceful in her melting weakness. Graham's grace emanated from a strong gravitational center. Consequently she influenced a new image of womanly grace, which women convey with a wider range of strength, sometimes with piercing intensity and force. And she influenced a new image of manly grace as well. Men began to dance from their own strong center of gravity. Grace became more than a pretty bauble on brittle points.

In a more playful vein, Steve Paxton, an early postmodern innovator, extended grace in dance by creating a form of improvisation based on the minimal concept in giving and taking weight in contact partnering. Androgenously paired in any combination of gender, contact partners involve a spontaneous play of energies as they easily (but sometimes with amazing speed) lift, catch, support, and bounce off each other. This often has the effect of the serious rolling and tumbling play of animals. When it works, a magical grace is created, which grows out of an open center. Or perhaps it is a vulnerable and gracious space, opened to a play of powers, a stance of "responsive openness," as Drew Hyland calls the play stance.[7]

So our understanding of grace may change; new examples of dance bring us into new relations with constants. Contact improvisation is not necessarily clumsy just because it is not balletic. Rather, it exhibits a different kind of grace. Dance constants are not subverted by new forms. Rather, all original dance works are unique inventions upon constants, even when they take opposition to them. We are only aware of an opposition, it stands to reason, in light of what it opposes.

Countering Definition

EXPRESSION: ACTION AND CONTENT

As a defining constant, the term *expression* has a twofold meaning in dance. First, expression in dance is the *for-other saying* of dance, a phenomenal feature of its structure, which it holds in common with all arts. *To express* is an action verb. *To dance* is also an action verb. The act of expressing in dance is synonymous with the movement medium of dance. Human movement is expressive action. In other words, dance is transitive. It is at once expression being done and expression being transferred.

Second, expression in dance is *content. To express,* then, moves from its phenomenal position as an action verb to the nominative position of *an expression,* one which has been accomplished and named according to some qualitative content. Or we may think of this as a shift from the act of dance to a marking of its content. It is significant that this is only a shift in attention, since the unique content of each dance is created in, and inheres in, the action. When we view dance as expression, we make this shift and thus understand the unity of action and content. Expression is action and content; but we should not lose sight of the phenomenal perspective, namely, that in prereflective consciousness, action and content are one.

DISCOVERY STANCE OF MODERN DANCE

Expression as subjective content (psychological, emotional, symbolic, and so on) has been closely associated with modern dance, from Mary Wigman's bold expressionism at the root of modern dance to new expressionism in the 1980s, with its dramatic emphases through such artists as Robert Desrosiers, Pina Bausch, Suzanne Linke, Doris Seidon, and Wendy Shenken. Yet the expressive content of modern dance has always existed in dynamic tension with formal (structural) considerations. When formalist considerations come forward, expressive content is tested. The nondefinitional (creatively open stance) of modern dance has encouraged radical explorations of a formalist-expressionist aesthetic tension. The formalist pole grew out of a concern for the act of dancing, or the formative object of dance, while the expressionist pole emphasizes expressive content, or the expressive subject of dance (as I show in the last two sections of this chapter).

While form and expression are both essential to all kinds of dance, in modern dance they are open and not essentialist terms. To explain this, let us return for a moment to what was examined in the introduction as the existential context of modern dance—its disposition toward nondefinition. Even the designation *modern* prefigures an orientation toward the new, a rejection of the past as it may definitionally delimit and bind us to essentialist philosophic or aesthetic models. For this and other reasons stated, I have been prompted to relate modern dance to existentialism, to call it a discovery form of dance, and also to see that ballet, in comparison to modern dance, emphasizes aesthetic formalism and valued tradition (especially in its formalized movement vocabulary), while by no means being totally bound by them. Certainly the ballet has also demonstrated both formalist and expressionist tendencies, as the difference between George Balanchine's abstract formalist ballets and Antony Tudor's development of the psychological expressiveness of the body through the formal syntax of ballet shows.

Modern dance opened the expressive ground of dance to a fuller range of subjectivity in general by opening up a new range of movement possibilities and felt (or psychic) states intrinsic to the movement. Nevertheless, we recognize that feeling in modern dance is expressed through an aesthetic formulation of movement. We also note that even rigorously formalized ballet has some expressive content, if only in the innate expressiveness of the dancer's body. Form and feeling are points of tension and emphasis in dance (as in all art) and not divisible entities. Dance exists through human movement, which is always psychophysical expressive form. In its original forms, modern dance opened up and pressed the limits of expression in terms of kind of movement expressed, its range of intensity, and its referential potential. It has tested expression as a conditional constant of dance ever since.

In this study, we have already seen that expression is not a simple term in dance; but rather than avoid it, I hope to clarify (and to challenge) some meanings it has acquired. I will strive to cut beneath dualistic views of expression to see that, in dance, content and action meld in the term. Expression interpreted simply as content may be countered as a definitional limit of dance. But when this happens (as I hope to show in the next chapter), the basic unity of action and content shows itself. That is, *without expression there is no dance.*

Yet true to its nonessentialist stance, modern dance tests such claims, limits, or definitions. In the process, it is forever reinventing dance and thereby leading us to several questions. How far can perceived limits be pushed? When they are successfully pushed, what results? An expanded limit or a redefinition? Related to this, do value-given constants remain, or are they replaced by their opposites? This I eventually address to some extent through late modern dance as represented by Merce Cunningham, since he emphasizes form to the intentional exclusion of symbolic expressiveness and organic sequencing of movement. Directly to the point is a consideration of postmodern deconstructive dance, which pushes the lower limits of both expression and formalized technique through minimalism, pedestrian movement, and denial of expressive ecstatic movement as represented in mainstream modern dance and ballet. Of course, not all postmodern dance fits this description; oppositions have also been at work within its evolution. The early postmodern styles were polemic in relation to dramatically expressive styles, which, I believe, were and still are misinterpreted as "self-expressive." Later styles surpassing the postmodern period turned toward expressionism once again, renewed through its rejection and questioning—as we shall see in the next chapter.

HOW, NOT WHAT

While deriving from an open and antidefinitional stance, modern dance still falls within a view of dance constancy. An art that takes nondefinition as its stance (or call this an experimental and creative openness, if you will) nevertheless, in order to be meaningful even on its own terms, has to attest the arrival of points of definition. Thus it is not correct to say that modern dance has not achieved clear definitional stances. But neither should we ignore that it concentrates—as a point of definition—on constantly rediscovering dance.

As a consequence, there are modern dance techniques but not one modern dance technique. Because of this, modern dancers study the human body and its movement potential. In the process of scientific study and aesthetic experiment, they produce a view of dance (and dance technique) that has more to do with learning *how* to move than with unquestioned imitation of movement styles or the incorporation of a codified movement vocabulary (the substantive *what* that ballet technique stipulates in its practiced vocabulary of movement).

Teachers of modern dance technique often incorporate several styles of moving (yes, even technique has style) with a view to the qualities that inhere in the movement produced by particular artists. For instance, the movement of Limon can be described in part through its weightedness, lyricism, and fullness of phrasing, that of Erick Hawkins as it treats extremities with a tassellike ease, and that of Cunningham according to its sharp precision and sudden changes of direction. These are defined ways of moving embedded in, not imposed upon, individual movement styles.

Modern dancers make choices about movement, since they do not have a constant vocabulary of prescribed movement. Certainly they borrow from the ballet and learn from it. If they have recourse to any movement constancy, it is through the continuing concern to create movement (and thus new styles of moving) out of the endless variety that may be played upon basic locomotor movement (the fundamental transfers of weight between the feet as they move the body through space) and axial motion (possible motion from a fixed base). Technique in modern dance is less a means for establishing a vocabulary of movement than a preparation of the alert, alive, and responsive body.

The Expressive Subject

Because of its seeming lack of defining essence, modern dance also has to take thoughtful positions toward creativity. In its striving for origination, modern dance encounters its primary aesthetic potential as a nonessentialist (unbounded) art, grounded in freedom and individuality. At the same time, it incurs its sharpest danger. I agree with Hawkins that "the error consists in believing that because it is possible, it is desirable."[8] The importance of this is also stressed by Paul Kuntz, who concludes that "by itself sheer novelty is as ruinous as repetition by itself."[9] Ballet risks boring us with repetition, and modern dance risks boring us with novelty. In addition, the danger is increased in modern dance that freedom may dissolve into a lack of standards, low expectations, and an anarchy of individualism and eccentricity.

The positive side of the modern existentialist expansion of both philosophy and art, as it answers a need to challenge well-ordered logical systems in philosophy (being first an attack on Hegel's essentialism) and settled aesthetic standards in art, is its achievement of new expressive forms within a concern for humanizing values — acknowledging human anguish, the accidental, and the irrational in life. The danger of this expansion lies in its potential to destroy meaningful form altogether. The existentialist reliance on intuition and subjectivity through its attack on reason, to balance the Western analytic and scientific scheme of values, was perhaps the most alarming.

In *Irrational Man,* where he writes extensively about links between modern art and existentialism, William Barrett says that "Modern art has been an immense movement toward the destruction of forms—of received and traditional forms. The positive side of this has been an immense expansion of the possibilities of art and an almost greedy acquisition of new forms all over the globe."[10] Now the existentialist movement may be simply viewed as an effort to recover the existing individual as a thinking, feeling whole. Carl Jung's psychology had already demonstrated that Western, one-sided, objectivized consciousness of the world would have to produce a compensation.

In dance, modern artists creating from a stance of existential openness answer the need to affirm vital unpredictable human existence in all of its subjective complexity. Its early expressionist themes, through the work of Mary Wigman and Martha Graham and later Anna Sokolow and Daniel Nagrin, were often as dark and anguished as the literary existentialists, who opened philosophy and psychology to the problems of the unconscious and the subjective, along with the vagaries, hazards, and responsibilities of freedom.[11] The following brief portraits of the existentialism of Daniel Nagrin and Anna Sokolow may serve to illustrate this parallel.

DANIEL NAGRIN

In an interview with Daniel Nagrin in 1976, I asked him what being an existentialist meant to him, since he was the one dancer I knew who had directly identified himself with existentialism. Being an existentialist means "not knowing," he answered concisely, then reiterated, "living with uncertainty, accepting the paradoxical truth that it is impossible to know."

His 1968 concert-length solo, *The Peloponnesian War,* casts modern imagery against a reading of Thucydides's monumental history and a score by Eric Salzman and Archie Shepp. It is one of the clearest examples of subjective existentialism (and its antiessentialist philosophic stance) in modern dance.[12] Its illogical juxtaposition of obscenities, nobility, absurdities, and dreams, its grab-bag nature, its teetering at the edge of things, its recognition of perennial human problems, and most certainly its open

Daniel Nagrin in *Peloponnesian War.* Photo: Carol Stein.

and unfinished nature bespeak the concerns (and subjective style) of existentialism.

When questioned about the existential nature of this dance, Nagrin commented that he was constantly breaking style in the piece, doing and undoing at once: "Every time I did something, I undid it. I wanted to shake people who are addicted to the romantic premise that they can arrive at absolutes. *Complete, total,* and *ideal* become the new obscenities. Romantic idealism is at the root of fascist ideologies. When we have to be right at any cost, we're in trouble."

Asked how he felt about existentialists being accused of nihilism, he replied that "becoming uncertain is not a negation. If people will become hesitant and less certain, they will become more compassionate and loving. Existentialists understand that they see the world from where they are; who they are makes a difference, and what they look at colors their vision. We can't see everything. Human beings all too typically see what supports only their own identity. Being an existentialist means allowing for differences."

Nagrin further explained a statement he had made in class, that if we dancers don't live with danger, we're nothing. "The creative person lives on the edge of the abyss, ready to fall. You can't find out what's possible without risking death or injury. The creative act carries you to a place where you don't know, actually, whether you can do it or not – it carries you to a point of physical risk!" The tone of Nagrin's comments recalls Friedrich Nietzsche's famous dictum "live dangerously," and the image of his fallen tightrope walker:

> After a while the shattered man recovered consciousness and saw Zarathustra kneeling beside him. . . . "I lose nothing when I lose my life. I am not much more than a beast that has been taught to dance by blows and a few meager morsels."
>
> "By no means," said Zarathustra. "You have made danger your vocation: there is nothing contemptible in that. Now you perish of your vocation: for that I will bury you with my own hands."[13]

We were reminded that, while the existential aesthetic has been delineated for other arts, no one has written about its appearance in dance. Sartre writes of the "literature of commitment." Samuel Beckett, Jean Genet, and Eugène Ionesco's theater of the absurd initiated existentialism in drama. Paul Tillich writes of the "courage of dispair" in contemporary art and literature. In poetry, T. S. Eliot's *Wasteland* is an existential expression of the decay of civilization. In *Irrational Man,* Barrett explains the scattering of time-space values inherent in the existential aesthetic with examples from painting and literature. And in music the loss of a fixed tonal center (first through the music of Schoenberg) can be seen as a parallel to the existential theme of the broken center. I asked Nagrin how he would characterize the existential aesthetic for dance.

He put his answer in terms of both movement and the performer's relationship to the audience. "The romantic gesture assumes the existence of the Holy Grail, and indicates it. On the other hand, the existential gesture asks the audience to join with the dancer in paying attention to an inexplicable mystery. . . . An existential artist requires the involvement of the audience, saying come and help me, let's work on this together. The existentialist doesn't expect everybody to be interested in his work. . . . He has no right to expect to be popular." This statement bore directly upon Nagrin's interest in existentialist authors. He professed a liking for Camus and said that he had read some of Nietzsche but that Sartre's technicality did not appeal to him.

Finally we touched upon how his teaching and his choreographic work with others reflect his existential standpoint of not knowing. "I don't expect the people I work with to look like me," he emphasized. "What I perform is mannered by my person. The people I work with do not pick up my style. . . . What I project to others is a shape that is inherently amebic. It has to be filled out by the person who does it. . . . I like to be surprised by what my students do."

When Jennifer Dunning interviewed Nagrin in 1982, he was still going strong in a dancing career lasting over three decades.[14] He moved, she says, "with the intense, precise deliberation of an animal." When she remarked on his unmistakable style, he reacted in anything but formalist terms. "It's got nothing to do with form or content. . . . It's got to do with giving a damn about other people."

He also explained his early work with Helen Tamiris, his mentor and one of the founders of modern dance. "She was self-defeating in terms of history and schools, because what she was doing was working from the moment. Each class was different. There was no schema, only that you were constantly thrown into yourself." This disposition to work from individual resources and not according to established aesthetic models explains in concrete terms what I call the existential context of modern dance—its defiance of essentialist definition.

In 1978 Nagrin premiered his dance adaptation of *The Fall*, from the novel by Camus. Here he shows that dance is not just for nymphs and fairies in forests primeval or gardens of youthful feminine beauty. In the stark conclusion of *The Peloponnesian War,* his stripped and aging body tenders a sense of finitude impossible to youth. Age is not caricatured; it is finally the existential heart of the matter.

ANNA SOKOLOW

In 1980 I interviewed Anna Sokolow. Although she does not directly associate herself with the term *existentialism,* as Nagrin does, her concerns, like Nagrin's, are those of committed, subjective existentialism. Certainly her works demonstrate *sorge* (care), as Heidegger sees the core of existential authenticity. Yet, like Heidegger, Sartre, and other literary existentialists, she has been accused of nihilism. She told me she resents the label "mistress of gloom and doom," which belittles the real purpose of her work, which is "finding meaning in life." "Why" she questioned, "should it be a crime to be sad?"

Her dances, echoing a central existential theme, recognize that "within life there is death." Her comments recall Carlos Castaneda's mystic and existential writings on "death as a teacher." She spoke of them and of her appreciation for the Day of the Dead in Mexico, expressing empathy for people in whom "death cannot be brushed aside."

She acknowledges the importance for the artist of "going within oneself to find out the truth." Being accepted or being a success do not matter. "I was never a joiner. I was never a conformist. I'm a loner. I can only do what I feel in dance. Is it wrong to do what you feel, or do you have to please somebody who's going to buy a ticket?"

Sokolow believes her own struggles in life are reflected in her work, which has grown out of "a search for beauty" and "a yearning and desire to make things." She offers no apology for confronting the brutal realities of loneliness, emptiness, and fear in *Rooms* (1955), *Steps of Silence* (1968), and *Dreams* (1961).

She is not an advocate of the aesthetics of detachment, movement for movement's sake, or art for art's sake. Like the existentialist authors who ask "why is there something instead of nothing," she is passionate about the dancing that grows directly from that something. This is reflected in her description of a teaching incident: "I asked a student who was showing me her dance, 'What are you trying to tell us?' And she replied, 'Nothing.' Another student asked, 'What's wrong with doing nothing?' I told them to get out. I don't want to teach Nothing—I want to open the door to Something."

The Formative Object

We do not aim to *express*—we present this event before you.—Merce Cunningham

KING, FENLEY, STREB, CUNNINGHAM, NIKOLAIS

Later forms of modern dance parallel the second (objective formalist) phase of existentialism in its incorporation of phenomenology, particularly in its concern to return to consciousness of *things in themselves*—the object seen clearly (purely) for what it is. Formalist dance in its focus on movement for itself—or the formative object of dance—illustrates this, beginning with the work of Merce Cunningham. *Pure dance* has stuck as a label describing nonrepresentational dances performed for the sake of satisfaction in the movement itself.

Dancer Kenneth King associates his work with phenomenology.[15] He wants to dance about what cannot be known, thus reminding us that dance, in its movement essence, extends beyond what we typically call knowledge. Phenomenology, as we saw in the first chapter, exhibits a concern for describing the object of awareness as it appears immediately to consciousness, reducing it to its essential form. In 1986, when King and I talked about his work and its relation to philosophy, he explained that he started to dance as a teenager, when questions about death loomed large for him. "Dance is the art which reveals the unknown, or what can't be known through any other means." He believes that dance is a phenomenology of movement—that the phenomena of consciousness (which he relates to Jung's collective unconscious and its archetypal images) are distilled in human movement and inscribed in dance.

Maurice Merleau-Ponty's book *The Visible and the Invisible* has influenced King's thinking about dance.[16] "Gesture punctuates the invisible," King says. "The invisible space around the gesture is its eidetic contour." His dance for Buckminster Fuller, *Critical Path* (1985), is a geometric abstract of motion. One is aware not only of the architecture of the work but the traveling of a critical human path as well.

Dancer Molissa Fenley admits taking up new existentialism, through its incorporation of phenomenology and nondualistic positivity, in dance that reaches for the "peak moment." Such works as *Eureka* (1982) and *Energizer* (1982) speak to the will to go beyond the normal, and beyond the self. These works, she says, were motivated by Colin Wilson's philosophy.[17] Her works are stylistically abstract; but in contrast to King's abstraction, they paint with explosive splashes of motion rather than lines and synergetic networks.

In another way, Elizabeth Streb's dances also represent the formative-object phase of existentialism. As her dances are pitched into dangerous feats of accomplishment, they exemplify for me the existentialist image of *being thrown,* holding form and formlessness, creation and destruction, in dynamic tension. In her athletic dance games, high-risk movement is literally thrown into a deft manipulation of equipment. Poles, balls, hoops, ropes, are relentlessly moved, not just with the hands but with the feet, the head, the entire body. *Polevault #5* (1981), *Ringside* (1982), and *Target* (1983) are strictly choreographed dances; yet the threat of possible failure is built in. Performed mainly without music and as virtuoso task games, her dances are concentrated in the formative moment, seeming to point out the spontaneity that all good dancing rides on — or rides in the middle of.

As she told me in an interview, "I don't always achieve what I'm after, but when I do, it's like being in the middle of a wave." This I believe, effectively describes the formative, present-centered moment of dancing, as the dancer focuses her self in her actions, not watching her self and her actions from the outside.

When dance revolves around expressive action (rather than expressive content) and the formative moment, as it does in Streb's work, what then is being expressed beyond the movement itself — if, as I hold, dance is more than movement? I asked Streb if she felt she was "expressing anything" in her dances. Her answer states well the bondedness of self, motion, and expression: "I strive to achieve a pure focus, ridding myself of everything but that move, that act. I think that everything I am as a human being comes out then, at those moments. It involves so much emotionally, physically, and psychologically to do it."[18]

Merce Cunningham is perhaps the clearest example of formalism in recent modern dance. He was the first to reveal movement as the inmost formative object of dance in his radical rejection of dramatic representation. His work *reduced* dance (to use the phenomenological term) to its movement essence.

Yet if this study of the body in dance has yielded anything so far, it is that even formalist dance such as Cunningham's is innately expressive and meaningful because it exists through the innately expressive human body. Cunningham clearly recognizes this, noting that dance is done by people, and people are not abstractions.[19] Even Alwin Nikolais, who openly eschews self-expression in dance—focusing attention on multimedia mixes of shape, motion, light, and sound—nevertheless recognizes expressive intent in the great range of expression deriving from the interplay of the psyche and the physique, which the dancer must learn to control.[20]

POINTS OF DEFINITION

In the next chapter, I consider further how all dance, no matter how purely abstract or formal, refers us beyond its movement medium. I have been developing the thesis that dance is expressive, that dance is more than movement. Human movement mediates as it becomes affective within us, or meaningful to us. The movement material in and of itself is simply raw material until it is shaped within its presentational (expressive) purpose. It comes alive as art when it brings us to stand in the open of its unique saying (to recall Heidegger)—when it brings us within its own scope of expression. This is my thesis, which should become increasingly clear.

In summary, modern dance has reached various and contrasting points of definition as it has taken an open, discovery stance (a nonessentialist or existential position) within the general defining characteristics of what we know and have valued as Western theater dance since it originated with the Greeks. New forms of dance do not, I contend, redefine dance. They bring us into new relations with valued constants, which are themselves open to interpretation as they are brought to our attention anew in original works. Within the broad defining outlines of dance, modern dance exhibits the same tendency to shift between formalism and expressionism that other historical dance forms exhibit, but it stretches our understanding of both form and feeling through its unsettled nature and causes us to look more carefully at these as interpenetrating aspects of dance. Now we can turn to a closer consideration of expressionist and formalist tendencies, as they create an aesthetic tension in dance.

7

EXPRESSIONIST-FORMALIST TENSION

Aesthetic-Historic Tension

Plato succinctly states two areas of interwoven aesthetic values realized through dance: "One department of dancing is the presentation of works of poetical inspiration with the care for the preservation of dignity and decorum; the other, which aims at physical fitness, nobility, and beauty, ensures an appropriate flexure and tension in the actual bodily limbs and members, and endows them all with a grace of movement which is incidentally extended to every form of the dance and pervades all intimately."[1] Thus he sees that poetic expressiveness as well as beauty and grace of form are the purposes of dance.[2]

Selma Jean Cohen makes similar distinctions. She argues that dances have been meaningful in various noninterchangeable ways throughout history: "We know that the Greeks and Romans wanted their theatre dance to serve as a kind of language. Augustine claimed this as the source of its value, for he declared that merely graceful motion pleases only the senses, leaving the mind unaffected. . . . The Renaissance looked for symbolic values, while the eighteenth century returned to the idea of dance as a kind of drama involving actions and passions, though with lurking digressions intimating that the delights of airs and graces might be even more important."[3]

Cohen says that in general practice dance shifts between "imitation" and "pure movement," as reformers call for dance to return to one or the other of its "true functions." She relates these terms to Nelson Goodman's distinctions between dances that denote and those that exemplify and states that these may be seen as two types of dance at the extremeties of a continuum "from nearly realistic denotation to exemplification of forms." She observes that contemporary styles almost run the gamut and that "we had better beware of asking any one of them for a kind of meaning more appropriate to another."[4]

Cohen and Goodman make primary distinctions in yet other ways. Cohen takes a broad historical perspective. Goodman shows that all art has some level of referential content, regardless of whether it emphasizes denotational content (pointing out something directly through representation) or abstract forms, functioning as "a sample" of something (pointing it out indirectly), such as a rhythm, a pattern, or a shape. So-called pure art also functions referentially (often through exemplification); it also has subject matter.[5]

Aesthetics historian Katherine Everett Gilbert, in writing about "mind and medium" in the early modern dance, notes that it was Aristotle who set a standard for the double orientation of art as analyzable structure (form) and psychic expression (feeling).[6] Form and expressiveness are also contrasted in the Greek gods Apollo and Dionysus: Apollo is the god of all plastic powers; through him measure, reason, and pattern are formed. Opposing Apollo is Dionysus, the god of song and dance; through him our bond with nature is forged, symbolized in the rapturous approach of spring. Friedrich Nietzsche wrote of the aesthetic tension between the two gods in *The Birth of Tragedy.*[7] Thus we might understand that the expressionist-formalist (subject-object) point of aesthetic tension, introduced in the last chapter, has a deep, historical, and mythical source. Expressionist and formalist theories have typically supported one aspect of art or the other, often articulating important points but missing the whole (as we considered wtih Arnold Berleant).

To accept that all dances are meaningful whatever their aesthetic character or emphasis is to accept that all dance contains at least some primal symbolic potential—and perhaps many other varying levels of referential power. I have already accepted this by describing dance as a projective poetic saying that is more than movement.

Goodman and Susanne Langer, who both draw from Ernst Cassirer's work on symbols, hold that art does function symbolically—that it refers us beyond its immediate material.[8] Louis Arnaud Reid criticizes and defends some points of Langer's work.[9] He states that art functions symbolically in a general way to create new meaning in the manner that full ideas also symbolize. It is not the single word that symbolizes in language but its integral sense within a full idea. He emphasizes the formulative function of the art symbol and differentiates the use of the word *symbol* in art from the common use of the word. Thus he focuses on art's unique formulation of experience and away from Langer's association of symbols with concepts. The "aesthetic symbol" is for him a new construct "embodied" in the work. In spite of some differences, Reid and Langer both see that art symbolizes in a more general way than language does.

Goodman's distinctions between art that symbolizes through denotation and art that functions through exemplification help to explain varying ways in which art refers us beyond its material manifestation. The difference between the actual appearance of the art and what it brings to mind is important. In representational dance, the dance movement is necessarily unlike what it represents. The difference between the movement and what it represents renders representation a possibility. To Goodman, "denotation is the core of representation and is independent of resemblance."[10]

Neither does Goodman view expressive properties as occurring through resemblance or imitation but rather as properties possessed by a work—the qualities belonging to it. He states that expression and representation do not function through "imitation" but rather through "intimation."[11] And he argues convincingly that what is deemed "pure" or nonsymbolic in art nevertheless functions symbolically as it exemplifies or stands as a sample of whatever it shows forth as heightened in our consciousness. "Whoever looks for art without symbols, then, will find none—if all the ways that works symbolize are taken into account. Art without representation or expression or exemplification—yes; art without all three—*no*."[12]

Form and feeling—or form and expressive content, if you will—are necessarily a part of each other. While they may be described as properties of a work, they do not comprise the work. They are partial ways of looking and describing, which are of value to aesthetics (as we take works apart) but not to the aesthetic experience (as we perceive whole gestalts). Do we not, rather, enter into a world that the art work makes vivid for us within its own created essence, a world where meaning emerges only from the whole and not from single parts? Such worlds are possible because *art makes meaning:* that is, art worlds are not life worlds, but create meanings of their own. Both worlds become more vivid as we cross the distance between them. Their meanings are of a different order. It is only by virtue of the difference that we can associate them at all, through apprehending likeness (exemplification) or direct (denotational) connections.

I agree with Reid that a work of art creates and embodies something unique to it. It engages us precisely because it is not derived from something preexisting outside of it; rather, meaning builds through the artist's discoveries as he creates a unique work. Reid discusses "expression" in art in terms of "the emergence of creative embodiment," which he calls an "aesthetic embodiment" in some medium.[13] I have already considered that to embody a dance involves a forming of our own given embodiment toward an aesthetic embodiment, an embodiment that Reid describes as "new embodied meaning."[14] I also agree with him that this new created meaning is "integral with the formed medium and yet transcends it."[15] Meaning in dance is integral with the body and its motion; yet the dance work in its entirety transcends this medium as it becomes a meaningful whole.

I am disputing extreme distinctions between form and expressive content (sometimes called feeling), while continuing to pursue general questions about dance and expression. With Goodman, I believe that expressive properties are integral to and possessed by dances; with Merleau-Ponty, that these properties are primal in the bodily lived substance of dance; with Jacques Seranno, that they appear on a continuum from descriptive form (at the initial pole) to created form (at the terminal pole); and with Martin Heidegger, that they are poetic, projective saying.[16] The created form (at the terminal pole of expression) or the projective saying of art (its standing in the open) can also be thought of in Reid's frame of reference as the fullness of the work in its created embodiment. Its unique embodied meaning (a meaning embodied in the work and also transcending it) arises out of its fully created nature. Form and content are not divisible at this point.

Yet distinctions between form and expressive content have divided dance into its Apollonian (formalist) and Dionysian (expressionist) oppositions. These we might see as aesthetic oppositions and also as enduring historical oppositions, created by the distinct intentions artists take toward their medium, intentions that operate to renew dance (and art) in general.

Langer paints feeling in masterfully large brush strokes, relating it to mind in her major work. For her, expression, form, feeling, and mind are inextricably involved in one another, and art is a special case in which to observe this: "The prime function of art is to make the felt tensions of life, from the diffused somatic tonus of vital sense to the highest intensities of mental and emotional experience, 'stand still to be looked at.'"[17] Feeling, or sentience, is art's domain; we live art through the affective, through moving out toward the art work and being moved by it. Art becomes more meaningful as we relate it to our world at large and use it cognitively.

Yet, expression, or feeling, has often been narrowed in dance to refer to overtly expressive (or hot) qualities in movement. Expressionism has come to identify styles of dance characterized by a passionate intensity, the most prominent historic examples being Mary Wigman, Kurt Jooss, José Limon, and Martha Graham. Given such an identification, artists can intentionally emphasize either form against feeling or feeling against form.

The question of whether one can succeed in emptying art of expression (or of expressive feeling) is relevant to our fuller understanding of the term *expression* as it has acquired meaning in the historic shifting between expressionism and formalism in dance, especially in view of various styles that have emerged from these broad categories of aesthetic emphasis. Coolly abstract, or even cold and remote dance certainly is not without referential content, feeling or style. Langer properly speaks of the expressive quality of a work as its "feeling." She further states that the achievement of sensuous or poetic quality is what characterizes artistry. Beauty resides in quality of expression: "Every kind of art is beautiful, as all life is beautiful, and for much the same reason: that it embodies sentience, from the most elementary sense of vitality, individual being and continuity, to the full expansion of human perception."[18]

As I look now at some narrow stylistic terms of expression, I will continue to press toward the larger sense of what it means to express in dance, and to stress the view I have been developing—that action and content are one and that style is a marking of the whole character of a work.

Moving Against Expression

The antiexpressionist school of postmodern dance moved against expressiveness (or overtly expressive styles) in mainstream modern dance and ballet. Merce Cunningham had already cooled down expression in modern dance. The early postmoderns who succeeded him tried to neutralize it (depersonalize it altogether) and to move against it.

They had their reasons, perhaps best stated by Yvonne Rainer, who became disillusioned with the modern dance of her day—which, by the early 1960s, had moved away from its earthbound beginnings toward the polish and aerial heroism of the ballet. She repudiated this in what Sally Banes has called "a strategy of denial." Rainer's most quoted manifesto says "NO to spectacle no to virtuosity no to transformations and magic and make-believe no to the glamour and transcendency of the star image no to the heroic no to the anti-heroic no to trash imagery no to involvement of performer or spectator no to style no to camp no to seduction of spectator by the wiles of the performer no to eccentricity no to moving or being moved."[19]

To Banes the beauty of Rainer's *Trio A* (originally performed as *The Mind Is a Muscle* in 1966) resides "not in ideas of grace, elegance, dramatic expression or even of nature, but in the material truth of its coexistent presence and distance." And she saw the possibility that the cycle of conflict between technical dance and expressive dance had been broken through the introduction of dance that was "neither perfection of technique nor of expression, but quite something else—the presentation of objects in themselves." She felt that a new definition of dance (not simply a new style) had appeared.[20]

While something new in dance undoubtedly appeared through the postmodern, I argue that it was not without style, but was rather a stylistic departure from the highly developed technical modern dance represented by Cunningham and the psychological and dramatic-expressive dance of Graham. At its foundation, postmodern dance employed deconstruction of overt dramatics and repudiated the dictates of established techniques. Minimalist and pedestrian styles emerged as a result. It is also claiming too much for postmodernism to say it redefined dance, since postmodern deconstructive styles have been superseded by a regeneration of technically difficult and even overtly expressive styles, which nevertheless are influenced by the postmodern challenge to technical and dramatic-expressive dance traditions.

The attempt to present our unadorned steps for themselves alone was begun by Cunningham. Although he used technically developed dance movement, he removed any pretext of denotational symbolic content, allowing the movement to be seen for itself. While rejecting established techniques, postmodern dance extended this focus on the movement medium of dance by making conscious use of the pedestrian. Functional everyday action was rendered nonfunctional danced action by being placed in a communal dance context—by being performed for-other—much as a René Duchamp ready-made is rendered art by being selected and exhibited as such. Because of this, the postmodern pedestrian style could be performed by untrained dancers, unlike Cunningham's technically based style.

However, there was a risk in pedestrian dance not present in the inert matter of Duchamp's found bicycle wheel, the risk of unintentionally projecting the self (and self-importance), not the intended dance—a risk inherent in all dancing, but which the trained dancer overcomes in learning how to focus on the performance of the dance.

Rainer was aware of this risk as she intentionally sought to depersonalize her dance. She moved, however, within a highly idiosyncratic style, creating out of the alert yet quiet ease of her own work body. In the sense that she retained an expressive (for-other) purpose and projected her dance as a revelation of the unconstrained work-body per se (and not just her own), her dance *Trio A* let us appreciate our own work-body in its understated elegance. She created in *Trio A* an innocent, worklike style, replete with soft arm and leg gestures, occasional relaxed lunges, balances on one leg, resilient floor rolls, little skips, a momentary hand stand, quiet foot tapping and head rolling, shoulder shrugs, hand clasping, and easy arm flinging. Her dance suggested that grace may also be released through the working intelligence of the subtly detailed body. This she achieved through opposing previous styles and denotational (direct, or hot) dance expressiveness.

It would be difficult to claim as Banes does that "the achievement of *Trio A* is its resolute denial of style and expression, making an historical shift in the subject of dance to pure motion."[21] The shift to pure motion has taken place often in dance. It was a formalist concern with the Greeks; in the early modern period, Mary Wigman termed pure dance "absolute dance"; later the so-called pure dance of Cunningham, Farber, and Balanchine followed. Nikolais's nonliteral abstract dance gives us another vision of pure motion with an intensified depersonalization. Formalist dance, like formalism in the other arts, is often linked with purity of motion and depersonalization. Any attempt to purify a medium by emphasizing its formal (objective) characteristics either on a high technical level or on a pedestrian level has to produce some stylistic consequences if anything with a unique identity is to result.

Postmodernism in its minimalist manifestations moved away from explicit movement and toward the implicit in movement. It also displaced technically difficult movement, in terms of the extended and ecstatic body, with consciously pedestrian or understated movement. As an attempt to zero in on the mundane and to blank feelings and emotions, it was fraught with stylistic implications. But it is impossible to erase the affective, because we live it bodily. We live and breathe within the constantly changing landscape of our senses and our emotions. Neither are these separate from our ever-expressive moving body. Blankness itself (as in stillness, boredom, silence, waiting, white) holds expressive tension. Feelings attendant upon these qualities are produced in us as we merge with such qualities in our aesthetic experience of them. Louis Dupre explains that the aesthetic experience is a perception colored by a subjective disposition; consequently, "the merging of the self with its object is usually referred to as a *feeling*."[22]

The thingness (or objectivity) of things is alive with style and colored with feeling. Even architecture, which may be the most structurally objective of the arts, is full of expressive tension (feeling) and stylistic identity. If our ordinary walking can also be taken as an object, a thing in itself (a movement object), then it must be apparent that there are many individual styles of walking. Walking is full of style, as it speaks of the person. Each person's walk expresses him. That which is familiar about him clings to his walk and pervades it. I can frame such a walk and attend to it as a dance. However, such intentional framing of the ordinary soon loses its power, and my appetite for a transformational walk, which carries me beyond the familiar and mundane world, returns.

If we believe, with Maxine Sheets, that "*each dance creates its own inimitable technique*,"[23] we would view dances that lack typical technical virtuosity as, nevertheless, having inherent technical requirements. If, as I claim, dance movement is created, performed, and presented *intentionally*, it supposes some level of being able (technically) to *do* the movement and some level of being able (expressively) to *present* the movement.

In spite of their easing of technique and explicit expressiveness, postmodern dancers were aware of some technical and expressive requirements of dance.[24] They used the same formulative and learning processes that have always gone into dance but also new and looser styles of moving.

Undoubtedly, postmodern dance stimulated a revaluation of technique and expression, enlarging and expanding a definition of dance—much as the early modern dance had done. But it could not displace technique (skilled movement) and expressiveness as valued qualities in dance, since these impinge upon the entire lived realm of the affective—or aesthesis—which is always present within the body aesthetic. Neither could it redefine dance simply on idiosyncratic stylistic bases nor on mundane movement terms. Dance carries its history with it. To intentionally suspend or oppose that history requires a consciousness of it, a deep familiarity with it. Moving against phenomenal basics or value givens in dance has the effect of sharpening them, as basic.

Saying no to involvement of the performer and spectator and no to style may not be so easily achieved in an art that is for-other and is performed through a bodily lived material. A dance could only be without style if it were totally without form or dynamic. I wonder if Rainer's attempts to depersonalize her performance presence in *Trio A* through "workly concentration and withdrawn face," did not translate as a matter of style rather than as a breakthrough wherein "personal style or idiosyncrasy fades."[25] Did it not appear as highly idiosyncratic, and even more personal than a dance that accepts a simple giveness of the self, self superseded in the performance of a dance? Did not the withdrawn face begin to invade dance and to mark the postmodern style? And did not workly concentration enter stylistically into the movement—successfully through founding artists like Rainer, who could show us work as revelation, and unsuccessfully through countless neophytes who adopted either the work formula or the work style but could not hide lack of imagination behind the withdrawn face? The polemic eventually degenerated from mundane dance into vacuous mundane behavior, and a sense of accomplishment faded from dance.

No amount of pretended concentration will engage an audience. Dancers who engage us are skillful with movement. They possess technique and are expressively imaginative.

GAINING AND LOSING

In minimalizing, cooling, or blanking expression, antiexpressionist postmodern dance posed both a gain and a loss. When an element is minimalized, it is singled out for attention through understatement. When we are conscious of an intent to blank technical skill and expressiveness in movement, they stand out as conditions by which we recognize dance. In contradicting these vital dance values, minimalist dance (tending toward nondance) contra indicated them. In its early forms, postmodern dance also provided a unique view of the values embedded in our workaday body-of-action. Through both exaggeration and understatement, Steve Paxton gave us the various ways of our walking. Pedestrian dance became popular in many college and loft performances. While the values of our ordinary acts were being championed, a danger was posed in the loss of universalizing and vitalizing qualities, which I hold are necessary to the aesthetically valuable in dance.

This point becomes increasingly important as we consider that the health of a culture depends on what it accepts as the best in art. In dance a culture affirms its collective and vital body; and it cannot be claimed in good conscience that an unexpressive body is an aesthetically vital or healthy body or that a singular pursuit of low-energy, easy, pedestrian movement is in any way developmental. It might be claimed that art and biology are separate issues. I claim that they should not be. In terms of dance, an understatement of the body, which poses no vision of vitality, is a metaphorical if not a real loss of the vital body we have always valued in dance for mutual aesthetic and biological reasons. In addition, there can be an arrogance and a short-sighted self-involvement in understatement, just as there can be in overstatement. As understatements, minimalism and pedestrianism solve nothing in this respect, and they pose problems of their own.

Problems were posed by postmodern denial dance (or nondance), as it extended into education and its objective intention turned to mute blankness. Art functions to vitalize and give aesthetic form to our native expressiveness, not to blank it. Education should also vitalize. The attempt to destroy dance values embedded in vividly expressive movement (which extends the body's capacities and indeed indicates its reach toward the world and others) pointed out the vividly expressive as a quality by which we recognize dance. This it did through negation. But as it championed the ordinary, it threatened to become a cult of the mundane—retreating from the problematic and developmental sweat of skill, high energy, and vivid expression.

Laszlo Moholy-Nagy speaks of expressiveness as a biological necessity: "Art is the most complex, vitalizing, and civilizing of human actions. Thus, it is of biological necessity. Art sensitizes man to the best that is immanent in him through an intensified expression involving many layers of experience. . . . No society can exist without expressing its ideas, and no culture and no ethics can survive without participation of the artist who cannot be bribed."[26]

Maurice Nathanson also speaks of the relation between mundane everyday expression, art expression, and biological expression. He views *expression* as a formative term, in the encompassing sense in which I am using it. As such, the term permits us to understand a fabric of meaningful relations between art and morphological, biological, and physiognomic enterprises. Nathanson believes (like Merleau-Ponty) that we are at every moment caught up in interpreting the design of our mundane world, which is originally significant in itself. The art process is analogous to this, but it stands out against a backdrop of mundanity. Art moves out from a world of intentional consciousness, personal history, and a human existence in nature; likewise, expression, while it moves toward a world, also moves from a world. Such movement may then function to return us to that world and to our source in the material sphere, "the domain of nature."[27]

The human being, as body, does not grow through inexpressiveness, whether of feelings or of ideas. Antiexpressiveness (to the extent that it becomes expressive as an active denial of expression) is another case. As polemic, an antiexpression cannot escape taking on what it is against. A successful disputation is expressive. Considered definitionally, antiexpression *is* expression but, curiously enough, expression against itself; it might be written as expression-against-expression. Its potential to vitalize (and to be valued aesthetically) thus derives from contradiction.

The human being grows through expression—moving in accord and moving against. Expressiveness tends outward as an elaboration of structure and feeling. The upright posture offers more freedom of motion than crawling. Falling down and jumping into the air are possible from this position. Testing and risking the body are fundamental to growth. They are means of formulating vital experience. We see this clearly in the child as it learns new movement, which tests its powers to control and direct energy. It is also apparent in the learning of clearly defined dance forms. When one element has been mastered, another becomes a challenge.

Yes, technique is seductive—a seduction repudiated by the early postmoderns—and seductive in a developmental manner, given a reasonable and not a manic attachment to it. Growth in technical skill occurs through an increasing mastery of movement difficulty and range of expressive nuance. Crawling is also expressive, as Simone Forti's dances show, but it is expressively limited—limited to the floor and to symbolic meanings inherent in crawling. On the other hand, human movement capabilities far exceed crawling and other pedestrian forms. Health and vitality depend on the elaboration of a full range of movement possibilities and expressive potential, on problems solved, and difficulties overcome; in short, on challenges of skill in both movement and idea. The human being develops through elaborating and extending expressive values, not through hiding, blanking, or diminishing them.

Efforts to blank expression may, however, elucidate and locate it. We have considered (with Merleau-Ponty) that expression is qualitatively intrinsic in the nature of the body, in movement, and (it follows) in the nature of dance itself. In this sense, we may say that *dance is expressive by nature.* Expression is an aspect of its human material and, in addition, of its presentational modality. Expression cannot be blanked without removing the dancer herself. In *New Untitled Partially Improvised Solo with Pink T-Shirt, Blue Bloomers, Red Ball, and Bach's Toccata and Fugue in D Minor* (1965), Rainer tried to do just that by painting her face black ("to eliminate personal projection," says Banes).[28]

Such postmodern experiments pointed out the dangers in overpersonalized dance, but (as we noted in chapter 2) these concerns were not new; Graham also objected to "self-expression" dancing. Artists who make history never lack a perspective of the intrinsic abstract and depersonalizing (universal) nature of all good dancing. Since dance is abstracted (formulated) expression, we can also say that *dance is abstract by nature.* It is formalized and stylized movement, having undergone a creative process. Because of this, in dance the self is not pointed out, nor does it pause to admire itself like Narcissus. Rather, in all good dancing, past and present, the self is impersonal, anonymous, lost to the larger purpose of the dance. The necessary abstraction of all art is the process of objectification required in the rendering of any style. This is also true of style in dance, be it the balanced and lifted style of classical ballet, the lyric modern style of José Limon, the ritualistic patterned style of Laura Dean, or the worklike style of Yvonne Rainer. A face painted black may symbolize the removal of the personal, if that intent is clear. Then again, it could have the effect of simply calling attention to itself.

Depersonification through material manipulation is certainly not new to dance. Masks and painted faces have been typically employed in dance theater and dance ritual. They are used to emphasize or to deemphasize features, freezing the character to allow the person underneath to shed his characteristic persona (mask) in order to become the fixed archetypal mask. Consider Mary Wigman's use of masks in both her solo and group dances and Alwin Nikolais's masking and painting of the entire body in tubes and materials. Masking and painting effect a dissolution of the personal into the general, but they also mark and intensify characterization and theatrics; they do not obliterate them. The mask is a device to free the dancer from the self. In a very real and tangible sense, the dancer can become that timeless other in the mask. The mask has a mediating influence on both performer and audience, as they subconsciously identify with its anonymous frozen outline, its all-in-one.

For the sake of contrasting postmodern impersonalized work (at least its impersonal intention) to a possible opposite (logically, an intentionally personalized work), it is difficult to come up with an example of the latter. Daniel Nagrin's eccentric characterizations and faintly autobiographical work, such as *Poems off the Wall* (1981), come close, but even here the dancer triumphs over the person. Abstraction, or aesthetic transformation, is an essential qualification of all theater dance art. But even so, a range of expressive intention from the personal to the impersonal is possible as an aspect of aesthetic style. Feeling can also be extended or intentionally withheld as a matter of style and degree, but it cannot be totally blanked short of removing the dancer altogether.

Intentionally antiexpressive art (whether it achieves this intention or not) risks being interpreted as against-other, since expression is not just stylistically manifested but is action and content, indivisible — the means for relating to, or reaching, the other. Antiexpressive art risks being intensely private. By definition, denial dance must deny the audience, and Rainer's manifesto indicates the truth of this. But we might well bear in mind the importance of the artist's implicit incorporation of the other.

In a less combative moment, Rainer speaks much as any dancer might who understands the expressive in terms of the other in her task: "I like to think that I have a careful screening process operating to exclude personal material that applies uniquely to my experience. What passes my screening must somehow be identifiable with probabilities of experience of you, the audience. Surgery, no; illness and thoughts of suicide perhaps; love, pleasure, rage, self-doubt, yes."[29]

I have already stated that an audience is usually ignored in the sense that its presence is assumed. The communication of the artist and the audience is not direct in any case; the dance mediates between them. And the artist does not ask for a response to the work but simply presents it. The manner of this presentation becomes an aspect of style and can vary widely. Consider for instance the confrontational presentation of some of Bertolt Brecht's theater work, or the end of Anna Sokolow's *Opus '60* (1960), when the dancers shout at the audience in angry acknowledgment. In contrast to confrontational acknowledgement, withdrawal dance simply withdraws, leaving the audience wondering whether its presence is marked or even necessary. This can be the effect of neutrality when it tends toward vacancy or negates the other.

I witnessed years of blank, smugly cool, walk-away dances throughout the postmodern period. This formula for avoiding feeling (and for not being square) became widespread. Was it an attempt to overcome poverty of the spirit by expressing it? Or was it impoverished art? There were probably examples of both. Audiences walked away from dance as dance walked away from them. Walking away and looking away became characteristic, almost stylistic, in these dances. Dancers habitually walked away and looked away from each other onstage. *Cool* gradually became *vacant.* The effect was isolation, but not strikingly so, as in many existential works—only vaguely so. Where in Cunningham's work accidental connections and disconnections between people were important, postmodern dancers could not afford to make any lively connections if denial of moving and being moved were to be pushed to its extreme. Objectivity, thingness, and finally dull presence began to consume the dancer.

Anna Kisselgoff questions whether the label *postmodern dance* still has validity, since by 1981 it was being applied to such a broad range of work.[30] She noticed "a new expressionism" emerging in dance, stating that "the human body is, after all, ideally suited to express human yearnings."[31] Similarly, Jack Anderson describes a move to dance drama in the works of such innovators as Johanna Boyce, Arnie Zane, and Senta Driver.[32]

Kisselgoff muses that postmodern dance might even include Cunningham, himself, who is supposed to be the point of departure for the Judsons' 1969s avant-garde, antipsychological aesthetic. Virtuosity (the element early postmoderns rebelled against in Cunningham) was returning in what Kisselgoff calls the systematized dancer. Systems of movement were emerging in the works of Lucinda Childs (permutations of patterns), Laura Dean (reduced patterns aiming toward a ritual effect), and Molissa Fenley (patterns used to show gradations of speed and energy).[33] She contrasts the new formalist concerns of these dancers with the earlier formalist concerns of minimalism:

> Unlike the earlier attempt to clarify through the minimal, the new structures are difficult to follow. A formal device is to construct self-obscuring structures, each superseded so quickly that the eye cannot retain the work's organizing principle. Formalist concerns remain central but there is a new swing toward overt expression of emotion. Narrative and personal recollections, albeit fragmented and nonlinear, are back. Those who profess an interest in Asian religions concentrate on the self. Psychology may yet return under another guise.[34]

It appears that expressiveness, which early minimalist postmoderns sought to cool (or disguise) in their attempts to drain dance of expressive feeling and to depersonalize dance in new ways, reasserted itself, renewed through those very attempts. Noel Carroll believes the early experimentalists were successful in removing "the expression of feelings" from their choreography but not in removing "the expression of ideas." He recognizes that "the historical character of dance plus the specific (contrastive) relational structure of the anthropomorphic metaphors associated with existing dance make it practically impossible for anything that is dance not to suggest some broadly anthropomorphic properties."[35]

The postmodern dance became a vehicle for a revaluing of technique and expression in dance. But it is not at all clear that in any of its phases it eradicated expression or expressive content in dance (how then feeling?) or redefined it. Rather it grew out of modern dance (against it), just as Cunningham grew out of (against) the modern dance he had experienced with Graham. Moreover, postmodern dance produced various styles difficult to combine into one, although, the style inherent in the ease and unremarkableness of sneakers comes close (as Banes suggests in the title of her book *Terpsichore in Sneakers*).

WHAT IS NEW

Postmodern attempts to redefine dance according to ordinary rather than extraordinary movement could not succeed as nondance or as antidance and still be dance. Not until negations become part of our individual and cultural understanding of what constitutes dance can they surpass the status of being non (nothing) and anti (against). Which is to say, they have to become positives in that constitution to become part of it, establishing a public level of confidence in the artistic value of the work. New works may show us dance constants in a new way; they do not erase them. The burden of proof lies always in the work itself.

For this there is a reference. Existing and acknowledged dance works provide the collective and public reference in establishing dance constants—a code distillation. When new works receive public attention as valuable work, the reference expands, and the code expands thereby. The reference does not reverse itself to become what it is not. Because we can accept the work of Iannis Xenakis or Phillip Glass as music, does not mean that we believe Bach's work is no longer music. New examples do not replace old ones. We recognize the new in reference to the old according to kind, and through some level of community agreement (establishment of family resemblances).

In modern dance, *new* has often been mistaken for *better*. But if new were necessarily better, art would be too easy, not worth our attention, and of no lasting value. To be new in terms of individual inventiveness, and at the same time of genuine worth, is much more difficult, engaging a total commitment of the artist's individuality—but with no loss of history. History imposes the impersonal truth, invoking the artist's suspension of self-importance.

For new work to be comprehended as art, value must be realized (given reality) through it. Aesthetic value has independent worth. Works of art, old and new, are not in competition with each other, because the created values of art are self-contained (realized in the integrity of the object) and unique to that object. In the intended object of art, value either appears at a vital and recognizable level or it does not. When it does, its reason for being is complete.

Deconstruction and Regeneration

Opposition to dramatic expression and formal technique in dance (beyond original polemics) eventually lost purpose and power. There are some things in dance (as in all art) that can only be done once, after which they lose our interest. Once a radical statement becomes clear, particularly if it pushes lower limits through devolution, its lower terms eventually disappear, which is what happened to the postmodern mundane aesthetic. It degenerated into hints of movement, movement indicated rather than executed, movement more talked about than performed—and finally movement disappearing. Steve Paxton's *Transit* (1962), in which he "marked" or indicated movement instead of expending full energy in performance, and Yvonne Rainer's *Ordinary Dance* (1962), a work accompanied by an autobiographical monologue spoken by the performer, were *original* polemic deconstructions, no doubt influencing the years of spoken and indicated dances that followed. A tension of vital oppositions faded in the aftermath of these and other original postmoderns until finally, neither form nor expression carried the work.

During the sixties, negation of technique and overt expression, and pointless, vague, ingroup "nondance" became common fare. Avant-garde composer Steve Reich comments that "for a long time during the 1960s one would go to the dance concert where no one danced followed by the party where everyone danced. This was not a healthy situation."[36] Dance, he believed, needed to return to the human desire for rhythmic movement performed to music. Nondance (a term used loosely before the postmodern label became prevalent) simply defined itself out of existence. A nondance is by definition not a dance. What else could it be? Nevertheless, there it was in front of us, staring blankly past us, seeming like it might be something, or would like to be, or thought it was, depending on the particular nondance one happened upon. Dance ruminated in hollow lassitude. The challenge was for audiences to decipher what might be new and valuable but perhaps not apparent to their eyes, or to admit a case of the emperor's new clothes—a lack of substance parading as a matter too difficult for all but the most astute.

In response to the degeneration that followed the first vital deconstructions of highly technical and overtly expressive dance, a dance regeneration was forthcoming in the late seventies and early eighties. This happened in part through vivid and rhythmic minimalism (Laura Dean), acknowledgement of poetic expressiveness—even of message—through well-delineated conception (Senta Driver, Carolyn Carlson, Wendy Shankin, and Doris Seidon) and a decisively overt, and often absurdist, new expressionism (German choreographers Pina Bausch and Susanne Linke). There was also a rediscovery of clarity and distinctness in the clean geometric abstracts of Lucinda Childs and the fluid movement of Trisha Brown, who had both been with the postmodern movement all along and had the technical resources to call forth some upper, as well as lower, limits in movement. Meredith Monk, whose work has consistently engaged a total theater concept, also was associated with the postmodern period. Yet her dances never deny drama or expression; they grow out of her belief that "theater is a place where the psyche is activated."[37] Her classic piece, *Education of the Girlchild*, a ritual of growing up female, has outlasted its postmodern classification.

Nina Wiener's mystic *Wind Devil* (1983) and Johanna Boyce's full-evening work *With Longings to Realize* (1983) recall the continuing thread of expressionist sensibility constantly recurring in modern dance. Once again the thunder of powerful movement performed with speed, accuracy, and inventiveness appeared in the solo work of Elizabeth Streb, Molissa Fenley, and others. Like Cunningham, Laura Dean extended meaning through mystical detachment; but unlike him, she achieved it through movement simplification, spinning, and ecstatic repetition. Kai Takei, early in the postmodern movement, developed primal imagery, seeming to probe the unconscious while extending it consciously. The work of these artists is stylistically unlike any of the modern dance that preceded it, yet it has a basis in ritual, psychic life, myth, and mystery close to the founding earth principle of modern dance (as we shall consider in the next chapter). Such work was influenced by all that had gone before, including Anna Halprin's community rituals in San Francisco and

Los Angeles, which finally turned more toward social work than art. In an article in 1984, Anna Kisselgoff wrote about the return of "emotion" in dance, and how it was being dealt with in the works of Gina Buntz, Peggy Lyman, and Elisa Monte.[38]

Through such work – primarily of women – the mythic earth principle, which exerted such a strong pull on the early moderns and the original postmoderns, is being perpetuated, but in tension with a constructive technical and virtuosic reach. Preceding this regeneration, the original postmodern repudiation (and deconstruction) of established dance is as important as the destructive side of Shiva's cosmic dance (associated with his female side – the burning ground of the heart, the dissolution of ego), which renders new creation possible.[39]

As a whole, the postmodern period turned dance upside down, just as early modern dance and late modern dance were revolutionary through opposition to accepted aesthetic standards. It becomes increasingly clear, however, that polemic postmodern dance did not succeed in erasing either expressiveness or virtuosity as valued qualities in dance. Nor did it redefine dance. Valued properties were even more apparent in attempts to push their lower limits. Pedestrian, task, and work styles emerged, which express ease, withdrawal of dramatic expressiveness, and inward concentration – at first with aesthetic vitality and often within the desirable negativity of righteous protest.

Postmodern dance is in its most telling aspect a deconstructive (and involutional) art in *protest of power ascendency*, especially of the dominance of technological, military, and industrial power exerted destructively against nature.[40] Thus the early postmodern relaxation of *techne* – ascendent (extended and airborne) technique in particular – and its protest against the Vietnam War.

Cunningham and Koans

LETTING MOVEMENT BE

Like the postmodern devolved styles, Cunningham's dances also express concentration and withdrawal (perhaps the better word in his case is *detachment*). But the stylistic result is not the same. His movement images are highly focused in technical virtuosity, clear movement delineation, and precise execution, not to mention chance methodology, through which he has been linked to the archetype of chance, as it appears through the chance method of consulting the *I Ching*, the Chinese book of wisdom and changes. Cunningham imposes no attitude of denial or opposition, but neither does he give his art any specific emotional ground. His dance is indifferent to being anything but itself; it magnifies the nonlinear and poetic nature of the movement medium, suspending performance facades so that the dancer's face might simply reflect the movement. Neither preening solicitation of the audience (which the postmoderns objected to) nor withdrawal through an intentional distance from the audience (which many postmoderns turned to) are evident in his aesthetic.

He lets the movement be. Movement is valued for itself and presented with a conscious attempt to delete artifice and dramatic illusion. To this point, Cunningham is also deconstructive. The audience seems invited to free-associate within his highly technical, abstract, and unpredictable dance. I believe the latter quality relates his work as closely to the single-pointed simplicity of Zen and its freely associated, mind-releasing koans as to the mathematically balanced and richly imagistic *I Ching*.

Cunningham sets up a dialectic between the intellect and the unconscious, as he plays methodological games. At the same time, he engages the yielding (yin) earth principle, accepting chance as the determining factor of his game plans. Thus he affirms the unconscious (through chance) but also works against it, intellectually employing it in his own methodological schemes.

The effect of his imposition of many layers of chance is to disperse or scatter the movement, an effect that paved the way for postmodern monochromatics in the works of formalists like Lucinda Childs, which occurred late in the postmodern development, almost as a return to the abstract formalism and high technical achievement of Cunningham.

MEANING AND NOT-MEANING

More than most, Cunningham's dances cast perception in the active mode, requiring the audience to assign the dance's meaning or nonmeaning and raising questions about meaning and meaninglessness in dance and art. At a time when the arts were grappling with the meaning of meaning on their own terms, his dances were atypically meaningful, or meaningless.

In a 1963 article, Walter de Maria says that "meaningless work is obviously the most important and significant art form today." He defines meaningless work as "work that does not make you money or accomplish a conventional purpose. For instance, putting wooden blocks from one box to another, then putting the blocks back to the original box, back and forth and so on, is a fine example of meaningless work." He warns that caution should be taken against getting any pleasure from the work, or pleasure could become the purpose. Sex then, if pleasurable, would not qualify as meaningless work; nor would a dance, if pleasurable to any extent at all. On de Maria's terms, a dance performed with purposefulness or vitality would, therefore, not qualify as important or significant art because it would be meaningful work. Neither would a dance done for others, or even within view of them, be important or significant art. Meaningless work (significant art) would have to be done alone. Otherwise, one would risk the danger that others might find meaning in it or that they might ascribe to it the meaning of meaninglessness. He saw meaningless work as "the new way to tell who is square."[41] Get the meaning?

Clearly, Cunningham's dance is not meaningless on these terms, nor could any dance that fulfills some purpose not mean something. I have held that the dancer moves with an aesthetic purpose; that his movement is meaningful within the imperatives of his dance as he formulates and finally projects the imaginable (or possible). Further, his dance exhibits a communicative (for-other) purpose. Its material is innately expressive, as well. The dancer's art may dwell within the intrinsic expressiveness of movement, as Cunningham's does—accruing meaning nevertheless, because human movement cannot be fully abstracted; it is always reflecting a human condition. Cunningham also acknowledges and works within this condition, even though he declines to *impose* subjective content. He never told his dancers what his dances were about. However, they suspected he had specific ideas concerning content, and they formulated their own ideas about the dances.[42]

MOVEMENT IS THE MESSAGE

I have said that dance may point beyond its movement medium, being intentionally symbolic when it unites us with a narrative, an event, or a state of being that can be descriptively marked in some way. Graham's dance dramas come to mind here, and even some of Twyla Tharp's distinctly allusive dances in vernacular styles of music and dance—jazz, ragtime, and country-folk—which are pointed out anew in her oblique connection wtih them.

Cunningham's work, on the other hand, stands in contrast to work that makes intentional connections. Roger Copeland holds that Cunningham's work is disconnective, stressing a perceptive alertness and at the same time a detachment from the world.[43] In this, it fulfills the function of training perception, which media theorist Marshall McLuhan sees as the function of art.[44] Cunningham's work is not denotatively meaningful; rather *movement* (its medium) *is its message*—to recall McLuhan again. But clearly, it is not enough to leave it at this. Further questions follow quite naturally: What kind of message is movement? What is Cunningham's movement like? If it does not denote anything, what does it exemplify? It is obviously not just any movement whatsoever.

I remember being assigned in a composition class with Cunningham to come up with one rhythm in the lower half of the body and another in the upper, a problem not unlike tapping a binary rhythm with one hand and a ternary rhythm with the other, except that it extended to the whole body and required movement invention. Polyrhythms are apparent in African drumming and often in the dancer's relation to the music in African dance. However, this compositional study posed a polyrhythmic problem to be solved intellectually and technically within the whole body complex, requiring an objective creative stance. I do not think Cunningham explained it that way, but it had that effect on me. In solving the problem, I was required to move against my organic grain, so to speak. My disposition to move quite naturally in a simple, rather than complex, rhythm had to be suspended as I worked on the problem. But as Copeland says, Cunningham's work may have posed a question about what is natural.[45] And indeed, I have found that most any movement, once you figure out how to do it and it ingrains through repetition, begins to attain a degree of naturalness, although I have to admit that some movement feels more natural to my particular body and that my preference for familiar movement plays a part.

Cunningham's work becomes meaningful, I believe, as it engages and frees the intellect through bodily lived sources. Like a random number table in motion, it has a leveling and dispersing effect—evoking the qualitative steadiness of meditation (difficult to sustain amidst the theatrics of John Cage's sounds) entered into like a Zen koan riddle. (I do not know that Cunningham followed Zen or any mystic religion, but he did tell us in composition class that he employed chance to get away from his own movement dispositions.) What is the sound of one hand clapping? What is Mu? What was my face before my parents were born? There is no logical answer. Yet both intellect and intuition are engaged toward their solution, the former finally giving way to the latter. What Zen master Philip Kapleau says about koans explains Cunningham's dance as well: "Those who grasp their spirit know that koans, despite the incongruity of their various elements, are profoundly meaningful." They point us beyond I and not-I to the "Mind's inherent purity."[46] I also relate Cunningham's employment of chance to purify his work "of himself" to the import of the koan. "The import of every koan is the same: that the world is one interdependent Whole and that each separate one of us is that Whole."[47]

It would also seem that the koan may apply to dance in general, since dance, like the koan, does not function as a literate (verbal) sign. "The aim of every koan is to liberate the mind from the snare of language."[48] We have seen that this is true of dance as well. I have said that dance is preliterate poetry. I could add that, like the koan, a dance cannot be explained except through demonstration; its meaning lies in its performance and our perception of it. If this is right, then Graham's dances are certainly as close to the koan as Cunningham's are, but his scattering of movement calls attention to movement itself, disclosing it as the inmost formative object (the medium or substance) of dance. Thus Cunningham points out the inherent beauty of human movement. Freed from the compulsion to say something, perhaps he allows us to see the Zen of all dance—that its saying is in doing.

Movement for itself, like mystical emptiness and like the existential void, is not meaningless. It is a clearing, which stills speculative activity, allowing the mind to rest that it might shine, as mind. What originally seemed a negation in Cunningham's departure from dramatic and intentionally symbolic action in dance proved to be a clearing where his dance could shine for itself through the intelligent, extraordinary, and versatile body. Carolyn Brown, Cunningham's partner for many years, achieved this kind of clarity in his dances; she compares them to puzzles.[49] Indeed, it is in their puzzling character that I associate them with the mind-releasing, transformational, koan riddle. Mind is evoked in Cunningham's dance, but (as is the way of all dance) through its bodily lived source.

Because he concentrates on the dancing body, Cunningham has been termed a purist. His aesthetic derives from the beautiful forms and pathways the body can draw through space and from an indeterminate unfolding of structure, which lends it complexity and a keen intellectual edge. His movement style is a curious mixture of the classical ballet (emphasizing infinite reach, taut erectness, airborne trajectory, and turned-out lines of fully stretched limbs) with the less rule-bound more earthbound modern dance (as it developed introspectively and encouraged a freer use of the body). Cunningham reconciles the formal vocabulary of ballet with the tolerance and freedom of modern dance in his unique movement style.

Pictures, created in 1984, is a good example of Cunningham's fusion of ballet and modern dance and of his embodiment of mystical paradox and quietude, as well. While this is a recent piece, it remains very close to the inspiration behind all his work. In it we see his continual striving for a pure focus on the human body, in its motion and in its stillness. But it is stillness rather than motion that pervades *Pictures,* as intermittently throughout, dancers connect with each other in delicately held balanced designs or in huddled masses, forming the shapes (pictures), which coalesce at random.

While *Pictures* is more visual than kinetic, its pictures are, nevertheless, embroidered with bursts of virtuosic ballet kinetics. These are most brilliant against the bodily designs held with sublime disinterest at their points of arrival. In the journey between these designs, dancers execute a contained, careful trudging, unreasonably interrupted with leaps and turns, pivoting slowly around at an arbitrary point, descending to a kneeling backward crawl, hands and knees supporting the cleanly placed locomotion to the back. The music for the work, *Interspecies Smalltalk,* by David Behrman, maintains a distance from the dance, filling the still pictures with haunting sounds. The effect of the whole is of muted elegance, since the stage light is designed to alternately light then shadow the dancers against the backdrop.

Toward the end, Cunningham himself enters, and moves unobtrusively across the back of the stage. He remains there for some time as part of a pleasantly shifting background, eventually entering into the picture making more actively. The final picture forms as dancers exit at odd ungoverned moments, leaving Cunningham holding a female dancer suspended more or less horizontally, and relaxed, in his arms. There is a peaceful repose in this picture, as he holds her there quietly – dispassionate but alert and attentive, as though he might be expecting someone to speak to him at any moment.

Many things could be said about this image. Perhaps "platonic" describes it best. For me it holds composed platonic stillness, androgyne completion, and vivid awareness – even in the sense that Plato (like the mystics) believes it better to be at rest than in motion.[50] In this work, as in other Cunningham dances, there is a single-pointed stillness shining through the nonsensical whole, which like the koan brings about unexpected revelations of ourselves in our spiritual being.

Cunningham has expressed his desire not to "impose" his dances (and their meaning or nonmeaning) upon the audience. Rather we are left to discover our own meaning in them. Whereas audiences once walked away in disgust from Cunningham's contradictions, present audiences have found a way in through the movement itself. As I heard someone say of a recent Cunningham concert, "I feel washed clean by this dancing."

I have held from the beginning that, in some sense, all dance prizes movement purely for itself. Cunningham allows us to see this more clearly.

Transformations

Although Cunningham founded his dance company in 1953, it was not until about 1964 that the American public began to appreciate the Eastern paradigms of mind release and ego surrender, which guided it. He does not strive to express himself in his dances but rather to rid his work of himself in letting, rather than making, the dance happen. Thus Cunningham changed perceptions of what dancing can be about and opened dance art to the grace of letting go, of willfulness, a grace that permeates all dance affected by him.

Art evolves by means of change and by tests in the public domain, the domain that is art's other in the largest sense. Art functions to move a large and culturally biased other beyond its complacency – to keep it free. Art is tested in the public domain because that is where it is valued (or disvalued): valued first as an end in itself and second because it grows out of, and actualizes, personal freedom and, in its largest (ideal) measure, affirms everyone's freedom. Therefore, its tests should be exacting; what passes as art is the measure of a society.

Vital culture depends on vital art. Our vision of vitality, of our own vital body, is shaped in our dance. Audience responsiveness depends on vital and inventive dance, which draws forth visionary intelligence. The image of the dancer as strong (able), graceful (centered in action), well proportioned and beautiful (poetic in action), exists with interpretive modifications historically and cross-culturally. There is reason for idealism in the constants of dance. The health of a culture rests to a great extent on its concept of the healthy body. On this the health of dance also depends. Ideals are formative. There is nothing formative in the nonexpressive, the sloppy, the weak, the meaningless, except as they serve to sharpen and contraindicate their opposites.

Aesthetic exaggerations of purposelessness may remind us of our condemnation to freedom (as Sartre puts it) — of our human agency and innate purposefulness, the meaning embedded in our very bones — of the compelling urge toward life exhibited by the marvels of the body's interlacing systems, an ineffable complexity within an expressive unity (as phenomenology, science, and art are showing). To be free is to choose. We may choose between purposefulness and its opposite, vitality and its opposite. Dancing points out volition perhaps more directly than any other art because of the immediate demands it exacts of the body when it moves beyond the ordinary. When nothing is risked beyond the ordinary, it is the ordinary that we mark. Ordinary movement will be perceived (it stands to reason) as ordinary movement. But dance is not ordinary movement; it is movement that has undergone a creative transformational process.

Radical subjectivism holds that the look of the viewer can transform anything into art. This meta-art attitude can be adopted, but to adopt it is to choose it. We cannot ignore that subjective departure from the concrete object of art occurs in some phase of aesthetic perception, but the choice to create in the mind what is not in any way elicited by the object is a choice to ignore the object and to dwell in the privacy of oneself. The thought that I can make anything out of the objects I perceive has its culmination in pathological narcissism.

Dance expression arises out of a tension between ordinary and extraordinary movement. Movement and its intrinsic expressiveness is transformed through the imagination (inner vision) of the artist and his mastery of his medium. When we merge with his vision as we move out of ourselves toward the dance that has elicited our response (our feeling in favor of it), we become part of the transformation. Of course, transformations are not unique to dance; they are the results of that which we call art, or subjective realizations of aesthetic worth. As such, they are also subjective standards, which we commonly call upon in measuring the worth of a work. We should expect to be changed, to be renewed, and to be vitalized by that which we are willing to call art, and by dance which we are willing to call art.

So far, in the discussion of a tension of opposites, I have added to the definition of dance that, as art, dance is movement that has undergone some meaningful transformation. It is thus that it holds the transformational power to move us beyond self and beyond the ordinary. Dance becomes meaningful (its uniquely embodied truth becomes apparent) at this vital level. Our high expectations of dance are warranted if we understand that in dance we are perfecting our vital body of earth and world — of form and expression — and (as I shall finally venture in this study of opposites in dance) our mythopoetic body of male and female attributes, of nature and culture, of earth and heaven.

8

MYTHIC POLARITY

Because thou lovest the Burning-ground
I have made a Burning-ground of my heart—
That Thou, Dark One, haunter of the Burning-ground,
Mayest dance Thy eternal dance.
—Hymn to Kali, which sings the adoration of the mother aspect of Shiva and the dissolution of the ego necessary to creation, recounted by Ananda K. Coomaraswamy

Female-Male Archetypes

Female-male mythic archetypes generate a plethora of polarized oppositional complements, reflected in various ways in our dance. These I consider in this chapter as yin-yang, Dionysus-Apollo, earth-heaven (mother-father), and nature-culture—still in sight of expressionist-formalist aesthetic tensions and values. First I consider the mythic significance of the founding and recurring expressionist principle of modern dance, its Dionysian, earthly, female, and existentially open essence.

Genius of the Heart

The new abstract and new expressive dance of the late seventies and continuing in the eighties accounts for the past and uses it. It owes a lot to the postmodern attempt to see dance anew. In its technical and abstract aspects (as in the works of Lucinda Childs), one can see the effects of Merce Cunningham but not his methodologically imposed detachments and disconnections. As it incorporates postmodern rejection of highly evolved, established techniques but not postmodern anti-expressiveness, this new dance is closer to early modern dance, regenerating the female earth mythic principle through organically derived intuitive expressiveness. Once again, dancing from the heart, or *The Genius of the Heart*, is important, as the title of Deborah Hay's dance, created in 1980, indicates.

Regarding this, we might remember that in its origins modern dance did not place a premium on technically exacting movement skill. This entered gradually through the incorporation of Rudolph von Laban's objective studies of movement, which tempered Mary Wigman's work.[1] The work of Laban and Wigman eventually became the foundation for Hanya Holm's technique, exacting high levels of skill and systematic use of paths of action in space. Doris Humphrey, Martha Graham, and José Limon eventually created individually stylized techniques also emphasizing movement skill and rhythmic fundamentals, which reached high levels of challenge. However, the root of modern dance is not predominantly technical. Loie Fuller's extravaganzas of "free" and "flowing" movement, Isadora Duncan's embrace of the "soul," her imitation of "nature" (in such simple movement as the swaying of trees, the rushing and ebbing of waves), and Ruth St. Denis's revelation of the cosmic "spirit" of dance attest to this. Modern dance was at first a revolt against the artificiality and affectations of ballet, which subjugates the body's natural expressiveness to codified movement, or what the female founders of modern dance conceived of as empty abstract movement.

Perhaps nothing better symbolizes ballet's removal from the primal earth principle and resistance to gravity than the strapping of the female foot into virginal pink and heaven-bound toe shoes. The early moderns bared the female foot and restored its sacred connection to the earth. They relaxed the elogated spine of ballet, allowing the hips to move and the torso to undulate. Nudity, freedom, eros, and nature were revered. The rigors of formalized technique came later.

It is not without significance that choreographers of note are typically male in ballet. Nor can we ignore that modern dance accomplished a feminist revolution in terms of authorship in dance and the arts in general. *In no other art* are at least half of its famous composers (its artist author-makers) women. The field of modern dance in choreography and performance, both professionally and in education, has been created and sustained by women in very large measure.

The founders of modern dance were women. In the background is Loie Fuller (1862–1928). Founding the American dance revolution, Isadora Duncan and Ruth St. Denis were both born around 1878, grew up outside of the mainstream of society, and were "indoctrinated into dress reform and Delsarte and defiant feminism."[2] The important German root of modern dance was Mary Wigman and her student Harold Kreutzberg. Wigman's work was coming into prominence as early as the 1920s and was introduced to American audiences in 1930.

Certainly men have been involved from the beginning, but in far lesser numbers, and often in association with (or in aesthetic rebellion against) dominant female figures: in the name melds of Humphrey-Weidman and Denishawn, we note the lesser order of the male. Daniel Nagrin was associated with his mentor and wife Helen Tamiris; Erick Hawkins with Martha Graham; Merce Cunningham, Paul Taylor, and Robert Cohen all split off from Graham. Mary Wigman carried Rudolph von Laban's aesthetic theories into artistic vision, forming the expressionist foundation of modern dance. Hanya Holm brought Wigman's art to America, where it took firm root. And modern dancers still look to Isadora Duncan as the revolutionary (even feminist-pagan) inspiration behind their art.

Ruth St. Denis is known as "the mother" of modern dance in America, beginning its lineage through the school she formed with her husband, Ted Shawn. Shawn sought to found a dance that would exploit the full potential of men. The enduring influence on his work was Ruth St. Denis. Her quest for a new kind of dancer also became his quest, at once spiritual and theatrical. In both endeavors, St. Denis was inspired by ancient cultures and mysticism. Elizabeth Kendall writes that the art of Ruth St. Denis was "half-conscious. . . . It came from the natural performer's unerring instincts for putting herself and her audience into another time and place – Egypt, the Orient – simply by acting out that time and place with costumes and movements. Lacking a dance education, she invented one, a kind of dance pre-history culled from her visions of antique and sensual civilizations and some scraps of information from public libraries. But she believed it. She never doubted she was giving her audience an ideology as well as a performance."[3]

The emerging independent woman of the twentieth century created "natural," "aesthetic," "creative," "expressive" dance, which could speak to her deeper meaning and to the freedom she sought. She thus also rejected the nineteenth century dress code, which severely restricted her movement and impaired her health. The art she founded became a "prime symbol" for woman in our time as Kendall points out in her book on the founding of the new dance art, and the influence of the mothers of the founding artists. Kendall deals with the social climate that encouraged the new art and the restrictive dress code that engendered a search for solutions to the problem of women's health, a search lending impetus to modern dance as it turned toward an "older instinctive wisdom" lost to modern civilization.[4]

Perhaps it is no coincidence that in modern dance the most highly technical, abstract, and technological dance (late modern dance, arising roughly in the fifties) is dominated by two men, Merce Cunningham and Alwin Nikolais. They provide an important formalist balance to the dominance of the feminine expressionist principle. Technique triumphs in Cunningham's dance; abstraction, clean geometry, and purity of action prevail, through which modern dance moves closer to the sublime and chaste impersonality of the ballet. A dazzling array of technology and mixed media, supported by an armada of high-technology light and sound machinery, sustains Nikolais's work, moving modern dance closer to the theatrical spectacle of the ballet, but within a fresh vision.

The stereotype inherited from ballet is that women dance and men choreograph. The idea that it is all right for men to dance without betraying their masculinity is a relatively recent result of the feminist revolution. (The other side of this revolution is that sport, which has been considered the male province, has opened up to women.) Freed from the pretty pastel aesthetic of the classical and romantic ballet, men have also been able to explore and express the broader aesthetic palate of their maleness in modern dance. In professional modern dance today, the number of male choreographers and performers may almost equal that of women. However, in studio and university classes, women are still the majority. When speaking of the Next Wave Festival in 1983, Barry Laine offered this note on gender: "Of eleven programs of produced choreography in Next Wave's three years, only one featured male choreographers (Bill T. Jones and Arnie Zane). Where are more of our innovative young men?

Can we conclude that modern dance is still dominated by female creativity?"[5] Similarly, Roger Copeland asks, "Why is modern dance dominated by women?"[6] Jennifer Dunning, writing about the many guises of women in dance today, says that "women have reigned nearly supreme."[7]

MYTHIC POLARITY

The aesthetic of modern dance is not restricted. It was founded by a feminist liberation of the body and its belief in a free range of expression. Thus modern dance developed an existentially open discovery stance, questioning male and female stereotypes in dance, opening up new experiences of the body for both men and women and new creative tensions between the female and male archetypal polarities within the body. These polarities are illustrated in myth, most broadly in the mythic principles of earth and heaven. They may be understood as complementary, sometimes dualistic, lived oppositions.[8] Among the historic and aesthetic tensions in dance, this one, as it relates to our mythical body of female-male attributes, may be the most instructive for an age in quest of a fuller realization of all human capacities.

Carl Jung, Joseph Campbell, and Friedrich Nietzsche all hold that myth has its origin in the human body, implicating male and female polarity. Jung elucidates male-female mythic polarity in his concepts of anima and animus, and Campbell, in his "wall of pairs of opposites."[9] He reminds us that "the human mind in its polarity of the male and female modes of experience, in its passages from infancy to adulthood and old age, in its toughness and tenderness, and in its continuing dialogue with the world, is the ultimate mythogenetic zone—the creator and destroyer, the slave and yet the master, of all the gods."[10]

We saw in the first chapter of this section that it was out of the Dionysian dithyramb that both dance and drama sprang as theater arts. We also considered that art grows through formalist and expressionist, Apollonian and Dionysian, tension. Nietzsche's thesis is "that art owes its continuous evolution to the Apollonian-Dionysian duality, even as the propagation of the species depends on the duality of the sexes, their constant conflicts and periodic acts of reconciliation."[11] He is persuaded that the dramatic dithyramb and Attic tragedy are the sublime achievement and goal of the marriage of these Appolonian and Dionysian urges in art.

From Nietzsche, we learn that Apollo functions to effect "individuation" in art and dream, while Dionysus effects "mystical jubilation," which "breaks the spell of individuation and opens a path to the maternal womb of being."[12] They are both necessary to artistic realization, as the unseen subjective Dionysian and the visible formative objective Apollonian coalesce, as the actual, waking I (the self) is unselved in art to reveal the larger I dwelling in the depths of being.[13]

Art is abstracted from the actual I, the personalized body. This requires an Apollonian shaping. In contrast to the enthusiast, the artist is capable of condensing Dionysian insight and its intoxicating inspirations into clear aesthetic images—feeling into form. In the process, an inner dialectic arises between the technically formative and the turbulent sea of aisthesis, from which art grows. *Neither aspect alone is adequate to produce art.* Yet we do observe that art may emphasize either an Apollonian or a Dionysian spirit.

According to its founding principle, modern dance emphasizes the female (Dionysian and ecstatic, intuitive and inward, integrative and monistic) earth archetype. However, in the formalist, abstract, and technical phases, it is tempered by a necessary opposition through the male (Apollonian and rational, intellectual and outward, individuating and objectively formative) heaven archetype. In the mythical feminine, there is vulnerability, yielding transparency, spiritual freedom, and dark enchantment. In the mythical masculine, there is the firmness of form and shape, heroic power and light, and the objectivity and dualism of differentiation.

These qualities of Dionysus and Apollo are readily recognizable as polarized male and female attributes, not ascribed to people exclusively on the basis of sex but analogous to Jung's concepts of anima, the female side of the male, and animus, the male side of the female. We might also think of these female and male attributes as yin-yang complements in the human person—polarized qualities of consciousness in constant flux, allowing for movement, change, and transformation.

In his work on myth and psychology, Edward Whitmont explains these qualities as related modes of consciousness: "The Yang way, utilizing primarily the left hemisphere of the brain, strives from center to periphery. It is separative, analytical and abstracting. The Yin way, corresponding to right brain activity, draws inward toward the center. It moves toward unity, identity, patterns, and analogy. The former represents a male and animus consciousness. The latter constitutes the feminine and anima consciousness which we are now more and more recognizing as equal in importance to the analytic male trend."[14]

While dance — all dance — may be based in the female mythic principle, as David Levin suggests,[15] certainly dance also belongs to men. Many men, in their own ways, have found the inner way, the yin of all true dancers, a way increasingly open to them without the stigma of effeminacy, the ennobling, feminine genius of the heart, which Nietzsche praises in the god Dionysus: "the genius of the heart who silences all that is loud and self-satisfied, teaching it to listen; who smooths rough souls and lets them taste a new desire . . . the genius of the heart who teaches the doltish and rash hand to hesitate and reach out more delicately."[16] Nietzsche's dancer Dionysus, whose name and deeper female essence we take here as symbolic of the founding essence of modern dance, is an earth god with maternal regenerative female qualities.

We learn most directly about the female aspects of Dionysus from Marija Gimbutas. In a study of the forces behind Western civilization, Gimbutas states, "the primeval Dionysus is saturated with a meaning closely related to that of the Great Goddess in her aspect of the Virgin Nature Goddess and Vegetation Goddess."[17] Gimbutas points out that vestiges of prehistoric, matriarchal, mythical images are part of the cultural heritage of the West, persisting alongside the newer patriarchal values that began with the Indo-European subjugation of old Europe and developed thereafter in the teachings of the Greeks. Old European values were concerned with utilizing both the feminine and masculine as creative forces. The old European values — centrally, the Great Goddess who effects passage from death to life — were not entirely lost: "transformed they enormously enriched the European psyche." Dionysus is a complex symbol connecting prehistoric and historic Europe, allowing the nurturing female ethic of the Great Goddess to survive through a patriarchal era. Charlene Spretnak also speaks to the qualities of the Great Goddess and examines the literature on the subject.[18] Whitmont symbolizes Dionysus as son, lover, and consort of the Great Goddess. As she returns in the consciousness of modern times, so does the repressed Dionysus return to free the deep feminine and its wisdom in ourselves.[19]

YIELDING DESCENT

In the return of the Great Goddess, modern dance has played no small part. Apollonian formalism does not provide the foundational aesthetic principle of modern dance, although it provides an apparent aesthetic tension to the dominant expressionist principle, even in the beginning. The work of Doris Humphrey (1895–1958) has strong formal properties; still it was guided by a search for physical or natural laws of movement, her concern to move from the inside out and to find a balance between Apollonian and Dionysian sensibility. Her famous work to that point was *Two Ecstatic Themes* (1931), conceived as Circular Descent in "the curving, falling forms of the . . . intoxicating experience of Dionysian release," and Pointed Ascent, "a frantic attempt to regain the security of Apollonian stability." This dance is based in Humphrey's theory of fall and recovery, inspired by Nietzsche's representations of Dionysus and Apollo.[20] In contrast to the formalism of ballet, Humphrey's formalism does not defy the earth; it acknowledges it by affirming the laws of nature and by falling and spiraling into the earth. This spiral of the body into the earth, which finally entered the language of modern dance through Humphrey's technique, draws upon one of the oldest mythic symbols, the timeless spiral dance of the Great Earth Goddess.[21]

Spiraling, falling, and yielding to the earth are not motions common to the classical ballet, which seldom gives in to gravity. The grace of ballet is not primarily of the earth but of spirit and air. The grace of modern dance is born of the sensuous, life-renewing serpent spiral, ancient symbol of the feminine deity and her transformative wisdom. True to its existentially open founding essence, modern dance also explores air, mist, water, and fire. But even as it makes use of air and light, the spiral connects modern dance to the earth. At the genesis of modern dance, Loie Fuller in her aerial play with light and color composed her famous first dance, the *Serpentine* (1890), out of a continuous spiral design, moving her silk skirt in a wavering whirling mass and falling finally to the floor as the silk enveloped her.[22]

Indeed the open exploratory stance of the emerging modern dance encouraged an accepting aesthetic which honored all the elements. But most important for our times, it revered the body's sacred female earth, formerly denied a place in classical ballet.

The mundane aesthetic of the postmodern period, beginning in the sixties as a protest against the codified techniques developing in modern dance and the ballet technique informing these, again moved close to the earth source of modern dance. Kei Takei's *Moving Earth* is just one case in point: "The first thing you notice about her dances is the absence of traditional dance technique. There are no pirouettes, jetes or contractions. Instead, what you see are dynamic qualities: tense, rigid, limp, flopping, lunging, flinging, frenzied, gliding, somnambulant, sagging, ponderous, heavy, earthbound dancers."[23]

By the 1980s, neoexpressionist works were emerging in such artists as Pina Bausch, renewing the expressive essence of modern dance with its origins in the work of Wigman, Graham, and Kurt Jooss. The mystical essence of St. Denis was returning (although not so literally) in such artists as Laura Dean (or perhaps it had been retained all along—certainly in Erick Hawkins). Even Cunningham, despite his highly technical focus on movement for itself, was acknowledging the mystical, with his use of chance and the *I Ching,* as well as the Zen-like koan riddle his work seems to pose. Finally, Isadora's innocent pagan spirit returned in such openly ecstatic works as Debora Hay's. Hay states well the motivations behind the postmodern relaxation of technique: "breath is movement and movement is dance and anyone can dance."[24]

I liken the early modern dancers' desire for a rebirth of the natural body (in "natural dance," as it was often called then) and the postmodern dancers' pragmatic inclusive aesthetic and negation of technological power (protesting war and established authority) to the descent of the primal Sumerian earth goddess Inanna into the depths of earth, a symbolic death and rebirth bringing forth life manifested in the fruits of earth. Thus Yvonne Rainer's *no* to dance theatrics[25] and imperative to start over again—the same imperative to create from inner sources rather than established techniques and manners that the female founders of modern dance faced. Istar (Babylonia), Isis (Egypt), and Demeter (Greece) are Inanna's counterparts in myth. She is associated with the qualities of her grandmother Nammu, described in ancient fragments as "the mother who gave birth to heaven and earth," probably the oldest "universe creating deity" of which we have written record.[26]

The earth goddess is also associated with the transformational power of Shiva's feminine side, Kali (noted in the hymn at the beginning of this chapter), with both her terrible and enlightening, her destructive and regenerative, powers. Here is the deconstruction or descent of ego, which her dance upon the funeral ground represents, as well as the mystical and existential abyss of irrationality, unknowns, and nothingness. Kali is the dark goddess, time and night, ever-joyous dancer releasing souls to bliss, an aspect of the great mother Devi and of Shakti.[27]

The feminine mythic principle also relates to the hidden reservoir of the unconscious, or *maya*—suffering, illusion, concealment, and revelation—the mystical concept that began to inform Western philosophy first through Arthur Schopenhauer and then through Nietzsche, as he anchored his philosophy to the myth of eternal return. Finally, it began to influence psychology through Jung, with his view of the collective unconscious as well as his investigation into its transformational powers. Jungian analyst Joseph Henderson relates that Jung and his followers became increasingly aware that the unconscious contains archetypal images, which are creative and integrative as well as destructive. And two characteristics of the unconscious long known to both Eastern and ancient Greek philosophy also became apparent: (1) repetition, the symbol of eternal return, and (2) the tendency for an image "to turn into its opposite and back again," recalling the play of creation and destruction in Shiva's cosmic dance.[28]

Along with the positive aspects of the feminine principle, modern dance opened a view of the female mythical negative (the terrifying face of Ereshkigal), the side that Sylvia Perera describes as "the destructive-transformative side of the cosmic will." Perera explains that "Ereshkigal is like Kali, who through time and suffering 'pitilessly grinds down . . . all distinctions . . . in her indiscriminating fires'—and yet heaves forth new life. She symbolizes the abyss that is the source and the end, the ground of all being."[29]

The earliest modern dance work to look into the fierce, and fatalistic range of the mythical feminine is probably Wigman's *Hexentanz I* (Witches Dance, 1914), a dance that dares to be grotesque, explosive, and undomesticated. Wigman explores the diabolical in this and later witch dances (though there are also pastoral moods apparent in the pictures and titles we have left of her works).

Tiel Tiele, who worked with Wigman and taught at the Wigman school in Berlin for eighteen years, remembers German expressionism well. I have often heard her recount the search for a deep sense of self and for honesty in action, which characterized the work. That this did not entail raw self-expression but was tempered by a strong concern for form is also clear. Wigman's contributions to the dancer's poetic use of space through an understanding of both its objective and mythopoetic qualities are well known. In my study with her in 1965, I was aware of her easy familiarity with Laban's objective movement theories but was also aware that the metaphorical, poetic, and intuitive grasp of movement informed her perspective first and foremost. A search for the truth of oneself, as this might be communicated to others and understood in a universalized expression, characterized the teaching of the Wigman school. The last time I saw Tiele teach (in Canada in 1979), I observed how closely she scrutinized the students' belief in what they were doing. She was not looking for beautiful surfaces but for convincing expressive depth. At the same time, she cautioned, "be objective."

Today we are experiencing a revival of expressionism. Brutal self-destructive forces in the inflation of both male and female mythic archetypes—especially as these come into conflict—are exposed in German choreographer Pina Bausch's neoexpressionist dance dramas. The violence of our times is enacted here in brilliantly formulated, erotic, emotional (Dionysian) imagery. Bausch locates the violence we cannot expiate unless we are willing to look upon it, just as we look upon the wild destructiveness of Dionysus when the joy of his ecstatic dance turns to fury.

In being all things, Inanna-Nammu-Ereshkigal are monistic, integrative, and transformational. They are like modern dance, esoteric, both beautiful and ugly, sometimes fluid, and sometimes stuttering, wild, and distorted. If modern dance has not always been pleasant and beautiful, at least it has been down to earth, erotic, often mystic, seldom sweetly romantic, highly individualistic, incessantly experimental, and subject to radical change. Thus modern dance is founded in the wisdom of the receptive, all-containing feminine earth.

In the absence of a singular guiding aesthetic view, technique, or stipulated movement vocabulary (and within the hazards of such freedom), modern dance has developed an extremely diversified aesthetic field, allowing explorations of the joyful and playful as well as the diabolical. Paul Taylor's works, for instance, seem to grow out of the allowing noncensorship of modern dance, as they range through an entire spectrum of values, from the bubbling child's play of *Esplanade* (1975) and the deep romance of *Roses* (1985) to an exploitation of the incest taboo in *Big Bertha* (1971). The exploration of themes from nature have not been limited to women in modern dance. Men like Erick Hawkins have been concerned with the nature of the body and have dared to dance with pliant softness and transparency, as in *Geography of Noon* (1964). Like Graham before him, Hawkins also draws upon the reverence of Native American cultures for the earth.

Steve Paxton, in the postmodern period, founded contact improvisation, an intuitive form of dance based on spontaneous giving and taking of weight between partners androgenously paired and impossible to do with the vertical ballet spine, since it is experienced through a constant forgiving adjustment of one's body to that of the other. And Cunningham, while highly technical, formalist, and intellectual (or anti-intellectual), nevertheless, affirms the yielding yin through his incorporation of chance in structuring his work, thus "letting happen" the dance, relinquishing ego in the process. In another manner, Nikolais's works also descended from an egotistical position. Since the dancer's personae is submerged and often hidden, no one stars in his dances; all are a part of the total vision. Certainly his work has also drawn upon the rich imagery of a suprapersonal consciousness, or a "collective unconscious," as Jung calls it. Despite their high technology and mechanics, Nikolais's works evoke primordial organic life, as the amebic *Noumenon* (1953), with which he is so closely associated, shows.

Jung sees the constructive aspects of the unconscious and its psychic energy as well as its destructive potential; thus he interprets the shadowed side of consciousness and the dark female principle in a positive way, reversing the common and prejudicial disposition to view darkness as negative and emphasizing the integrative function of the unconscious: "One has to be able to let things happen. I have learned from the Orient the lesson expressed in the words *wu wei:* 'not-doing'; not 'doing nothing,' but 'allowing.' Others have known of this, too, as for instance, Meister Ekhart when he speaks of 'yielding oneself.' The dark spot upon which one stumbles actually is not empty but is the Bestowing Mother, the Images and the Seed."[30]

Similarly, Zen master D. T. Suzuki speaks of an inward way of seeing, of "consciousness becoming acquainted with itself" by means of the "unconscious." As I understand the Zen koan riddles, they work through the unconscious to bring about such transformations on a spiritual level. Suzuki links them to psychology as well. The unconscious, he states, lies quietly in consciousness, becoming active as it announces itself through consciousness. He also reverses our common disposition to speak of the unconscious rising to consciousness by lateralizing the two terms. "Zen would not object to the possibility of an 'unconscious conscious' or a 'conscious unconscious.'" Therefore he speaks of consciousness turning inward (the directional image is not up and down, but inward and outward), of "consciousness coming to its own unconscious," a "homecoming": "This is the seeing of one's own 'primal face' which one has even before birth. This is God's pronouncing his name to Moses. This is the birth of Christ in each of our souls. This is Christ rising from death."[31]

Indeed it might be more positive and less dualistic to call the unconscious or the subconscious *inward consciousness.* The integral dancing moment in all dance demonstrates (as Zen does) that, in the truly inward way, contrasts between inner and outer disappear, as Suzuki explains the nondualistic way of Zen.[32]

Body of Nature and Culture

If modern dance is founded in the wisdom of the yielding feminine principle, it is nevertheless also founded, as all dance is, in our polarized mythical body of yielding and striving, yin and yang, expression and form, female and male. And, as all dance, it is grounded in our body of nature and culture.

Culture (which in contrast to nature must exert itself to form a sphere of action) is the province of the male (yang) and associated in myth (demonstrated strikingly in the *I Ching*) with heaven (the creative). Man is powerful through active consciousness, intellect, and an upward and outward heroic surge of forces. The female (yin) is powerful through earth (the receptive), the yielding unconscious, and nature. Her mythic directions are descent and inwardness; her attributes are intuition and vision. There are destructive potentials in exaggerations of either primal power or mythic pole. The male when cut off from the female leads to the manipulative aggressions of war and the compulsion to dominate. The female cut off from the male leads to madness.

Fear and repression of the feminine have not allowed us to realize its positive transformative wisdom, its peace. The most destructive mythic symbol associated with the feminine may well be Kali, Shiva's destructive side, but as noted in the hymn of Kali at the beginning of the chapter, this side is wrought in the burning ground of the heart as ego dissolves. Here self-assertion (both male and female) gives way to self-realization. These are characterized in the opposing qualities of "will" and "will-surrender" by Ananda Coomaraswamy. Self-assertion is the evolutional "path of pursuit," while self-realization is the involutional "path of return."[33]

In Joseph Campbell's perspective, the male represents *culture,* the ascent of power, competition, and war-like gods, while the female is associated with *nature,* peace, compassion, and transcendence. The female is broken by nature, as she is "broken by menstruation" and "given" in birth. The male is broken through culturally instituted puberty rites.[34] Ruth Underhill also points out that the mysteries of menstruation and childbirth are rooted in natural manifestations of power, as are the rites of protective isolation surrounding the mysteries, whereas male rites are primarily a social affair, rationalized finally in theological systems. The mysteries of menstruation and birth are as persuasive as death—and are still sources of religious awe.[35]

If this sounds like biology as destiny, the determinism that Simone de Beauvoir so rightly objected to in *The Second Sex* (the first existential view of women and feminism), then perhaps we need to be reminded that lethal threats to the biological chain of life now require a deeper valuing of the primal goddess, who is devoted to all living things. In the female mythic symbol there is reverence for the earth: receptivity, peace, giveness, surrender of ego, and the transformational powers of birth. The finality of death, which so occupies the male atheistic existentialists, appears in a different light when paired with the reality of birth—a reality that women are not likely to overlook.

In her study of the data of biology, reproduction, and femininity, de Beauvoir explains the view of Heidegger and Sartre that "the real nature of man is bound up with death" or with man's finite limited state. She points out the correlative side of man's finitude: "The progress of his life through time creates behind him and before him the infinite past and future, and it would seem, then, that the perpetuation of the species is the correlative of his individual limitation. Thus we can regard the phenomenon of reproduction as founded in the very *nature* of being" (my italics).[36]

Campbell equates the male with death and the female with birth in his pairing of opposites in myth.[37]

In many ways, such myths no longer have a literal application. Women are no longer slaves to their nature. Neither are they slaves to the species—nor is the body (understood simply as biological) enough to define femininity. Now women can choose to be *more than nature,* and men can choose to *find their nature.* Still, myths hold important archetypal polarities, and they teach us much about ourselves in terms of the history and archetypes of consciousness, as Jung and his followers have brought to our attention.

Body of Earth and Heaven ☯

As Henderson studies the significance of "the wisdom" of the female deity, he concludes (as Jung and others do) "that all men and women capable of mature reflection upon their psychic constitution discover that they are basically two in one, male and female."[38] This is the most immediately communicated significance of the earth-heaven, yin-yang symbol. The yin-yang interlocking symbol holds the female and the male as counterparts of the whole. It is not, however, empty of creative tension but holds the interest of individuality in its dualistic inner shape and exchanges of color. It is not a neutral symbol. It is full of action inside; yet its round surface bears the surface neutrality of the earth, the moon, and the pearl when their darkness meets the light. It seems an appropriate mythological symbol for a time when modern man needs to find the genius of his feminine side, just as modern woman seeks the light of her own appropriate self-image in the strength of intellect as well as heart.

Our body of earth and heaven can also be visualized in the Lakota Indian Sun Dance Tree, a symbol that holds the male-female polarity within a transcendent androgynous whole. The Sun Dance Tree—the axis of the universe—survives from ancient times. Its top, open to the sun, is the male principle. Its foundation, rooted in the earth, is the female principle. The tree is modeled on the sacred pipe of the Lakota and is also compared to the human body.[39]

In the apotheosis of the male-female god—the jewel (the male) in the lotus (the female)—the wall of pairs of opposites is shattered.[40] Campbell relates this meaning of the bisexual god in the union of the Buddhas and bodhisattvas of Mahayana Buddhism with their own feminine qualities; in the compounding of darkness and light in the womb; and in the vision of God in Genesis 1:27, wherein God creates man in his own image, male and female. Campbell further speculates that "the wise realize, even within this womb (of time), that they have come from and are returning to the father; while the very wise know that she and he are in substance one."[41] Thus we might visualize the commingling of darkness and light in the creation of our body of earth and heaven, of heart and mind, of nature and culture, of night and day.

Our body of earth and heaven is our body of mythic tension, our body of dance. It holds a tension between vibrant powers that Rilke's poetry sings of as "pure tension" and "music of the powers!"[42] It is lived through effort and ease—it suffers and exalts the rhythms of nature; yet it is also a product of its culture, its time, and of individual will. Dance allows us to experience the body's natural powers as well the body's acquired culture. Dance exists in a pure tension between the body's nature and its culture, its yielding earth and active heaven.

In early modern dance it is not difficult to observe a giveness to nature through the release of the body to gravity. The floor work of Graham and the groundedness of Wigman's work attest this. Doris Humphrey sought to build a technique true to nature by acknowledging the pull of gravity. Beginning in the following generation and continuing into the present, Erick Hawkins founded a quest for beautiful movement—sound and healthy movement—through the study and application of kinesiology and a sensitivity to "our animal energies."

The postmodern mundane aesthetic searched also for something true to nature but in an entirely different way. In the best of postmodern dance there is ease, not vapid but graceful, in giveness to the earth and acceptance of nature in an attempt to *find* dance anew, putting ordinary everyday movement with untrained dancers in a dance context. The radical disposition was not to *make* dance, which is of course an act of culture. "Happenings," popular in all the arts in the sixties, stand in contrast to cultural (man-made) artifacts. Happenings happen; cultural artifacts are consciously created.

Yet, as it exists in a tension between nature and culture, dance is transformational. Viewed in terms of culture, the notion that "anyone can dance," however true this may be at a certain level, threatens a loss of the virtuoso qualities we rightly prize in dance and a loss of creative tension as well. Dance carries creative tension in it through the human body, which is coextensive with nature but is nevertheless also a product of culture. We learn our movement as a development of will and within the dramatic duality and reciprocity between the voluntary and the involuntary, as Paul Ricoeur explains. "The unity of willing and movement which breaks up when it is thought itself includes a certain duality, a lived duality. The bond with the body, even though indivisible, is polemic and dramatic." Underneath lived tensions and dualities is a basic unity: "Every voluntary hold on the body repossesses the body's involuntary usage. . . . Voluntary motion of the body does not present itself as a native power of an *imperium* over an inert body, but as a dialogue with a bodily spontaneity."[43]

I dance with the natural body I have been given and also with the body I have made myself into through will and creative effort. My nondance, everyday body has also been accrued through will and influenced by my nature and my culture. Dance triumphs over nature as an act of culture; yet the irony is that nature never leaves it. Aesthetically vital dance returns me to my nature. At the same time, my natural endowment of body is extended through the creative (cultural) act of dancing. I dance within my own nature, creating out of it as I yield to it and as I strive to create beyond it.

While art is coextensive with material nature and bodily lived nature, it opposes nature in the sense that it must be intentionally enacted. Nature acts within and upon us. Conversely, in creating art we are actors, participating together to create culture and extend nature. Yet vital art is not created wholly through cultural contrivance or willful doing. Nondoing (yielding) is as important as doing (acting). I could even say (and make mythological sense) that the vitality of art lies in its *recovery of nature,* its yin-yang meld of nature and culture.

It is thus, when I have learned my dance and know how to do it, that I can say it has become second nature to me. Art recovers the nature from whence it sprang when it achieves spontaneity of expression. Spontaneity and nature are equated here, since they are both in accord with the unquantifiable lived moment when striving ceases and grace appears. This is the present-centered moment, the vital moment of both art and religion. This is also the transformational moment symbolized in the waxing and waning of the changeable feminine moon and in the emergence from the depths of the sea of the perfectly formed androgynous pearl, cultured in the pearl oyster who (according to Chinese mythology) "concentrates wholly upon its yin force."[44] This moment of unification, which Martin Buber calls I-thou, is a symbolic recovery of yin, or the spontaneous yielding that gives birth to the creative. The *I Ching* represents heaven, the creative, as male, yet attributes creation's coming into being to Earth, the receptive, the all-containing female yin.

Heaven and earth also meet in the mythic symbol of the world mountain. In Sumerian myth, the goddess of the world mountain of heaven and earth is personified as Nammu.[45] It is she who gives birth to heaven and earth; she is by nature integrative. The Aztec god of duality at the summit of the world mountain (the place of duality) is personified in Ometeotl, a "transcendent-immanent dual divinity."[46] Our body of earth and heaven may be envisioned as an extension of the world mountain. We dance its mythopoetic rhythms, revealing its tranquil composure and also its ecstatic dualities.

It is when we are present centered—at one with the world and free of conflicting dualities—that we dance its grace. Then Kali, the energy of the universe, melts into Shiva's heart, releasing his cosmic dance of creation.

PART III

SIGN FOR LIFE

Sondra Fraleigh, Michael Youseff, Pamela Trippel in *Debussy Dances* by Sondra Fraleigh (1979). Photo: June Burke.

9

ACTS OF LIGHT[1]

Metaphysics has nothing in common with a generalization of experience, and yet it could be defined as the whole of experience (*l'experience integrale*). – Henri Bergson

Thus far, I have been describing dance as purposeful expression, a description I will continue to develop. I have also considered that dance has subjective content (that it is of our sentient selves), that it has objective structure (discernible form), and that these are interrelated in the tensions and polarities of our dance. In these concluding chapters, I consider the lived ground of dance and what the dancer signifies (signs) through this ground. This leads to a further concern for the nondualistic unity of our lived world – our one world – and the proof of this unity that our dance offers. When we understand our purposeful action – our acts – in light of our embodiment, all dualisms collapse, and the metaphysical in our purposeful undertakings appears to us.

Dance and Metaphysics: One World

René Descartes's metaphysics, which Gilbert Ryle calls "the myth of the Ghost in the Machine," dominates western concepts of body and mind. The body in Descartes's dualistic scheme is material: it functions as a machine to execute what the mind wills. The mind, then, is immaterial, invisible, inner, and mysteriously ethereal. Bodies are situated in space, but minds being invisible extend beyond physical categories. It is common to express body-mind divisions by saying that bodies belong to the physical world, the external visible world, and that minds belong to an unseen internal world, each mind being invisible and insulated from others. Ryle points out that this antithesis of inner and outer are construed mainly as metaphors "since minds, not being in space, could not be described as being spatially inside anything else, or as having things going on spatially inside themselves."[2] Ryle exposes the absurdities of this ghostly concept of mind as well as the two-world view of body and mind it produces. Armed with clear academic English, he demonstrates the problems of Descartes's metaphysics. He shows knowledge, will, emotion, sensation, imagination, and intellect to be occurrences within the single indivisible world of persons.

In opposition to Descartes's metaphysics, Ryle assigns mind no privileged position, nor does he identify mind solely with intellect. "There are many activities which directly display qualities of mind, yet are neither themselves intellectual operations nor yet effects of intellectual operations. Intelligent practice is not a step-child of theory. On the contrary theorising is one practice amongst others and is itself intelligently or stupidly conducted." He finds mind in "knowing how" (knowing how to do something) as well as in "knowing that" (knowing that something is the case). "A person's performance is described as careful or skillful, if in his operations he is ready to detect and correct lapses, to repeat and improve upon successes, to profit from the examples of others and so forth. He applies criteria in performing critically, that is, in trying to get things right."

Moreover, in getting things right, a person is simply regulating his actions; he is not involved in two processes, one of doing and another of theorizing. Moving with a purpose does not necessitate, as is the common supposition, thinking or theorizing before acting. It does involve the exercise of mind and intelligence in fulfillment of that purpose. "The clown's trippings and tumblings are the workings of his mind, for they are his jokes; but the visible similar trippings and tumblings of a clumsy man are not the workings of that man's mind. *For he does not trip on purpose* [my italics]. Tripping on purpose is both a bodily and a mental process, but it is not two processes, such as one process of purposing to trip and, as an effect, another process of tripping."[3]

The clown's antics and the dancer's performance are not unthinking or unconscious acts; neither are they habits. They are skilled and purposeful formulations and presentations. They are skillful in thought and action, but not as two separate things. Skill is action done purposefully and well. That is, skillful action involves fulfillment of known goals, it is not merely done habitually; and it must be done well. The clown and the dancer are performing their wit, their intelligence, and their artistry. Their movement displays their judgment; it is not prefaced by it. They are not thinking and doing; they *think what* they are doing. Of the skilled performer, Ryle says, "He learns how to do things thinking what he is doing, so every operation performed is itself a new lesson to him how to perform better."[4] The clown and the dancer are not sleepwalking, dreaming, or on automatic; they are striving to meet their goals in performance, and using their training—their store of knowledge and practice—as they perform.

This pragmatic explanation serves as an initial illustration of our single world of mind and action, but it does not explain the wonder we experience when our purposes in action are perfectly fulfilled; when, as we considered earlier, our movement attains a freedom from striving as intention is dissolved in it. For instance, in a dance that I have rehearsed, learned, and know how to do, I have expectations and hopes. I hope I will perform it well; but more, I hope that as it unfolds in the movement I set into play, I will be taken by the whole of it, be free in it, and that it will lead me beyond my ordinary boundaries, as it takes on an exhilarant life of its own.

Similarly, a writer may be taken by the exciting unfolding of an idea. He may then experience something new, something that had never occurred to him before, extending his boundaries in the process. Although the idea "came" to him, we know nevertheless that it is his idea, one that he himself set in motion. At the same time, the idea is not the result of a struggle, for it has come seemingly of its own accord—as a gift. He experiences spontaneity and freedom in it. But, like the dancer, he has prepared himself for this idea to come. He has learned his craft, rehearsed it, and knows how. He does not want his writing to be labored any more than the dancer wants her dancing to be. He wants to express his idea with ease and clarity. He does not want to chase the idea. He wants to catch up with it—to be in it—to fully express it in the writing of it. He cannot will such freedom, but he can prepare for it. He also seeks the gift of grace in his work.

The dancer and the writer may both experience an ecstatic merging with their own transformational actions, as they move them beyond the ordinary. They seek the "clear place" (Hawkins), the "clearing," and the "lighting" (Heidegger). In fact the extraordinary is not beyond the average reach. It is there in life and in ourselves, whenever we extend our reach and move to meet it.

Martin Heidegger grounds metaphysics in being—as being-in-the-world rather than beyond it. However difficult, baroque, and obscure he may be, Heidegger has had a profound effect on modern philosophy.[5] He influenced a view of the immanent transcendence in "average everydayness," the transcendence in the being of beings, who are essentially beings-in-the-world.[6] "Being-In-The-World," he says, "is a structure which is primordially and constantly whole."[7] "Falling," he says, is both a motion and a proof of our existential mode of being-in-the world.[8] "Authentic existence" is viewed in terms of our existential "fallenness" and its temporal character.[9] "Time" belongs to the totality of being, or is "the horizon of being."[10] *Falling* is Heidegger's motional and temporal image for existence in its everydayness. Authentic existence is not seized above or beyond falling, but within it. "*Authentic* existence is not something which floats above falling everydayness; existentially, it is only a modified way in which everydayness is seized upon."[11]

Heidegger obviously came up against the limits of language in saying what he wanted to say (as Ludwig Wittgenstein recognized).[12] The very style of his writing indicates this. His disposition to turn nouns into verbs and verbs into nouns to suggest unceasing movement and ever-expanding time and space embues his writing with an abstract yet dancing quality. It seems he wanted to dance being with words. A thing (anything and everything—entity and phenomenon) is not merely a presence—it "presences" as a "presencing." The "ing" in being seems to guide the ongoing dancing quality he seeks. Like a dance, our being-in-the-world is of motion, time, and becoming.

I read Heidegger's philosophy much as I view a dance—as expression in the making, as a celebration of our ability to express. Heidegger perhaps says being in the same sense the dancer *dances* being. Certainly dance provides the symbol that permits him to see the gathering in all things—the gathering that all things are. He describes our one world in its primordial manifestation—in its "worlding"—as a gathering dance of the fourfold nature of all things: a round dance of earth, heaven, divinity, and mortality—a dance of "the worlding of the world."[13]

Now, does he mean us to make sense or nonsense of this image? Or is he simply inviting us to live in the unsayable nature of our own "worlding," as a dance is lived beyond the limits of language? He reaches for dance and for mythic images in his attempt to say or to express being, directly. He also uses movement imagery to express more general concepts—to impart the feeling of them, the sensations that ground them. Thus everydayness is conceived through the physical phenomenon and the image of falling; and the unfinished, unsettled nature of our lives is conceived through "thrownness."[14] He borrows from Rilke the image that being is a "venture," describing its further movement as "a release flinging (beings) loose . . . a daring."[15]

This strange way of talking appeals to me as a dancer. I might just as easily have picked it up from dancing as from Heidegger, since he describes being in movement terms. He describes being, poetically envisioned through Rilke, in its wholeness as life, nature, and the open. This is not life strictly biologically conceived; this is the *phusis,* that which arises.[16] The image is one of spontaneous movement, seemingly out of nowhere—a perfect description of the spontaneous essence of dance, the open, unblocked, unboundedness we love in dance as we seem to live and understand our own arising in it. This is the quality Heidegger seeks to give word to. He describes what we dance: the arising, falling, throwing, binding, releasing, flinging loose, and gathering of life.

In dance, we pay attention to our own throwing, gathering in, falling, and arising. Unlike the athlete who throws a ball, a discus, or a javelin (and herself in the process), the dancer throws only herself. She relates to no object, and she has no objective outside of the throwing. Her throw will not accomplish anything beyond her dance. Thus she discovers how many ways of throwing there are. Twyla Tharp originated a wonderful thrown way of turning, wherein the head, arms, and upper torso begin the turn as a throw-around, and the lower body and legs are taken along for the ride, the legs joyfully catching up with the original throw and moving past it before the turn abates. We see this turn a lot in her energetic and piquant *Push Comes to Shove* (1976). We recognize in it the vitality of our own thrown turning and oblique playfulness, whether we do the turn or not. In Jerome Robbins's beautiful work *Dances at a Gathering* (1969), the communal gathering and fading of seemingly divine beings touched by mortal tragedies is satisfying to watch for itself, as a thing, in the Heideggerian sense of worlding—as is also the hazardous "ventured daring" of Elizabeth Streb's thrown solo dances. Both choreographers satisfy our recognition of ourselves as moving beings in transition. They distill and express our transitive being-in-the-world, Robbins through beautiful images that gather and fade and Streb by literally throwing herself into high-risk movement.

The view the dancer opens to us is of the lived and moving ground of being, the same view Heidegger endeavors "to open" (and "to clear") with his use of dance as a metaphor for the manifestation of being. He seeks to express the moving qualities of the experiences that bring being into focus for us—dread, curiosity, guilt, resoluteness, idleness, care, and so on. Heidegger wants to clarify an ontology, to express the meaning of being. When he comes to the dead end of analysis, he turns to the language of myth, to dance, and to movement metaphors. Of Heidegger's basic position, Michael Murray says, "If we reflect upon the background of any possible expression, expressibility as such, we are close to Heidegger's existential, transcendental concept of the world."[17]

Both Ryle, who provided an entrance into this discussion of the singular world of mind and action, and Heidegger take a nondualistic position on our integral being-in-the-world. Murray compares their work, pointing out Ryle's indebtedness to Heidegger, one that Ryle acknowledges.[18]

If we do not suppose we are split between two worlds—one physical and one metaphysical, one of substance and one beyond substance—metaphysics might be understood within a single world, where thought, intention, intuition, and action are not ultimately separate. Nature, or the living physical world whose shcema is inscribed in and through our unbroken wholeness, takes on a new complexion when metaphysics receives explanation within the life-world, rather than outside of it, as something ghostly pertaining to an unseen supernatural realm.

Lived Metaphysics

INTENTION

Making dances, performing dances, and interpreting the dances we see involves a lived metaphysics, one that functions in our single, unbifurcated world, where mind and body are continuous and where thinking, willing, moving, imagining, intending, intuiting, perceiving, feeling, sensing, and even transcending are continuous with the life-world. That is, dance involves us in the metaphysics of human movement. Because it has an aesthetic intent, it involves us in intentionally created movement, which is meant to be transferred from performer to audience and grasped immediately through intuition. It thus involves us in continuities of thinking, feeling, willing, and moving, as well as in imagining and intuiting.

The action of dancing is differentiated from habitually performed, functionally directed action, since it is intentionally performed, skilled action directed toward an aesthetic outcome. It belongs more properly to that class of actions performed intentionally and communally with concern for their outcome—those actions we call *acts.* Not all of these have an aesthetic imperative, but they are all purposeful—that is, intentionally done. Acts are things done in light of—in knowledge of—the doing of them. Dancing is not just any action whatsoever; it is intentional, skillful action with an aesthetic purpose. Yet it relates to and is derived from all of our actions as a whole, just as deeds are specific kinds of intentional actions performed in relation to our doings as a whole.

The acts that constitute dance in its full aesthetic transaction are not ghostly, invisible operations. They arise first through intentional exploratory stages in the creative processes of making dance. Finally, they are apparent in the intentional acts of performance as well as in the audience's active reception of dance. Intention in dance is not beyond or outside of the dance. That is, I do not imagine stick figures (or any other kind) dancing in my head as a fore-image of what I will execute in movement. Rather, I exercise my imagination intentionally, in the moment, as I invent movement (as a choreographer), as I perform it (as a dancer), or as I give it my open and undivided attention (as an audience). While I attend to movement in these various ways in dance, I am also attending to more—namely, the aesthetic qualities inherent in movement and invested in the dance. Certainly I do not think about all of this—I think of none of it—*I just do it.* Sometimes, however, the marvels in the actual doing appear to me full of metaphysics.

INTUITION

Either metaphysics is only this game of ideas, or else, if it is a serious occupation of the mind, it must transcend concepts to arrive at intuition.—Henri Bergson

Bergson, who laid the foundation for lived-body theories, explains metaphysics from within experience rather than from without. He identifies metaphysics with the intuitive, immediate grasp of things. He distinguishes metaphysical intuition from scientific analysis. It is by means of intuition and not analysis that one may possess a reality absolutely—by placing oneself within the reality, not by adopting a point of view toward it.[19]

Gabriel Marcel sees this phenomenon as a bodily lived consonance, or sympathy, with the world, while Martin Buber describes the same phenomenon as I-thou. Metaphysical intuition, Bergson describes as "an urge to movement . . . indefinitely extensible." He also sees it as "simplicity itself." Intuition lies behind analysis. Analysis provides knowledge proximate to reality and consists "in expressing a thing in terms of what is not it."

Intuition is the act that possesses reality: "An absolute can only be given in an *intuition,* while all the rest has to do with *analysis.* We call intuition here the *sympathy* by which one is transported into the interior of an object in order to coincide with what there is unique and consequently inexpressible in it."[20] Through intuition, the unique features of the world arise, but through analysis, objects reduce to their common elements. Bergson considers analysis as "the operation which reduces the object to elements already known, that is, common to that object and to others."[21]

Intuition is the light that floods an idea and lights our understanding, moving it from murkiness to clarity. Light is a good metaphor for intuition because of its seeming nonexistence and transparency. When I say something dawns on me, I mean that I have a sudden recognition of it; and I am using the dawning of the light, which ushers in the day, as a metaphor to explain my recognition. Light, like intuition, makes possible my seeing and recognition of the world. Finally, light becomes a metaphor for understanding. Thus I can speak of my understanding "in light of" or "in view of" something. I can *touch* and *feel* the world in darkness, but I can only *see* it when it is lighted. When I say "light has been shed on something," I mean that it has become clear to me, that I grasp it whole.

This insight (in-sight) — light, graceful, and effortless — is intuition. It lights our understanding and is the essence of dancing. It is of our dance when we merge with it. Dances are created and understood first through intuition — acts of light — and not through analysis. They are perceived first for themselves, as they are, and only second for what they remind us of. Dance is founded through intuition, always ready to mold itself on the fluid imagination, the fleeting moment, and our immediate grasp of the world in our consonance with it.

UNIFICATION

The dancer's movements are workings of her mind, will, intuitions, and imagination — for they are her art, neither automatic nor accidental. She dances with a purpose; she intends to communicate something to an audience, something the movement itself will convey. The audience perceives her dance through her movement as it conveys her intentions. In short, they see what she does and see the thought in it — not behind it or before it. If she moves softly, they see softness; if she moves sharply, that is what they see. The dancer learns how to fulfill her intentions in movement, how to move sharply or softly when she wants to. Moreover, she learns that soft is not merely one quality; just as Eskimos have many different names for snow, soft has many shades in dance. The dancer does not usually attempt to describe the many shades of her movement, she simply performs them (although in making and learning dances, analysis and description of movement do take place). The audience participates with her in the performance when it gives itself to the dance.

The dancer is not doing two things called *moving* and *thinking* (or even two things called *dancing* and *projecting meaning*). *She is doing one thing, which is dancing.* In the moment of its execution, her movement is of her thought; if it is thought of before or after, she will not be in the middle of it. She will not be centered in action. But she will still not be doing two things — she will simply be dancing poorly.

The audience completes her dance as they connect with it. In this connection are also the workings of thought, will, intuition, and imagination. Like the dancer, the audience is not, in its relation to the dance, doing four or even two things. It is simply attending to the dance, connecting with it, and (if the dance is good) finding fulfillment in it (all at once).

In dancing, and the communion between dancer and audience, there is a unifying metaphysic. The faster than light quantum jump of modern physics provides a metaphysical metaphor for the speed of the dance that passes between and through us, uniting the universe. In *The Dancing Wu Li Masters,* Gary Zukav gives an overview of the dance of life, which modern physics reveals in its mystical dimensions. "Quantum logic," he says, "is not only more exciting than classical logic, it is more real. It is based not upon the way we *think* of things, but upon the way that we *experience* them."[22]

Dance brings forward the metaphysical in the physical, the transcendent in ourselves, which is experienced when our possibilities are realized through expressive skillful action in unity with others and our world. Then obstacles and separations dissolve, and the field of our freedom opens up. Dance can be fully understood only within a metaphysical perspective and fully explained only within a mythical-metaphorical perspective, one that does not seek to replace the dance, because it ensues from it.

SIGN AND IMAGE

Only in metaphysics is there metaphor. —Martin Heidegger

Dance is a metaphysics of doing. It lives in the present-centered moment of its execution and through the immediate communion between dancer and audience. Assumed in these actions and interactions is a lived metaphysic and the metaphorical in it. The metaphorical presupposes the metaphysical.[23]

When we dance for others, we suppose that in the action of dancing itself—in movement per se—intentions may be embodied and communicated. Further, when our intentions are achieved and realized by the audience, something has occurred surpassing the fact of performance. Something of value has been transferred by means of movement and its theatrical environment—setting, lighting, and costumes.

Movement in dance, I have said, is valued for itself. But we have seen that dance is more than movement. It refers us to a wide range of phenomena beyond movement. This it does through literal denotation or through nonliteral exemplification. Broadly speaking, dance is metaphorical in the sense that metaphor involves us in transferred usages of expressions. In the strictest sense, metaphor operates through words composed into full gestalts (phrases or images) that refer us to something beyond the words. In its reference, the metaphor functions symbolically. It is an open, nonrestrictive symbol through which we interpret ourselves in our world, poetically. Not all symbols are poetic; the metaphor is, because it is open to interpretation and because it binds us to ourselves and our world in an open, metaphysical leap from the word to the world. It is in this sense that movement, like the word, functions metaphorically (and poetically) in dance.

Robert Frost explains the poetic essence of metaphor, its values and limitations: "Unless you are at home in the metaphor, unless you have had your proper poetical education in the metaphor, you are not safe anywhere. Because you are not at ease with figurative values; you don't know the metaphor in its strength and its weakness. You don't know how far you may expect to ride it and when it may break down with you."[24]

Dance uses human movement like poetry uses the word, not factually but imaginatively: that is *imagistically* and in the metaphysically open, nonrestrictive sense of metaphor. Even when a dance denotes something specific, it does so in an open, interpretive way. Agnes de Mille's *Fall River Legend* (1948), for instance, must deal with Lizzie Borden's murder of her father and stepmother interpretively. As poetry uses the word, dance uses movement, not for its singular beauty alone (what could one movement be, anyway?) but within a gestalt. Meaning arises from the whole and from the composed images, which are smaller units within the whole.

The singular word is called a sign. There is, technically speaking, no such thing as a single movement (as we shall later consider). Movement is by definition a never-ceasing. So how can there be one movement? In dance, however, we take a perspective on movement; we shape and design it and designate units in it in order to comprehend the structure of the dance and to perform it as a single, whole event. As a *whole*, the dance is—like the word—a sign. Dance is a sign for life—for our embodiment, our arising. It points to the whole of our existence, just as the word points to our expressive powers as a whole and, in a mythical sense, to God.

Units within the whole of the dance—its parts which nevertheless flow together and are continuous with each other in the whole—may be described according to their time-space configuration, or their world-line, as modern physics states the phenomenon of movement in time-space. These units may also be described according to what they point out or call forward in the imagination. Therefore we can call them dance images—images composed of movement in time-space that evoke something beyond their physical world-line. That something which they evoke we often call *meaning,* what the dance is about. The dance may also point out the character of the world-line, itself, by emphasizing abstract time-space values of human movement and by deemphasizing allusive values (as many of Nikolais's works do). Such dance is still symbolic in an open nonrestrictive sense, as it particularizes (since every dance is unique) and exemplifies a human world-line. Every dance traces its own particular world-line or space-time pathway, but some (like Nikolais's dances) serve as particular aesthetic manifestations of it. Because the time and space of human experience is lived through our body-of-motion (as we consider in the next chapter), dance imagery—even when it emphasizes abstract time-space values—is drawn from and points toward life.

Dancing always expresses something of our livingness. Conceiving and perceiving dance imagery involves us in transfers of meaning as we relate the dance and its imagery to our lived experience in general. (In the final chapter, we will see how this occurs in various ways with examples from several dances.) Dance reflects life; it is itself a ready metaphor for life, as Havelock Ellis shows in *The Dance of Life.*[25] The lived ground of dance—*the lived body*—is consonant with life. Thus dance has the power of signifying life: its imagery is of life (of the pure forces of nature and our own arising through them) and of living (of experienced joys and sorrows, of actually falling down and getting up).

Dances move. They do not speak as language does. They are not audible expressions. Yet they stand with other forms of nonverbal art expressions in the open of saying. Dance is like all human expression as Heidegger defined it: "a presentation and representation of the real and the unreal."[26] Dance presents movement, real in its measurable dimensions of energy, time, and spatial properties. However, the real, as quantifiable movement, does not sufficiently explain dance, because dance draws us beyond its movement manifestation and stimulates associations.

A dance may reflect human qualities of friendliness, agitation, desperation, or graciousness; yet these are also general terms, not exclusive to dance expression. Moreover, as they are intentionally embodied in the dance, these human qualities take on an aesthetic form. This is so even if the dance is improvised in performance (since works performed for others, even when improvised, are intentionally performed for an aesthetic purpose). These qualities are not conditions or states of being in the performers upon which they or we are going to act. We do not rush up on stage to console performers because of their desperation or to shake hands with them because of their friendliness. In this sense, the human qualities reflected in the dance are not really there. (Even when the performers wander in the audience, shaking hands, there is a sense of unreality in the situation.) We recognize these human qualities, however, because of our own experience of them. Dance can point them out by virtue of its distance from them. Dance is real only as dance—not as life. Because dance is dance and not life, it can point toward it. It can do this passionately (as in Martha Graham's *Cave of the Heart*, 1946), matter of factly (as in Yvonne Rainer's *Trio A*, 1966), humorously (as in Paul Taylor's *Cloven Kingdom*, 1976), ecstatically (as in Lar Lubovitch's *North Star*, 1978), or playfully (as in Twyla Tharp's *Eight Jelly Rolls*, 1971).

Dance brings the unnoticed flow of our fleeting existence into view. It gives expression to its many shades. It holds meaning as it draws from and points toward life. It is composed of our own livingness and refers directly to it. If dance is not life, it nevertheless is continuous with life through its lived ground, through the dancer, and through movement images drawn from our moving existence as a whole. Just as music and poetry transport us beyond sound and words, dance carries us beyond movement to its broader lived terms.

Life is the broader background against which art takes on definition and meaning. Life itself is full of interpretation. We learn quickly and easily that blue is not just one thing; it is sky, water, color, mood, eyes, loyalty (true blue), aristocracy (blue blood), it is part of purple and many more things. Similarly, when we interpret a dance, when we say what it has communicated to us, it is by means of our knowledge of our world—

its shapes, rhythms, colors, and movements—and by means of our experience and our powers of interpretation. The genius in the doing and the understanding of dance is ourselves.

Art and life exhibit common elements; this has been said often by many observers. Art has also been called life, but I think of it more as a sign for life—perhaps the clearest sign of the metaphysic that functions unnoticed in life. As art stands apart from life, we are allowed to see and to feel life anew, with new eyes and new bodies. *Art is not life.* This is precisely why it can point toward life. *Art is a sign for life.* It points out life's shapes, rhythms, colors, and movements.

Dance, Ellis holds, is the foundational art.[27] It is the most basic because its material is of the human being—or as phenomenologists would say, of the lived body. In some sense, all of the arts are of the body; they are accomplished through work, through movement, through a metaphysical dance. Dance ends in an aesthetic realization of human movement. It is the very stuff of life, and its moving essence underlies all creative processes. It celebrates life through its embodied essence. Dance exists through the life of the dancer; its material is synonymous with her life and our life even as it is translated and abstracted (or drawn forth) from it to take on a life of its own.

Daily Work

WHAT HAPPENS

To the universe belongs the dancer. Whoever does not dance does not know what happens.—Apocrypha, Acts of John 95:16–17 (attributed to Jesus)

Transcendence is not beyond the reach of everyday life. We begin to visualize the metaphysical within our reach through the very stretching of a reach. Metaphysical intuition, or the light of understanding, is not rare. It is given in the experience of our purposeful undertakings. It is part of what happens when we move purposefully—that is, with a goal in mind. Such action might also be called mindful action. Not all of our movement is so consciously directed toward a purpose. Work that is purposefully rather than thoughtlessly undertaken is mindful action. Such work eventually constitutes what we call our *works.* Works are the products of mindful action, which stand apart from work aimlessly or grudgingly performed, lost rather than built in the doing. Mindful work is creative. It is not only the basis for art, it is the basis for all our accomplishments. When work is freely undertaken with love, it is called play. In dance, all of these connections appear with phenomenal clarity.

We know what happens in our dancing. We move what happens, and we see it vividly. Dance is most intimately of life and its happenings. We dance that-which-is-there; we dance our own livingness. To use Heidegger's metaphors, we dance our "falling" and our "thrownness." Our "falling everydayness" is there in the daily lived reality of ourselves as we dance. Our thrownness is there in our perpetual leaping-away from our awaiting. Heidegger describes such present time and our presence (presencing) in it: "This Present gives us in general the ecstatical horizon within which entities can have bodily *presence*. . . . The Present 'arises or leaps away' from the awaiting which belongs to it."[28]

In dance, we capture the throw of our unfinished living, the event we are in, our intermingling with all that is and everything that happens. We attempt to catch and arrest this throw in all of our arts, to make time stand still, and to light it in our look. We seek to free time from its unceasing happening when we give it a particular form in a work of art. In dance, we feel and free our own happening as we give aesthetic form to it. The lived aesthetic of our own happening appears to us in the freely undertaken thing done. Dance is only that which is done freely. It lives aesthetically in the doing of work freely undertaken. No one can really make us dance, because dance is the essence of freedom. When movement is forced (in the sense of enforced), it is not dance. Dancing appears to us, then, as of our own free will in action freely undertaken.

The *real* in dance is that which we do freely and which we love in the doing. It is that which is accomplished in the actions we take, the *thing done,* which we see and value. In its largest measure, dance is what happens whenever we move to create something in light of our freedom and love the moving itself. Dance is the freedom, the play, and the gracious open center in fulfilling work.

Existentialism, perhaps more than the other isms, attempts to explain the real. Its very name indicates its concern for existence and what "is." It attempts to describe the experienced reality of being-in-the-world. In short, it attempts the impossible but stretches us in the attempt. Where existentialism has extended into dance, drama, poetry, literature, philosophy, and theology, it has become part of what is, just as everything is what is. We cannot capture, explain, or describe what is or what happens exactly the way we live it. We accumulate what is in our experience—what happens to us and what we make happen. In a curiously wonderful way, we can dance what is because dance is of life, of what happens in life, and of what we make happen in the movements we make. Indeed, all of our purposeful works are of life and of the same intentional action as dance. We move our works, as we dance them, into being.

We live what is, we move what is, and we dance what is. We create what is in art, science, politics, philosophy, religion, sports, through work and play. They are our works. Work is real. What is appears in all of our work, purposeful and otherwise. Everything we do is what is. What could be simpler? Yet when we try to isolate the "isness" of our doing, it recedes. It will not be held or grasped. But it is there in that-which-is-done. It appears to us most vividly in our acts because of their intentional character; acts involve the reality of conscious, purposeful action, built and not lost in the doing. Our acts stand apart from aimless work and from grudging work. They are composed of our daily work undertaken freely and with love.

ACTS OF LIGHT

In our dance as in our lives we clear a place and light it in our daily work. We set in motion the rituals of our daily existence in the doing of our daily work. It is out of those daily rituals intentionally performed that our works will be built. The best dancers I have known have spoken of their love of the daily work of dance—technique classes and rehearsal. Graham and Cunningham stressed that "to dance, you have to love the daily work." Rainer wanted to dance work. Viola Farber remembers her years dancing in Cunningham's company: "One afternoon, sometime in the fifties, I was the only student in class."[29]

If there is no pleasure in the work, it is not dancing. Zen masters and yogis as well understand the transcendent grace and light in the dance of daily work. One of the basic yogas is the yoga of work, in which work is freely undertaken for the pleasure in the doing rather than for the outcome. Zen topples the hierarchy of work, valuing all work equally and emphasizing the dance of work, the thing done with love, rather than the product of the work. This attitude releases the worker from an egotistical bondage to work and allows freedom and honesty in action. A Zenlike attitude engenders singular concentration on how something is to be done rather than on what it will be when it is finished. It is present centered rather than future oriented. The product then arises in qualitative concentration on the work at hand; the product takes care of itself in present centered work.

The transcendent metaphysic, lived in the present center (or the dancing open center) of work at hand, is recognized in many religions. In dance, we practice this metaphysic, as we do in all of our acts. In Ritual to the Sun, the final section of Graham's *Acts of Light*, the metaphysical potential in work freely undertaken is revealed. It is a celebration of the ritual of the daily work of dancing, shown through Graham's choreographic development of her daily class work. It begins simply, with the spinal breathing sitting exercises that open a Graham class. It gradually gathers a bursting strength and joy, unfolding an eloquent movement vocabulary, the result of years of dedicated work. The piece ends in a sitting resolution akin to the calm *révérence* that ends a ballet class. Graham's daily work is rebuilt, held onto, and lighted in this dance.

10

MOVING TIME-SPACE

To be a body, is to be tied to a certain world, our body is not primarily *in* space: it is of it. — Maurice Merleau-Ponty

There is at least one reality which we all seize from within, by intuition and not by simple analysis. It is our own person in its flowing through time, the self which endures. — Henri Bergson

Maurice Merleau-Ponty, Martin Heidegger, and Jean-Paul Sartre take a particular perspective on time, describing its lived character — its metaphoric and poetic dimension in experience, rather than its objective measure. Space, inseparable from time, is similarly conceived in its poetics by Gaston Bachelard.[1] Preceding their writings was Henri Bergson's exposition of our intuitive grasp of time.[2] These philosophers are interested in explaining time and space as experienced or perceived in subjective life. As I continue to describe the lived essence of dance in these last chapters, this will also be my concern. Here, I deal with time and space as they are lived and moved in dance, and describe the aesthetic (poetic) constitution of dance imagery in terms of time-space values in three contrasting dances.

Our Body of Time and Space

LIVED TIME-SPACE

Time, space, and movement are never separate except in analysis. Likewise, there is no such thing as one time, one space, or one movement except as we designate them according to how we live them, use them, build and compose them. (Thus we can speak of a room as being a space and of the time we met and a time when we will meet again.) Time, space, and movement are continuous with one another. Movement takes time; it is either fast or slow—an extreme of one of these or a gradation in between. Movement takes space, large or small—or in between. When we move, we are not doing two things, moving through space and moving through time; we are simply moving. All movement has rhythm and spatial design, at once and inseparably. Time is a concept; it is made concrete for us in moving bodies. Movement is also a concept made concrete in moving bodies. Immobile bodies stay time, space, and movement in our experience—they are stilled single points in our experience. Nevertheless, they have duration as they enter into our own unceasing changing. We live our unceasing changing and our still points as we live ourselves.

One movement or even one stillness can be only a point of view on concrete duration, a slice of our own duration, which is real and undivided lived duration: "Between positions and a displacement there is not the relation of parts to the whole, but that of the diversity of possible viewpoints to the real indivisibility of the object."[3] It is only when we stop to ask ourselves where we are that time and space appear to us objectively, as things in themselves. For the most part, we simply live time and space through the qualitative values of the time-space of our movement. Moreover, the living of them is not ordinarily measured or measurable in any objective way. Time and space are of the sensate, subjective experience of our everyday existence; time and space are also of our dance in its created time-space.

Sometime, however, in the creative process of dance, we become conscious of time and space as objects. That is, we take points of view upon them as we formulate the particular time-space of a dance. We decide just how much time a particular movement phrase should take, for instance, and what its rhythmic structure will be. Will it fall into square-fours or rounded-threes or will it simply ride on the rise and fall of a breath? Will its time be strictly performed, or openly interpreted in the moment, or improvised by the performer? Will we be making a point about time itself in the dance, or will we simply be using time subliminally to find the right (or honest) time in which a gesture really lives? When we ask these questions, we step aside from the dancing itself; we take a perspective on it.

When we rehearse a dance, we are trying to embody (incorporate) the ideal time-space in which the particular dance (movement) lives for us. When we step aside, we analyze; when we rehearse, we stop and start and ask questions of ourselves and of others involved in the process.

Behind such questioning and analysis, however, is the original intuition that sparked the dance. We work in light of it as we develop the dance. When the dance is there, when it is finished and we can perform it, only then do we know what it is. It sounds silly to say, but the dance is not there until it is there. That is, the dance does not exist in the mind or in the imagination until it is finished. We do have ideas and mental images about what the dance may be as we create and rehearse it, but the dance itself emerges only in the finished creation and performance. We have then created something that had no real existence before, something absolutely new and unique. And we have done it entirely through our actions and our choices.

Analysis tries to stop the time-space of movement to say what it is. Analysis immobilizes, but for a reason. It is part of understanding, but it is the immobile part. "What the immobile points are to the movement of a mobile, so are the concepts of various qualities to the qualitative change of an object. . . . To think an object, in the usual sense of the word 'think,' is to take one or several of these immobile views of its immobility. It is, in short, to ask oneself from time to time just where it is, in order to know what to do with it."[4]

In the dancing of the finished dance, the intuition that lighted its creation is recaptured. The dancer who has learned the dance becomes free in the performance of it. She no longer has to analyze any part of it, neither its space nor its time. She adopts a mobile perspective in performance. The dance only lives, in fact, through her movement. When she has learned the dance, it is there—and not before then. When she has learned it, she can *do* it. She then lives freely in the light of her dancing, not needing to visualize the doing. The thing that *was to be done* has disappeared.

In fact there never was any *thing* to be done except that thing that she does when the dance is finished. All is only possibility until then. In doing the dance, she is moving her own realized possibilities. She is performing whatever she has realized (made real) of them. She does not stop to ask what they are, because they are simply of the dance and of herself in it. When she has made the dance real through her doing, she experiences a release from the thinking toward it. Her thought is of the dance, erased in the doing.

She does not need to stop to ask where she is in space, or if she is in time with the dance. She has become its space and time. She is executing what Bergson calls "the mobility of the real."[5] When she has learned the dance, we say "she knows it." Then she is not involved analytically with its execution. She is involved intuitively and metaphysically in the dance, as we are also when we enact the dance with her in our active reception of it. At this point, we are living the time and space of the dance, not analyzing it.

We live space in the placement of the movement in space, where it goes, and how it is designed; but we live it as more than this. We live it wholly, as embodied space. The arch of a dancer's back imparts a totally different feeling than an arch of steel, plastic, or concrete. The arch of a dancer's back is formed of our own body-of-space. We feel the lifting and arching through our own embodiment — through which, in our lifted, back-arched leaning, we also feel the upward soaring and backward leaning arch of steel. Our body-of-space is the origin for our perception and understanding of space in general.

IMAGINED TIME-SPACE

How many regions in space have been inside me already. — Rainer Maria Rilke

The time and space we live is the time-space of dance, for dance is the embodied art, of life and our living of time and space through our movement. Yet dance is aesthetically intended and designed. It exists in whole gestalts of time-space and is composed of movement images that are products of the creative imagination. "Dancing," says Deborah Jowitt, "does not simply inhabit space, but carves and molds it — creating and erasing bridges, islands, continents of air."[6]

The creative process of forming a dance begins with the power to give image to movement, to give it life through the imagination. This power is not rare. Although it is probably in some part a matter of talent, it is also acquired and cultivated. It grows out of the experience of dancing, the development of kinesthetic awareness (of one's own motion in time-space), and movement imagination (ability to formulate movement through the use of imagination). The imagination is a bridge between the invisible (the movement urge, idea, or ideal) and the visible (the composed dance image).

Movement, space, and time embodied in dance take on the warmth of having been lived in through the imagination. They are experienced as human time (in the rhythmic play of feet), as human space (in a run through space, the reach of an arm, the drop of a head, the bend of an elbow, or a glance back), and as human energies (in the effort or ease of a leap). Movement, space, and time are only abstractions until they are embodied; in dance they can be experienced as lived, as lazy times or anxious moments are lived or as wide-open spaces or tightly closed spaces are lived. A dance may project the kinesthetic feeling and primal sensation of being free (in headlong runs) or of being bound (in restricted movement). A dance may call to mind specific time (past or future) and a particular place (natural or fabricated, as we shall see in Nina Wiener's *Wind Devil*).

Space given form through dance imagery is space lived through the imagination, held onto in the creative process, and finally given dynamic expression through the dancer. We experience this space through the dancer's performance as poetic space, space given an aesthetic form in dance imagery. Hence we may experience such space as both real and unreal. Because it arises through the imagination of the choreographer and the dancer, and because it requires the audience's imaginative grasp of it, the dance image functions to move us beyond the real presence of the dance. The dance image extends from the real to the unreal as it carries the imagination forward. It stems from the creative invisible imagination and becomes visible and real in the movement itself. Finally the image returns us to the invisible world of the imagination as we extend our own imagination out toward it. Bachelard writes that "space that has been seized upon by the imagination cannot remain indifferent space subject to the measures and estimates of the surveyor. It has been lived in . . . with all the partiality of the imagination."[7] Bachelard explains that the imagination moves us toward the future through its function of unreality: "To the *function of reality,* wise in experience of the past, as it is defined by traditional psychology, should be added a *function of unreality* which is equally positive. . . . Any weakness in the function of unreality will hamper the productive psyche. If we cannot imagine we cannot foresee."[8]

In effect, the dancer and the audience imagine (and foresee) together in the dance. They are both released from the realities of instrumentally purposeful movement, since dance, as art, is movement that is aesthetically intended and valued. They both live the space of dance as aesthetically constituted space when movement is danced or when instrumental movement is placed in a dance context.

When movement is aesthetically valued (when it stands out for us in its separation from the ongoing flow of time), it compels us beyond our ordinary comings and goings, either suspending or intensifying them. It releases us from the reality of instrumentally useful movement. The movement of dance really accomplishes nothing (beyond being itself) and goes nowhere (outside of the dance). However real its images are in terms of movement, as products of the imagination they move us toward the unreal, particularly in the leaps and bounds of imagination we take in making meaning out of the dance. In this we do not hang behind the dance, we *stay with it* and *go* where it takes us. It moves ahead, and we stretch toward it.

Dance can enable us to recall, or bring close, a particular property only by making it coincide with many others. Like a pebble dropped in a pool, the ever-widening ripples it creates in the imagination also belong to its action. We enter into the dropping and rippling of the dance not through analysis but directly, through our body's remembered experiences of dropping, diving, expanding, undulating, rolling, which we grasp in a flash, not merely in the mind or the muscles but intuitively and imaginatively, through our kinesthetically awakened, whole-body consciousness.

MOVING TIME-SPACE

In dance we live the poetry of time and space as we actually embody time and space in our movement, imbuing them with an aesthetic form. It is in this sense that we can speak of moving time-space in dance. We are in fact, in all of our movements, moving time-space; but in dance we give these specific aesthetic form. We create them as we formulate the time-space qualities of the dance, its envisioned poetry and rhythmic music.

The dancer moves time and space as she makes them move in her own movement. When she moves, time moves with her. When she is still, time stands still. When she reverses her motion, time reverses—or so it may seem in our perception. We live the time of her dance with her, much as she lives it — subjectively, experientially, musically, poetically, physically, and metaphysically; as both real and unreal, intuitively and imaginatively.

Certainly the time-space of dance is objectively measurable in choreographed movement. Yet this measure of exactly where the movement travels in space and its exact rhythmic structure is not what interests us in dance, neither as performers nor as audiences. Rather, it is the entire lived character apparent in the meaningful whole of the dance that engages our interest. We do not dissect the dance into its component parts as we perform it or watch it. We want to grasp it whole, in its unique character. We want to know what it is in itself, as we seek what it might reveal of ourselves. We seek to live more of ourselves in each dance or to coincide with each dance intuitively. We seek to move the times and places of our own lives, imaginings, and embodiment.

Dance may be measured in clock time. But we do not measure it as we dance it or watch it; we intuit the dance's time through our body-of-time. Dance is of time only as we experience it. We can understand the slow passage of time or that time passes quickly in a dance only out of our lived experience of time. It is also thus that the time of the dance may become a metaphor for a time remembered or a time forgotten. Time is the horizon for the ecstatic coalescence of the past and future in the present, as Martin Heidegger's works illustrate.[9] Dance captures time as it gives time repeatable structure in movement. In this sense, dance is silent music and poetry, though sometimes its rhythms can be heard as body percussion and as breath. When the time of a choreographed dance is finally stated (whether it takes the form of musically stated rhythms or poetic meter, whether abstract in style or representational, whether clearly composed or freely improvised), we can see, hear, and feel the time of it through our body-of-time — through our eyes, ears, and in our bones.

Poetics of Time and Space

Because the time-space values of dance have a lived ground embodied by the dancer, they allow us to look at life. And because these values are set apart from the unnoticed flow of our everyday existence, they allow us to notice what might otherwise go unnoticed. It is through the dancer's movement, since it is of our own body-of-time, that the lived moment, its unique place in time, and its meaning for us is noticed. Time and space are themselves neutral until we move them, as we constantly do. And they go easily assumed and unnoticed (hidden in our everyday movement) until we give attention to them. They stand out for us in our arts, indeed in all our purposeful acts, as in our dancing. The time we live is inseparable from the time we move: the movement makes the moment, as it makes each moment live in its unique and unrepeatable character. Dance makes this phenomenon abundantly clear. Below, the time-space values of three highly contrasting dances (works of Jerome Robbins, George Balanchine, and Pina Bausch) serve to illustrate.

Any good dance lends itself to a description of the time-space values embodied in it and their aesthetic (or poetic) essence. I link the aesthetic and the poetic because they both refer to qualitative substance, though in its narrowest sense poetry refers to verbal images. Descriptions of dance pursue the poetic essence of the dance—what is qualitatively there in the movement images, what they call to mind, what the dance opens to us through and beyond its movement. In this pursuit, descriptions of the lived qualities of time-space emerge quite naturally and inescapably, qualities that are in essence aesthetic or poetic. It is impossible to describe a dance without some reference to its peculiarities (poetics) of time and space.

Let us consider first Robbins's modern ballet for eight women on a classical Greek theme, *Antique Epigraphs* (1984), choreographed to Debussy's *Six Epigraphes Antiques* with his famous solo for flute, *Syrinx*. Like the music, the dance is inspired by French poetry about the life and myths of Greek antiquity, drawing in particular upon the spirit of Sapphic poetry. Together the dance and music create an atmosphere that is soft and coolly serene. The dance recalls the classical age of Greece with supple arm and hand gestures and simple flowing sequential lines of movement, ending often in the shape of a classical plastique, always with an easily stated composure.

Like the music, the dance elicits impressions of the classical style without copying it. It accomplishes this in sheer beauty of shape, balanced proportions, and understated elegance. It recalls Isadora Duncan's affinity to classical postures. Its time flows by softly, smoothly, transparently, in the fluidity of the movement. Each section comes into being and disappears in unfettered, unhurried time. The dance is stilled at innocent moments (seeming improvised rather than planned) in pliant arcadian friezes. Time and space are stilled or paused in the sublimely graceful figures.

(In the foregoing description, I refer directly to "time" and "space." In the next, these words do not appear. Lived and aesthetically constituted qualities of time and space do appear, however, simply through a description of the qualities that inhere in the movement.)

Balanchine's *Episodes* (1959), composed upon selected orchestral works of Anton von Webern, provides a stark contrast to *Antique Epigraphs.* It too is a modern ballet, but its movement images are highly abstract. We focus inescapably on the strangeness of them, making wide-ranging associations: the movement is spidery, it stutters. The images do not place us in a familiar environment; they do compel our watchful eye in their succinctness and microstructuring. The movement is masterfully detailed. (On seeing it again in 1984, after two and a half decades of increasing abstraction in dance, from Cunningham to Childs, I still thought it coldly abstract.) The work is broken into bits and pieces, each one minutely calculated and arranged—or isolated—against the rest.

The classical movement vocabulary is broken up and reassembled for detail, revealing its gestural basis through stop action, single gestures by one or a pair of dancers, which are repeated sequentially throughout the entire ensemble. Part of the work's strangeness derives from its inversions of movement: what runs forward often moves back along the same line to arrive at its beginning, like an inverted musical phrase or scale. We see this like a whole-tone scale because of the stop action, which lends each movement a singular weight and significance. Added to this sense of isolation and inversion is the upside-down position of the female body in many of the lifts. There is also a strangeness in the unnatural sprawl of the women, as they are manipulated through slow twisting lifts and shapes by their male partners. These deftly controlled, gradually spreading unravelings provide a smooth contrast to the icy fits and starts that begin the work and occur throughout the episodes in the sudden flex of a foot, an abrupt turn of a head, the quickened lift of an arm as an instant whole block, or in segmented movement. Singling out semitones of motion for their individual and equal effects, the dance derives its insular chromatics from Balanchine's translation of Webern's music (with its twelve-tone basis and strict dialectical rules) into movement.

As we might easily gather from the title, the time-space values of Balanchine's work are percussive, abrupt, and broken, rather than smooth and continuous; whereas in the Robbins's work, time-space is sequential and melting. *Episodes* breaks body space into tiny particles of motion and turns it upside down; *Epigraphs* blends and blurs it, cultivating unconstrained lines of motion that ensue naturally from the ease of an upright posture, smooth transitions, and simple walking. Neither work is narrative; both exemplify abstract time-space values and imbue them with poetic qualities. One is cool, soft, and transparent as moonlight; the other is cold and brittle as ice. In both dances, these qualities appear as lived and human qualities through the medium of human motion.

Pina Bausch's neoexpressionist dance drama *Bluebeard* (1977) provides an indelible contrast to the foregoing dances in its poetics of time and space. The abstractions of time-space values are somewhat evident in the clearly stated, historically allusive time-space features of the Robbins's work; they are overwhelmingly apparent in Balanchine's nonallusive, radical movement abstraction, which deliberately calls attention to minutely structured time-space in movement. In Bausch's work, time and space are perceived only subliminally, through the work's psychodramatic character and its daring plunge into the fearful abyss of compulsions, troubled dreams, and demons.

Bluebeard is brilliantly designed. Yet it is certainly not the abstract, formative, Apollonian principle that carries us into the work. Rather, we are drawn into a Dionysian expression (and expiation) of the all-too-familiar brutality and lovelessness that originally motivated the theater of the absurd — the same violence and alienation, portrayed without commitment to overcoming, that pervades mass media and popular movies in grotesque detail. Bausch's vision is curiously and repellingly derealized through aesthetic distortions and vivid stylization to remind us that art takes a perspective on ugliness, rather than wallowing in it. It recognizes spiritual poverty in order to overcome it, just as William Barrett states the aesthetic problem involved in modern existentialist art.[10] Similarly, theologian Paul Tillich views the "expression of despair" in modern art as "the courage of despair."[11]

Unlike the previous examples, *Bluebeard* does not derive from a close musical translation. Using only tape-recorded spurts of Bela Bartok's one-act opera *Bluebeard's Castle*, it develops an onslaught of movement metaphors for the psychological impasse between the sexes, for woman as victim, and for vicious circles of violence between men and women turned, finally, upon the self. Bausch is not concerned with choreographing the opera. Instead, she juxtaposes its imagery with her own, as she weaves Bluebeard's murderous abuse of his wife into a bleak vision of inauthentic existence—an inauthenticity best encapsulated in Sartre's term *bad faith*, his moral concept and symbol for the self-entrapment we experience when we do not act in recognition of our own freedom. In Bausch's work there is a still further admission of *no* faith between men and women—and no exit from the misery. The ugliness in the imagery rivets our attention to an amazing range and nuance of risked physical efforts, sculpted bodies, and skilled timing, which only dancers who are also actors can render. It is ugliness made almost beautiful, but not celebrated.

The dance exists in conflict between an anonymous She and He. Even though the point of departure is Bluebeard, he might be any man; and his wife might be any woman. As Anna Kisselgoff writes in her review of the work, "A fascinating aspect of Bausch's theatricality is that her characters look so anonymous and, thus, universal."[12] The universal is also emphasized in the metaphorically open nature of the work, as the large cast of men and women (all twenty-five of them) echo the sadomasochism of wife-killer and wife.

The images are, despite their emotional focus, also of time and space, as they are emotionally lived through times of trauma and long empty spaces of hopelessness. In the dance they are poetized in movement metaphors. In the first image, She thrashes along the leaf-strewn floor, lying on her back and using the power of her legs by drawing her feet up under her then thrusting her body ahead from the pressure of the feet and legs exerted into the floor, pushing the floor away. It is an absurd, almost comical movement. Children do it as they propel themselves on their backs in play. But in this tense thrashing there is only comically detached nightmarish desperation. Simultaneously, He listens to his tape recorder, flipping it off and on abruptly amidst his own fitful motions and posings. For no reason at all, He suddenly throws his full weight down on top of her thrashing, pinning her underneath. Still She manages to drag his dead weight around on top of her, her head flipping jerkily from side to side as her tossing and turning is crushed underneath him. In the second image, they do what might be a social dance duet, together but not really together, as she slips out of his arms over and over again with the same movement motif, alternating between instant stiffness and melting plasticity.

Images continue to flow quickly by, one after another, for two hours of excruciating physicality and emotional force. The rest of the cast enters, pacing in an endlessly slow and dull processional line. She extracts women from the line, placing their faces in held positions. They massage their hair. She reaches for his face. He pushes her down. Their duet dance repeats, with no forgiveness. She performs a solo with whipping circular motions of the arms, implicating the torso and head, finally reaching out with her arms, then pulling them inside a contracted, doubled-over posture and up to clasp the heart as she unfolds herself. This is early in the work, and *time* has not yet inured us to the violence. It is just the beginning of their ordeal.

11

MEASURE AND RELATIONSHIP

In *Time and Narrative,* Paul Ricoeur shows how time is experienced through the "poetic sphere" of metaphor and narrative, how it becomes human time.[1] My thesis is that dance also reveals time as human time and space as human space in its aesthetic (poetic) constitution of them in movement images. But certainly all the arts reveal time-space as lived in human experience. Dance does this through movement imagery, through structured figures of movement, in time-space. When we describe a dance or its movement images, we find ourselves also describing time and space in human (lived) and metaphoric terms.

When we look at dance specifically in terms of relations that hold within it, time and space again appear as lived and moved. Thus here, as in the last chapter, I am concerned with the dancer's moving of time-space. Here, though, the concern is specifically about relationship and its implication of measure.

Dance that has been given some kind of structure and repeatable measure draws relations of parts to wholes. It invokes our understanding of what it means to move with a purpose — to formulate, remember, and repeat such movement — and to move either in relation to others or alone. Measure is implicated in every relation, since a relation cannot exist without parts that are related. A part of a dance as well as one's part in a dance exist in some measure to the whole. I first take up this issue of parts of movement. Then I discuss several ways in which relation is lived through dance and how relationships between dancers symbolize our relationship to our world and to others. The latter returns us to dance as a metaphoric and poetic sign for life.

Moving Once

At certain points throughout the book, I speak about movement as though it can be segmented. I say for instance that every movement counts. This presupposes that there are singular movements, figures, images, themes, phrases, and so on, however we might conceive of a particular segment of a whole. I also describe some features of particular dances. This presupposes that I grasp singular, describable properties in these dances. Yet I also state the continuity and inseparability of time, space, and movement (turning to Henri Bergson's immobile perspective that analysis takes on movement). Certainly there is a diversity of possible viewpoints on movement. These are, however, *points* in time, *places* along the path of the real indivisibility of movement in our living of our own duration.

Concerning these points and places, the choreographer and dancer, in the process of choreographing and learning dances, conceive of, create, and commit to memory singular parts, which finally constitute the whole of the dance. They do not necessarily set out to make or perform parts (as they work toward a whole, which will supersede its parts), but at some time or another they deal with a part of the dance. As they make and learn the dance, they commonly speak of this or that movement, as though some such singular entity really exists.

In Louis Horst's dance composition classes, I was introduced to the thought that a movement motif—the smallest unit that will lend itself to variation in the development of a dance—should have three clearly stated distinct movements, each showing a different element or direction (a compositional principle he borrowed from music and translated into the dance medium). This fascinated me then and does now. What might one movement be, and what does it mean to move just once? Indeed, I have come to realize that composing and describing dance movement entail some conception of parts of movement and their relation to the indivisible whole of movement. Yet one cannot have a relation of parts to an *indivisible* whole; a contradiction presents itself here.

Like many choreographers, I often puzzle over what one movement is—when it starts, when it ends, at what point awareness of another movement begins, how minutely movement can be divided (if it can), and where division can occur in something that, by definition, cannot stop and still remain what it is. It has become apparent to me that, while dances do have distinct measure, we cannot measure them as science measures.

Neither does dance movement yield itself to logic, except as it creates its own internal logic. Dance is measured, created, and perceived imagistically and metaphorically in lived time, being of our lived motion and experience. Dance is of our bodily lived becoming. This becoming is perhaps best explained in Soren Kierkegaard's term *existential becoming,* which does not separate movement from reality but recognizes that motion is integral to reality, that motion is of our total existence and impervious to abstraction and logic.[2] In logic, everything *is:* in existence (as in dance), everything is a *becoming*—even the still points flow through time.

One movement (or a whole dance) is that which is made complete as such by its author and lived as such in experience. The following is a description of one such movement. It may show that deliberate movement (such as dance) draws our attention to the bodily lived nature of time-space.

I have a fraction of a dance (it is not long, but it feels whole, so sometimes I think of it as a whole dance) in celebration of arms. It is a three-second movement (more or less; I haven't clocked it) with a definite beginning and end. It is itself the beginning of a two-minute section of a dance. The movement is led by my right arm but implies the left in a curious way, since the left is conscious of not calling attention to itself. The right arm leads the movement by drawing a fluid singular line, which is followed by the rest of the body and is felt like the single horizontal flow of melody. It is not architectonic and layered. Its essence is its singular flow. This beginning movement, which I call a motif when I think musically or poetically, sets up an expectation and a flow toward a larger phrase, which in turn influences following phrases (or units or images, however they are thought of).

This movement is, therefore, central to the whole—the motive out of which this section of dance unfolds. It guides perception partly because it is an emphasized beginning. Not all beginnings are given emphasis, but beginnings and endings have in them the temporal emphasis that all lived beginnings and endings have. The choreographer may wish to diminish this given, but it is there to be dealt with. Since this beginning feels whole, I call it *one movement.*

The choreographer makes one movement by creating a coherent and comprehensible unit, which she limits by calling it *a movement.* What she refers to as a movement at one time she may subdivide as two or more movements at another time, depending on her conceptual framework, which can shift while making, remembering, and eventually giving objective repeatable measure to the movement.

When I first moved through my right-arm pattern, it was etched so clearly that I had no difficulty remembering it. It felt powerful and pleasurable, so I wanted to repeat it. In space, it created a stretched circle just overhead and roughly on a diagonal plane with a trail leading out of it in a horizontal attenuation. The end, or attenuation, was achieved by changing the out-pulsive dynamic of the beginning into a sudden in-pulsive, wrapping around, to unwrap out again. The end of the movement was prefigured in its beginning. That particular end could come from no other beginning. It could not otherwise be or feel like the same thing. The final position of the body, which is really transitional in the context of the whole, could certainly appear in other dance contexts. But it would not look the same because *it is not fixed position that defines dance.* It is the lived flow through presentness, containing the past and opening up the future.

Moving as One

We all have unique energies, no two of us are alike. Rhythm is the great leveler which brings us together. — Laura Dean

Dancing with others presents us the possibility of entering into the same lived frame of reference. When we are committed together toward the dance, we are focused in the here and now on a common project. Then the dance is no longer my dance; it is our dance. This is true of the audience as well, as they enter into the dance perceptively.

While I cannot know the body of the other as he lives his own unique rhythms and energies, I can know the body of the other as he dances it when we are dancing the same dance. Then we are moving a common presence, bound up together in the rhythm, space, and present time of the dance. Our success in performing the dance may not be equal, and our consciousness in meeting the challenge of the dance in bodying forth its forms may not always be the same; but we are engaging ourselves *as one* toward a unity of understanding through action. This is an occasion for knowing my body as known by another and for knowledge of another through unified lived-body purposing. It is an occasion for mutual fulfillment.

Present time is actual time, the only time in which the positive existential communal value of being with others is actual. The most basic meaning of being-with-others that dance illustrates is in unison dancing, made even more powerful when performed in a circle. The circle closes space and time in an eternal present and seals one to another and each to all. Folk dances performed in unison circles embody and symbolize being-with-others in the eternity of the moment. They heighten the moment of community and enclose the space of it. There is an equally valid way in which being-with-others is realized in concert dance—when communal value is embodied in the work and realized in the audience as they become bound up in the unison qualities and actual present time of the dance. The symbolic values of moving as one in unison and as one in time bear separate attention.

MOVING IN UNISON

There are two ways that I relate to the other in a dance that we perform together: moving *with* him and moving *against* him. The experience of unison movement has the effect of the universal. The same is in all. All are moving as one. Laura Dean's dances, which use unison movement in hypnotic repetitive patterns, often relating it to contrasting movements, illustrate this well. Many of her dances build in the manner of gradual process music, gathering complexity and layers of rhythms but maintaining a cohesion through a unifying pulse. *Sky Light* (1982) and *Transformer* (1985) are good examples. *Timpani* (1980), which she composed for two grand pianos, timpani, and six dancers, develops this sense of unity in particular, as throughout the dance individuals break away from and return to unison rhythmic patterns of percussive stamping and fluid arm gestures. These well-traveled pathways of movement carry us into their dynamic sweep, reinforcing the unison gestures and rhythmic repetitions. In contrast to the hypnotic unity and ongoingness of the dance as a whole, slow arm stretches caught and stopped with the final drum beat provide a surprising and satisfying end.

Unison dancing leads the self out of its solitary boundaries. In it, I am supported by something larger than self. My *I* can be lost in a larger *I*, my volume seem to expand. This is true whether I am dancing with one other or many others or whether I am participating in the spirit of unison dancing as an audience. In dancing with others in unison, I experience my body as expanding, as warm to the world and to others. Perfect unison dancing imparts this feeling most immediately, although dancing as one while performing differentiated motion has the same potential.

In dancing with others (in unison or as one), the self visually multiplies. The world expands. Self becomes lost in a plurality of one. Philosophers have long pondered the difference between the monistic one and the dualistic two. In dancing, as in poetry, they are not analyzed—they are experienced and expressed. Ralph Waldo Emerson expresses well the notion of many in one at the end of his poem *Xenophanes* (after the early Greek philosopher's monistic view):

> To know one element explore another,
> And in the second reappears the first.
> The specious panorama of a year
> But multiplies the image of a day,
> A belt of mirrors round a taper's flame,
> And universal Nature through her vast
> And crowded whole, and infinite paroquet,
> Repeats one cricket note.

In the same spirit, the little ballerina in the last row of many a corps de ballet takes her place to expand and warm the whole. Not recognized for herself, she multiplies it as impersonally as the anonymous artists who built the gothic cathedrals of the Middle Ages.

Indeed, in all action that is purely focused and impersonally performed there is something of the being-with of unison dancing. Ego dissolves with intention in the lived present. Intent is erased as it is reached in being-with (or dancing-with). Being-with is not being-toward; it is being-in, being inside the center. This is a point of intersection, a dissolution of selfness and otherness in the present moment of actual performance. The carpenter may become just as lost to himself in his work when he moves at one with it as the dancer may be. But the dancer serves to exemplify this purity of action for us, because her action leaves no material product behind; it is erased in the doing and lives wholly in it.

ETERNITY OF THE MOMENT

Dance is an art of present time—the now in the movement is the time of forever, a fully lived present, an eternal present. Eternity is a time and a shape, open, ongoing and never-ceasing, a shape without beginning or end. The time that goes on and never ceases is present time, since the past is time gone by and the future is time yet to come. The time of now is always with us and may be opened to us when we open ourselves to our own lived presence. The shape of eternity is circular, without beginning or end.

In dance, the present moment of eternal time and the circular shape of it coalesce in various ways. Between the dancer and the audience, the circle is completed in the moment of closure, when the dancer and the audience move symbolically as one. Then the I and the not-I blur—the acutely personal drops away. What is true of actually dancing with others can be taken as symbolic of the closure undertaken by the audience as they become one with the dance.

Unison movement immediately closes the lived distance between I and not-I. These distinctions dissolve as dancers actually move together. Likewise, linear time completely obscures when unison movement is repeated cyclically. Unison movement with rhythmic repetition is even more evocative of present time—lived as eternal time—when linked in the ongoing space and time of a circle. Such a circle is experienced as both moving and still. It is movement without beginning and end, which really goes nowhere in time or in space; it stays exactly where it is by repeating itself. This is not the differentiated existential line of finitude. The circular line never finishes. It may disperse and move into something else; but as long as it is a circle, it remains perfectly continuous. Circular movement is not the movement of existential becoming and dying away; it is the eternal movement of being.

Dance brings into view the many ways we experience time. Because its images are of lived time-space—time and space as we experience them—dance can capture life's ephemeral becomings, its changing contours, detours, zigzags, and abrupt halts. It can also project the lived experience of timelessness and the unchanging. For instance, there is a foreverness in the solidly held, unblinking opening positions of Anna Sokolow's *Odes*

(1965) performed in unison by a large cast of dancers, recalling the timeless ruins of ancient civilizations and the ancient in ourselves. José Limon's masterpiece *There Is a Time* (1956), drawn from the *Book of Ecclesiastes*, communicates both change and the unchanging. The circle dance, which links the successive sections of the work, symbolizes the eternal against which time and change may be perceived and lived. His dance demonstrates that the circle (as a shape) is more than a connected line in our experience of it. Limon uses the circle for its power to symbolize the cyclic nature of the seasons of life and to lend vision to time itself. As the work begins, the dancers stand in the circle of time; holding hands they sway almost imperceptibly—and only once—to the left then to the right. This gentle, still rocking returns to finish the dance but now is repeated continuously and evenly, side to side, back and forth, as the lights fade.

Pina Bausch used the circle symbolically in 1975, in a revival of modern expressionism and its intentional symbolism. The circle is a central image in her orgiastric and gripping choreography of Stravinsky's *Le Sacre du Printemps*. This dance is about time and the revolving seasons, particularly the lived time of spring in its greening and its madness.

Here the ritual return of spring approaches through the gathering of one large circle, which separates eventually into two sexually segregated groups, densely packed in clustered circles then in knotted circles. From this gathering of circles, spring bursts out, in the final female solo, like a wound. It is an explosive dance with stirring symbolism, performed in a bloodred dress against the stark black and flesh-toned group scattered on the stage. It is an image of spring personified in the dancer, the virgin body of spring, as she dances to exhaustion the awakening of spring and the rites of puberty, replaying the mythical time of origins, maturation, and sacrifice, the dying and reviving god, the circular intersection of life and death. Josephine Endicott performed this solo when I first saw it in 1984. "I really dance in *Sacre*," she told me, "I just dance until I can't anymore, I dance until I die."[3]

Mircea Eliade suggests that seasonal rites renew the cosmos and reorder profane time—that indeed sacred time and mythical time are circular.[4] They exist in the timeless sphere of the imagination and the human capacity for renewal, as the symbol is related to the emotion, the mythical paradigm to its human source.

Moving as Two

I am more sharply defined as an individual when I move in contrast to or against another dancer than when I dance in unison with him. My distinct separation from him is seen and felt. In such dance, where the dancer is distinctly seen against another in a duet or against many others in a solo, the singular individual presence of the dancer is intensified. She becomes more distinctly herself, differentiated from another or others. As she exists in a distinct contrasting relationship to another or other dancers, her otherness as such is also manifested. Dualisms and divisions appear, with all their possibilities of contrasted twos. These divisions with their degrees and kinds of oppositions may present themselves in dance in as many ways as they are lived emotionally or conceived of formatively.[5]

Contrast appears in any relationship between two dancers placed side by side who are not doing exactly the same movement at the same time, on the same side (right or left) of the body, or facing in the same direction. Some contrast appears even in side-by-side unison (that of right-left); more if unison movement is diagonally spaced or placed before and behind; still more if it is casually placed within subsets of the first symmetrical division of the space, with four lines crossing in the center. When two people dance as two and not in unison, contrasts and necessary oppositions are involved. However, it is significant that these oppositions are undertaken in the spirit of dancing together. Even though I may direct my dance oppositionally or apositionally against another, whether in facilitation of his movement or displacement of it, I also dance with him, since we are dancing the same dance and seeking a closure of the whole, the essence of the whole in each part. This is true when ours is a stylistically abstract relationship emphasizing the temporal and spatial qualities of movement; it is equally true when our relationship is evocative of an emotionally charged encounter.

Moving against another in a dance we do together always entails contrast. Contrast may appear even though no intentional apositional relationship or oppositional tension between us is implied, as in much of Merce Cunningham's work. It may also be sharply intended, as when extremely differentiated movement is juxtaposed. Nikolais's explorations of movement extremes often produce this kind of contrast. His light and sound inventions, which also explore extremes in theatrical presentation of dance, add to the contrast. Differentiations, whether intended or accidental, bring contrasts and oppositions to the fore.

Contrasts differ in degree and kind. Moving as two permits us to live through a range of oppositional tensions between self and other, assembling and dissembling as change occurs throughout the whole and as one kind of tension moves into another. Dance is composed more from an intuited flux and flow of oppositions between dancers than from an analytical calculation of them. Nevertheless, sometimes we stop to perfect a particular contrasting shape or tensional direction of movement and come to understand more fully what is in it, as we dance and live it.

There are at least four and probably more ways that I may dance against another (or others). (The other may indeed be others, who move against me in simple contrast or charged opposition.) These four I discuss briefly as *counterpose* (countered shapes, balances, and motions that push, lean, or balance against one another), *complement* (mutually facilitating motion between partners), *contrariety* (contrary lines of motion that either pass through and by each other or move to meet at or near the center and away again, but may not move in parallel), and *conflict* (movements that clash and strive against).

These are occasions for my body to exist against the ground of, and as ground for, another. These terms might be described as terms of oppositional withness, since all of these manners of moving against entail a tension of opposition, which partners undertake together and must cooperate in to achieve, a tension that may be sweet or bitter or bittersweet depending on the intention of the dance and the dancers' attitudes in fulfilling the intention.

COUNTERPOSE AND COMPLEMENT

Counterpose and complement have a lot in common; but if they merit different terms, we should be able to sort out some differences. According to kind of opposition, counterpose between partners in its simplest most direct form is a faced opposition, with partners either merely inclined toward each other (in the least degree) or vigorously pushing against each other (in the most degree). Counterpose is less direct when partners are not facing each other. A counterposed opposition reaches its stasis in a held counterpoise when equality of pressure toward or against is reached. Held counterpose might be easily held in either a symmetrical or an asymmetrical design from planted, sitting, or lying positions; or it might be precariously balanced and poised with partners leaning toward each other—each standing on one leg, for instance. It is not a true counterpose unless there is symmetry, not necessarily in the body shape or line but in degree of tension between partners creating a counterbalance of energy.

As the energy poised between partners gives way to visible movement between them in equalized give and take, counterposed motion may be achieved. This give and take might also take an antiphonal or conversational form of call and response—question and answer. Counterposed motion is not possible with perfectly parallel unison motion, although unison motion performed in a mirrored relationship may counterpose. (Mirrored motion is of course not necessary to counterpose.) I may counter my partner's motion with another shape of motion, in which case our individuality would be more strongly evident. I might achieve this, for instance, by pressing against and twisting into my partner's shape and line of motion while we turn together—I the twisting inside of the turn pressing out, my partner holding the outside shape and pressing in—with an equality of pressure exerted between us. Thus we would be countering and balancing the turn between us. This is entirely different from, for instance, twisting together in a turn facilitated actively by one partner and simply followed by the other.

We can perceive the differences in these two turns through our own lived tensions, although we do not often call attention to them and seldom have reason to. Sometimes, however, we do wonder at the endless ways of turning together. According to the present example, there are many more ways of distributing energies in twisting turns together, which would change the quality of the relationship immediately—alternating active and passive roles, following each other sequentially, and so on. It is significant that no matter how abstractly such relationships may be conceived or performed, they all have counterparts in life relationships. This fact is, after all, the point of going into such descriptions.

In terms of counterpose in dance and its equivalent in life experience, we might immediately think of ballet because of its many balanced and poised positions on point. But in its traditional forms, ballet does not emphasize a true counterpose of partnership, particularly in view of romantic manners inherited from the nineteenth century. Rather, it is typical for the man to mechanically facilitate the ballerina's poses. She is displayed; his facilitation of that should be as unnoticed as possible. With the advent of modernism in ballet, symmetrically counterposed movement and poses are more often seen. When the role of the male is not merely to facilitate the female, his line and dynamic relationship to her is more clearly marked.

Complement also requires individual uniqueness. *Two* must present itself clearly as *each one*. But individuality is valued less in complement than in other forms of opposition, since it implies a pleasurable perception of two as one. It follows, then, that whenever a contrasting opposition is perceived pleasurably as two in one, it is complement. However, another necessary ingredient of a true complement is polarity. Moreover, this must be a polarity of equal opposites. Such polarity we know through electricity, with its equal but opposite negative and positive poles, through biology, with its male and female, and through mythology, through its archetypal opposites. While individuality is necessary to complement, when one or the other of the two presents himself or herself so strongly that we perceive complete individuality, complement is lost. One is seen sharply contrasted against the other, rather than in a polar relationship of *with* as well as *against* in a tension that facilitates the motion of both partners.

In dance, when two presents itself as two distinct sides of a gestalt singularity (divisible yet cohesive) in contrasted polar and facilitating motion, a complement of partnership is achieved. When I move not merely in contrast to my partner (which most any movement differentiated from my partner's would convey) but to complement his motion, I am aware of my movement against his and equally aware that I am related to and bound up with him, in polar (equal and opposite) tension and attraction.

Pilobolus Dance Theater, which has a gymnastic (movement formalist) base, excells in the possibilities inherent in moving as two—extending principles of counterbalanced, cantilevered partnering to threes, fours, and more. Much of its early work focuses on architectural complement and counterpose of bodies. Later work explores other contrasting relationships of partners and their emotional equivalents, often in absurdly exaggerated figures. These figures seem to express Carl Jung's primordial body memory of the push and pull between self and other or self and world and of the struggle, balances, and releases between partners in birth, love, and death.

From their first and signature piece, *Pilobolus,* to later work, the theater has developed a most original statement of the powers of partnering.

In modern dance, beginning with the work of Pilobolus and Steve Paxton's contact improvisation, and especially apparent now in Senta Driver's dances, the traditional male-female contrast of strong-weak and lifter-lifted does not hold. Twos are freely conceived of and danced to elicit the strength, balance, bulk, and delicate ingenuity of both partners. In addition, partners of the same sex lift each other. To some extent, Jerome Robbins has broken the traditional mold of ballet in this regard, and George Balanchine's female dancers dance with uncommon strength and independence even when they are partnered. But in ballet for the most part, the male-female contrast and complement of male strength and female delicacy of line retains its classical distinction – the man lifts, the woman is lifted.

CONTRARIETY AND CONFLICT

When partners are perceived literally as moving against each other, antithetical lines of motion, extremes of tension, and polemic stances appear. Such abrasions of moving-against may be abstractly and dispassionately intended or emotionally charged. Contrary motion is most abstractly demonstrated in music, as two opposing lines of music simultaneously move apart or toward each other, either stopping short of center or moving through it and crossing to move apart again. Similarly, in dance I may fulfill a line of motion contrary to my partner's, for instance, when we pass in a straight line using the diagonal of the performing space or turn at the end of the line to dance through a single figure-eight path around that diagonal, tracing opposing sides of the figure, which will cause us to meet and pass again in contrary motion to each other. This may be compared to hands that approach and retreat, cross and uncross on the piano, or to lines of music that pass through each other when moving contrary to one another.

According to intention, contrary motion may become part of counterpose or of complement. Contrariety between partners or within a group may easily be achieved, according to the intention-of-against expressed in the movement. If partners perform contrary, diametrically opposed, motions, with intent to perform the movement in direct contrast to each other (such as the diagonal line and figure eight), complement results. It could be described as a complement achieved through contrary motion.

However, if partners perform contrary motions with intent toward a clashing impasse, conflict results. Conflict is expressed through a radical intention-of-against, projected in varying degrees, directions, and qualities of movement, with or without body contact between partners but always within a sense of the whole. The reference for the duality of appearance is singleness (the whole of the two conflicting parts). At least two are needed for conflict. (Conflict may be suggested in a solo if the self is divided against itself, in the same way we speak of "inner conflict" or being "broken in two.")

Conflict is easy to discern when the dancers express conflict literally, for instance in the simulated fights typical of musical theater dance as it carries forward a story line. But the work of artists like Martha Graham and Pina Bausch avoids such literal narrative, Graham by drawing upon the Greek myths to explore the psychological archetypes of conflict and Bausch by creating absurdly juxtaposed images and antistories, speaking to layers of conflict in our irrational dreamselves.

Three of Graham's psychological dance dramas illustrate her way of depicting conflict. *Cave of the Heart* (1946) dramatizes the legend of Medea, with its dualistic theme of the destructiveness of jealousy. Medea is the locus for conflict, as her jealous rage is directed against her husband, Jason, and the daughter of King Creon, whom Jason chooses over her. Here is a classic triangle, but still the central issue of pairs—duets of love, hatred, and jealousy that bring about the conflict. *Clytemnestra* (1958) faces the problem of "inner conflict." Will and spirit do battle as Clytemnestra questions her punishment for being "denied honor among the dead," Graham states in her script. In her program notes, Graham says she conceives *Clytemnestra* as a battle within the self, which releases an inner dialogue. In *Errand into the Maze* (1947), the heroine finds and faces the mythical Minotaur, a creature half man and half bull who devours human flesh; Graham refers to him in the program notes as the creature of fear residing in the heart's darkness. The heroine encounters the creature as her partner in the dance—confronting him in a struggle for life and igniting her transformational powers to emerge triumphant from the maze into the light.

Conflict is not always Graham's focus for duality, as the playful daring counterbalances and erotic complementation of partners in *Diversion of Angels* (1948) demonstrates. For Bausch, however, conflict is the primary focus. From her first attempt at dance drama in *The Seven Deadly Sins* (1975), through works like *Cafe Muller* (1978) and *Kontakthof* (1978), conflict as sexual and spiritual impasse pressed to its limits is her recurring and paradigm symbol. Hers are dissonant works, in which Sartre's metaphor "hell is other people" takes on special meaning. But she does not cross over into obvious self-expression or merely destructive behavior. Her works remind us as do Sartre's that all is not pleasing singularity. She moves us through the grating negatives that arise in relationships as poignantly as Sartre describes them and also leaves us, as he does, at a point of "no exit."

Other people are, of course, also the condition for recognition of individuality, for delicate and trying counterbalances, for the bittersweet tension of polarized complement, and for love. In their partnering, dancers embody our deepest bodily recognitions of ourselves in relation to others. It is not that they have figured out the truth of our relationships nearly so much as that their movement together—with and against—resembles it.

Moving as a Group

MOVING TOGETHER

The successful soloist declares through her presence the beauty of indivisible singularity. She is the whole undivided world in the moment of her performance. She marks it for us. Likewise, the successful group marks a whole and indivisible world, as it forms an ensemble that dances as one as clearly as any soloist does. Individuality may merge into the whole. Sometimes it is entirely lost, as in many of Alwin Nikolais's dances, where the dancer is unidentified. His dances submerge the dancer's individuality in visions of light, motion, and shape—from his early work *Noumenon* (1953), performed by three dancers enclosed in sacks of stretch material, to later works such as *Gallery* (1978), performed by ten dancers who seem like twenty as they multiply through the use of many masks and other illusions. Solos and duets do appear in his works, as in *The Mechanical Organ* (1982), but always highly stylized and seemingly not for themselves so much as for their contribution to the total vision.

Still it is obvious that Nikolais is aware of the contribution of the individual. At the end of the very curious and metamorphic *Noumenon,* the dancers, who have moved together in perfect unison throughout, sit facing forward and draw the sacks around them as they cross their arms in front of their chests, showing for the first time the natural shapes of neck and head. The human form is finally there and is emphasized when they remove the sacks from their heads as they are acknowledged in the bow—and we see their faces.

Self and individuality need not be entirely lost to the group, as Paul Taylor's dances often emphasize. In Taylor's early work, the long patrician lines of Bettie de Jong, the dexterity and drive of Dan Wagoner, and the vivacity and sparkle of Carolyn Adams are evident even in close ensemble dance. But just as in a good string quartet, the whole must supersede any one part, the self in dance must be submerged in the interest of the whole. While Taylor intentionally uses the individuality of his dancers (and declares their importance in his dictum, "up with dancers, down with choreography"), still they move as one in his ensemble work. Because the ensemble is more than an aggregate of individuals, because it is formed through some unifying principle, a tension arises between the individuality of the dancer and the requirements of the group, creating much of the interest that ensemble dancing holds.

A group dance moves as a single unit, a whole body, which assumes that even when individuals emerge from it in solos, they do so in context of the whole. Indeed, solo and group dancing stand in contrast in terms of number. *Solo* is one; *group* is a whole composed of more than one. *Solo* and *group* take their meanings in part from one another, by contrast. They differ in number; yet they are alike as singular wholes. When the soloist is successful, she draws us into the whole of the dance she creates. It is not self-importance that she marks when she is successful; rather, it is the dance in its unfolding. Likewise, dancers in a successful group dance transcend self toward each other and the world they make for us in their dance.

To move as a group is to move with some unifying factor. Unison movement immediately achieves this, but unison is not the only way group movement is achieved. Extremely individualized movement on the part of each dancer in a group may nevertheless be conceived of and operate as a functional part of a cohesive total. In much of Senta Driver's work (including *Missing Persons*, 1981), a strong sense of group emerges through assistive movement within the group. Assistive partnering occurs androgynously among two women and three men who move together in shifting relationships. There is, however, very little unison movement. The dancers in Driver's company move as a group not because they move alike but because their movement is functionally related, often with the mechanics of the group movement conspicuously exposed. This functional relationship can be seen in Driver's *The Black Trio* (1984), as it develops a complex interweave, a triangular language of signlike gesturing among three dancers, revealing assistive and resistive relationships.

Modern dance has explored the radical limits of group forms of movement to a far greater extent than ballet has. Driver's dancers roll together on the floor, deftly covering nearly the whole width of the stage. They push and bounce off one another with real (as opposed to hidden or idealized) effort – with weight, heft, and bulk of body thrown into the movement. The advent of modernism in all dance (modern and ballet) encourages new ways to move as a group – beyond the linear and geometric group arrangements of the classical corps de ballet.

Photographs of Mary Wigman's dancers in stony, statuesque choral arrangements, in molded laments, and in writhing piles attest an early concern in modern dance (or expressive dance, as it was also called then) to vary group dynamics. The emotional substance of Wigman did not lend itself to airy, open, classically ordered group movement. The group – its sacred and secular essence and the individual's relationship to the group – was most fully explored by Doris Humphrey. Following a more formalist aesthetic than Wigman's, she modeled a group work on an image from nature in her *Water Study* (1928). The group is unified in this work through the fluid, undulating essence of watery motion in harmonious groupings of dancers. With a very different result, and incidentally displaced arrangements of dancers, Viola Farber's *Tide* (1980) also uses water images for group motion, commanding a wide range of motion: free hurdlelike leaps following in waves upon one another; stretched, angular line connections of dancers, who hold together, stand, sit, and climb, upon each other, then break like the tide – or a tense moment – to reform at other angles.

In lyric modern dance styles, from José Limon to Alvin Ailey, group movement has developed choral qualities akin to singing – hence the term *lyricism*. In the opening of Ailey's famous work *Revelations* (1960) based

Tide by Viola Farber. Photo: June Burke.

on Negro spirituals, a group of six dancers commingle in a cluster like voices harmonizing in a closely knit chorus. Their overlapping arms slowly spread in a unison shape of the upper body; their backs and heads bend over the curving arms melting downward into the earth, each dancer maintaining a slightly different level in vertical space. The group's shape spreads and opens downward, the focus of heads and eyes descends. The arms open up a hollow, warm, encircling space. The backs and heads, bowed forward, form a descending curve. The feeling is one of spiritual unity. Even though the upper body takes the same shape in each dancer, the movement is not exact unison, because the dancers are opening the shape on varied levels, from deeply bent positions to standing. The unity of the group, however, is unmistakable. They move near and around unison, resolving often in full unison—as when they stand, reach, and gaze heavenward with upstretched arms, spreading open the palms and fingers of their hands to the audience. The opening statement of this dance achieves a profound sense of community; it is a poetic founding and grounding of the meaning of religious congregation.

EXALTED WORLD-BODY

Moving together as a group has to do with intention, not simply the number of people onstage. A group performs as a group through the cultivation of some common characteristic; in dance this may be accomplished in various ways—spatial, rhythmic, emotional—or it may be established physically through body contact. In two of Lar Lubovitch's works (*North Star*, 1978, set to Philip Glass's music, and *Cavalcade*, 1980, set to Steve Reich's *Octet*), all of the above characteristics unify the group of dancers. These dances ride on an ecstatic emotional pulse and breath rhythm (important at the inception of modern dance in its turning to natural rhythms of the body and away from total dependence on metric rhythms in music). The dances are further realized through an easy body contact (typical of postmodern dance) in connected lines of undulating motion, cascading nonstop waves, serpentines, and playful crack-the-whips. They are not difficult dances to understand, so simply do they display organic fluidity and pleasure in moving as an interdependent group-body. In *North Star*, solos, duets, and trios break from the flow of the group more clearly than in many other dances because of the repetitive waves of group motion that catapult them forward. The loose, soft, and swift abandon of the group as it moves joyfully together as one organism could never be choreographed with steps squared off on exact beats. Rather, the group must move spontaneously together as an interconnected world-body, moving in the moment—obviously according to some plan but within an energy created through the whole, as the dancers adjust naturally to each other, meeting the requirements of each moment. Even as it disconnects, dispersing the space in soft clean leaps, which cover the stage like flashing stars in the distance, the group—and its exaltation—remains the dominant theme.

If, in this brief consideration of moving (as one, two, and a group), it seems that I have wandered from the topic of moving time and space in dance, I should underscore the reason for describing various measurements and relationships which arise in the movings of dance—namely, that dance is an art in which we may understand the (human) lived character of time and space in their *interrelatedness*. Dance moves and makes worlds within our world. The worlds of dance are always temporal and spatial and are revealed through movement. Moreover, no amount of abstraction can ever fully abstract the human body or the relationships among dancers in dance. Because dance is of the human body, it is also of ourselves—of the times and spaces we live and move, as we live our world through our body in relation to others. This is the major presumption behind these chapters.

12

DANCE IMAGES

Of Life: The Dance Image

Because it is embodied, dance always reflects life. Dance imagery, no matter how abstract, has a lived ground: our lived body, our mythopoetic body, and our experience of time, space, and freedom.

In order to consider various forms that dance imagery may take and to underscore the lived essence of all dance, I will describe specific imagery in dance master works from different historical periods, which illustrate highly contrasting styles of modern dance. First I describe abstract formalist imagery in early modern dance in one of Doris Humphrey's works, then symbolic expressionist imagery in a well-known work by Anna Sokolow, in the second generation. I use Viola Farber's work to illustrate abstract impressionist movement imagery and to bridge the gap between late modern and postmodern dance. Nina Wiener's work typifies the expressionist regeneration period following postmodern dance. Last, Garth Fagan's eclectic aesthetic provides another view of the dance image and of the 1980s regeneration of the aesthetic values of historical modern dance.

Stylistic identifications of *formalist, symbolist, impressionist,* and *expressionist* are not exclusive to any period, even though early modern dance is generally characterized as expressionist and late modern dance, with Merce Cunningham and Alwin Nikolais, has a formalist focus. Doris Humphrey's structural formalism thus attains special interest as an exception to the expressionist current of her time. We have seen that stylistic designation refers to the general character of a work. It grows out of the artist's aesthetic intentions and influences the nature of the images he creates. There is no one way to conceive of, or to perceive, dance imagery. In analyzing dance images, one can only look carefully at specific works and draw some general conclusions.

I should note that the photographs, which provide a visual basis for describing some important aspects of the imagery, are not dance images—they are photographic images of the dance. But when photographs are good, they record the most telling moments of a dance; they freeze these moments in another medium.

In order to reconstruct or to dance another choreographer's work, a dancer strives to recreate the choreographer's aesthetic intentions—to embody them in performance. Thus the imagery that brings out the aesthetic intent of the dance—whether it is focused in qualitative properties of movement or designed to project, represent, or symbolize something else through movement—is crucial to the dancer's understanding. What the audience sees in the dance depends in large measure on the dancer's ability to express the intended imagery—to create it (through his own movement) as he understands it. As dancer Richard Colton of Twyla Tharp's company puts it, "it is the dancer's understanding of the choreography that the audience is seeing."[1] In the following, I describe imagery according to choreographic intention, as it is communicated to and embodied by the dancer, and according to my own impressions as audience.

HUMPHREY'S *PASSACAGLIA*

Doris Humphrey's *Passacaglia and Fugue in C Minor* (1938) is based on Bach's music and takes its title from his familiar work.[2] Like the music, it is melodic, developing flowing lines of movement, and it is also architectonic, building two or more voices or lines of movement at once. The dance, aided by a balanced rectangular set, gives Bach's music a visual architecture.

Susannah Payton-Newman, who reconstructed the work in 1979, believes that the dance captures the "spirit of architecture" in its "formality, solidity, and monumental nature—as well as its classical balance in relationship of parts to each other and the whole."[3] Still the material of the dance is human; it is not formed of wood or stone but of pliant and supple human motion.

Payton-Newman stresses that the architectural imagery of the work is

Figure 1. Photo: June Burke.

a result of the style of the movement design, particularly the shaping of linear and angular body designs: "The style is more linear and angular than curved in shape, although there are many curved pathways of movement from place to place in space. This style influences the imagery of the work as a whole."

Angular stylization based upon conspicuous departure from balletic line is carried throughout in the formalized designs of the body. Payton-Newman notes the importance of this: "The lines are close to many of the traditional lines of ballet but with slight differences, which make a great difference in the whole effect. For instance, the typical gently curving overhead arm position of ballet is changed by pressing the palms forward, angling the elbows out to either side of the head, creating more of a diamond than a circular or curved shape." We see a modification of this diamond shape in the silhouetted dancers shown in figure 1, a photograph taken at the beginning of the work. One palm is pressed flat forward with the other hand clasping the wrist, to create the firm-edged angular shape.

The beginning of the dance is unobtrusive and gentle, with contained heroic strength. It opens with the dancers turning slowly to the left from a shadowed profile into a gradually dawning light streaming from the side. For Payton-Newman, this beginning image develops "like a gradual process film, beginning with a single figure and culminating in the whole, catching and magnifying a slow slanting beam of sunlight on the faces."

Throughout the dance, she says, "you can imagine yourself as part of a processional through an old European town, looking up toward gothic spires sparkling in the sunlight, shifting from light into dark silhouette. The dance winds through old narrow streets, shadow and sunlight, and a skyline of overlapping shapes of tall buildings and churches. One can imagine bells clanging in full sound created in the swaying pendulum motion of the dance, or peeling softly in the distance in more delicate movements."

The dance refers to a period when symmetry was more explicit in architecture, she explains. "There is often a slope toward the middle of the stage in the imagery, with side support like cathedral buttresses. There is a strong sense of center and pointing upward. However, the work maintains a sophisticated use of symmetry."

Humphrey appears to employ symmetry to work in counterpoint to it, with a sensibility for the fine lines between powerful dynamic stability as one kind of symmetry and serene relief as another, achieving both of these in the work while avoiding "static death," Humphrey's term for the Apollonian extreme, a lifeless, tensionless symmetry without opposition. "Dynamic death" is Humphrey's term for the Dionysian extreme. She conceived of movement as existing in "an arc between two deaths."

In figure 1 we observe a subtle departure from the work's opening symmetrical design, even as the dancer in the light begins to open up a vertical line with her arms. Gradually, the dancer near her rises to meet and clasp hands with her. Then they move into the space together with exact pacing and with leaning akin to bowing, outlining a broad arc of space, which will demarcate the space of the dance and establish its community.

Figure 2 captures the sense of greeting, which infuses the piece, still retaining verticality and a momentary symmetry, complemented by the horizontal design of the arms. In an extension of this greeting, a solo male dancer opens the space out to the audience, thus extending the sense of community and belonging (figure 3). As so often occurs in the piece, whatever is enacted between the dancers is also given directly to the audience; and whoever moves out from the group also returns.

Figure 2. Photo: June Burke.

Payton-Newman interprets the soloists as catalysts for the whole: "Their movement is never isolated or out of touch. Whatever they do is eventually taken up by the whole." Relative to this, it is important that the Passacaglia and the Fugue both culminate in a celebration of community with all eighteen dancers moving in unison. "This is not the community for itself," she explains. "It doesn't look inward; it looks outward as its gift is given."

Payton-Newman remembers that José Limon often used the image of the gift in his version of the work for the American Dance Festival in 1960, her first experience of dancing in the work. (She drew upon Limon's directions as well as directions in the Laban-notated score when she rendered her 1979 reconstruction.) She emphasizes that the gift takes several forms, perhaps most strongly felt in the tolling of the bells as the entire ensemble of dancers move in unison to give away the movement (in the sounding and moving of the bells) in all directions – not just frontally. "We would be missing the point not to understand that the processional and the bells intone the spiritual quality of the piece. It is set in an imaginary place and time, an ideal one, a spiritual one. As a whole the piece starts quietly, building and gathering strength and affirmation. Finally the bells ring out

Figure 3. Photo: June Burke.

in so many ways that it is hard not to be swayed by them—as a dancer, or an audience."

The spirituality seems to result from a unity of dance and music, as the dance flows perfectly from Bach's music in rhythm, form, and dynamics. Bach composed the music for the clavicembalo, a form of harpsichord with two manuals and pedal, and in the severely exacting form of a constantly recurring ground bass, consisting of fourteen notes grouped in twos that constantly gather texture as they repeat. From a simple beginning, the music thickens and darkens as it accumulates voices. The dance parallels the music, drawing a great deal upon the formal repeated Passacaglia and four-voice Fugue of the musical form. The orchestral version often used for the dance was Leopold Stokowski's, a live performance recording, with coughing and other audience noises in the background. Payton-Newman feels that the organ version is too sweet for the stately unsentimental style of the dance. Thus the dance also draws a great deal upon the particular version of Bach's music used.

The form (and formalist values) of the dance is derived from the music but not wholly dependent upon it. The form and shape of stage space are also used to effect. The dancers take on the formal properties of the

Figure 4. Photo: June Burke.

stage while imbuing it with the warmth of their own human form. Payton-Newman indicates that they even move like the stage curtain, "as a waft of humanity, parting and closing the space, washing side to side." At these times and during their surging forward and then receding as a whole, we see their solidarity as a group most graphically.

Regarding Humphrey's formal structuring of group values, Payton-Newman says "this dance must have seemed to audiences in 1938 much like the sound of the first full symphonies. It was unbroken ground in terms of its power; the power of the whole was the power of each part in shape and architecture." We observe this in the strength of singular melodies, as solos and duets emerge from and return to the integrity of the whole. The whole engulfs the parts. The dance takes its power and central formalist imagery from the interdependence and functional poetry of the group, its architectural wholeness.

Figure 4 depicts the processional nature of the work, as the dancers move with taut arms angled at the elbow, trailing in long leaning strides. They trace a circular space and finally create two large circles, one inside the other, moving counterclockwise and in unison. At the same time, the soloists, with extended arms and lifted legs, provide a counterpoint and

Figure 5. Photo: June Burke.

carry the melody above the "ground bass" of the group. The dancer on a higher level in the distance provides a visual echo of the dancer in the foreground, which contributes to a spatial image of architectural leveling, or vertical stacking and ascension.

Figure 5 is a good example of a prominent image in the lyric variation, named for its fluid, singing quality. Six dancers are grouped, two against four, illustrating Humphrey's concern to keep the dance vibrant in spite of its symmetry, which she considered static and lifeless when overused.[4] The great sense of confidence that the work communicates comes not from symmetry but from a balance within the whole design. Interest is attained through an offsetting of symmetry, since symmetry is shown only momentarily in order to be contrasted or dissolved. Says Payton-Newman: "If you look closely, you will see that the work is not symmetrical, although, people have mistakenly interpreted it as such. The opening is completely symmetrical, but from the moment the first dancer stands and begins to move, the symmetry is offset. Thereafter, there is a constant concern for shifting groupings within the whole to gain a balance of parts over time without obvious visual symmetry."

Indeed one feels magical exchanges in the instant transformations of groupings throughout the piece; moreover, transitions are not apparent. Groups appear and disperse in an unpremeditated manner, as in Balanchine's formalist ballets—but with more weight and earth, since, unlike Balanchine's effortless formalism, the movement is grounded. Nor is Humphrey's formalism taciturn, sharp, and electric, as Cunningham's is. It is more deliberately sculpted and voiced, as can be clearly seen in the sculpted shapes caught in the photographs. The structure is not arbitrary, it is systematic. The visceral interweave of the piece makes it an interconnected system. We can sense and follow its system clearly, especially since the musical structure provides a systemic floor for the dance.

The movement of the lyric variation grows out of Humphrey's technical system, her derivation of movement from the falling and rebounding capacities of the body, creating ecstatic arcs of movement with weighted drops and held suspensions at the top. However, the effect of the whole in the lyric variation is not heavy. It is done by women and is set apart by its gentle qualities. Here the bells become elusive and distant. The floating top of the motion is cultivated.

The men's variation (not pictured) is much more aggressive. Payton-Newman describes the movement as "massive, with big jumps and deep bending." The fully extended arms open and close forcefully with tremendous effort. Clenched fists terminate the line of the arm—not threateningly, but with power. The image of the bell—now tolling strongly—is recalled once again.

All of the variations are short. Each has its own particular character. And while overall images guide the entire work, individual images guide each variation. Payton-Newman sees "a gathering of forces" throughout, each variation accomplishing this in its own way but "within a constant theme of greeting and an affirmative forward momentum."

Limon dubbed one variation "the chicken." Payton-Newman describes it as "fast clucking motion of the feet, supported on the top of the body through a held torso, which is oblivious to the small, fast footwork going on underneath." This variation, she observes, is also about "meetings, greetings, and partings." In short, about the community.

I asked Payton-Newman how true she thought Limon's version was to Humphrey's original. She answered that she was certain of differences but that Humphrey must have been satisfied, since she and Limon worked closely together (Humphrey was artistic director of the Limon company for several years) and she apparently did not alter his version. Limon's version may have been more heavily accented than most, according to Payton-Newman, who has studied softer versions. She points out that in the film *Four Pioneers* Humphrey's work is pictured in a lighter and smoother vein than the Limon version she danced in. "It is logical," she explains, "to suppose that interpretations will vary according to the particular character and physicality of the choreographer. Doris Humphrey was delicate and light in frame, while José Limon was large and dramatic."

In figure 6, the recurring image of the tolling bells reaches a climax in the tilt of the body and the pendulum swinging of the arms. But the dancers remain human in spite of the formality and objective structure of the dance: Humphrey does not let us forget they are people. The dancers are not bells; rather, the bells sound through them.

The gift appears repeatedly, also. In figure 7, the image has accumulated and intensified. Surrounding the dancer in the foreground, the other seventeen dancers move in unison, upstretched arms pressing diagonally forward with palms facing the audience. The hand is broad, spreading, and giving.

Figure 8 shows a moment at the end of the Passacaglia. The dancers have just performed what Payton-Newman calls "the squares," rhythmically deliberate processional striding, in which each dancer traces a square floor pattern, ending in the deep bow-lunge, seen here with the entire group inclined toward the side, shaped in a curved mass. From this, the final image of the Passacaglia, the dancers drop to their knees to begin the Fugue. The completion of the last image of the Passacaglia is accomplished both visually (in shape) and temporally, as the movement stills and the music silences. The change into the beginning of the Fugue is thus clear.

Closures and new beginnings are clearly focused throughout the work, since each variation is conceived as a unit. The imagery, then can be interpreted according to the whole and according to each variation. Or it can be interpreted in terms of specific small phrases of movement motivated by specific ideas. The ideas are strikingly clear in time, space, and movement quality and are not entirely abstract. They exemplify architectural properties and contain the potential to evoke a feeling of community.

The communal values inherent in architecture are founded in the dance. Part of our satisfaction in it derives from such subliminal associations,

Figure 6. Photo: June Burke.

Figure 7. Photo: June Burke.

Figure 8. Photo: June Burke.

whether we recognize them explicitly or not. Thus we see through this piece that dance imagery exists on varying levels of awareness. This is true for the dancer, and it is bound to be true for the audience. Certainly we do not all see the same things in a single work. But if the work is good, some clear image of it should impress the memory.

The leaping quartet from the Fugue is shown in figure 9. The picture catches the height of a leap, legs and arms etched clearly in their intended shape. The knees are bent and the body rides easily at the height of the leap with an upright torso. The arms frame the head, not in ballet's curved *port-de-bras* but with the palms pressed forward to add tension and strength to the angular shape. Expressions of strength, ease, and exuberance are not imposed upon the motion; they are conveyed only as the dancer attains her purpose *in motion.* She is the movement she performs, she unfolds the image to our view. The image is about her joy in motion—and about the joy we feel as audience in the leap itself. But this is not just any leap. It is stylized, one of a kind, composed, uplifted, and regally balanced in midair. The image does not so much symbolize these qualities for us (although it certainly may) but, in an immediate present, it draws us into these attributes as they are lived through, and in, this particular

Figure 9. Photo: June Burke.

leap. The image belongs to the work as a whole and to the work's stylized originality.

Throughout the Fugue the work gathers momentum. Although it starts quietly as does the Passacaglia, the Fugue uses the musical canonic form to accumulate energy and complexity in the movement and within the group. The conclusion is already foreseen in the beginning. As the dance builds, we are carried forward. This momentum opens up future time to us. It is not reflecting back, it does not hang on the rhythm—it drives toward a conclusion.

Only at the end are we released from this forward drive, as two soloists framing the community melt to the floor in a slow smooth inching slide, one leg straight forward, the other leg (supporting the weight) finally bending underneath the backward arch of the descending head and torso. Payton-Newman stresses that they must slide into this most vulnerable back-arched position, finally touching the floor with the top of the head and the elbows. She describes this final image as one of "gracious acceptance." Figure 10 captures various stages of sustained back-

Figure 10. Photo: June Burke.

ward falls sequentially cascading into the floor, which foretell this final image.

Payton-Newman stresses that acceptance is given specific imagery throughout the work, most compellingly stated in a section where the dancers walk across each other's backs. Dancers kneeling on the floor form a human bridge, not in a straight and obvious line but with dangerous and interesting displacements. There has to be trust and acceptance in the taking and giving of weight, as the bridge is traveled and feet are feeling their way like sensitive hands.

She notes that if we place all such specific imagery within an image that guides the whole, we notice that the dance is conceived overall as a procession: "People do arrive at their destination through the dance. In this there is great satisfaction. The fact that the procession is stated early in the piece and returns often in further developments imparts a sense of completion, of fulfilled destiny, in the same way that Bach's music does this in its very full developments of a simple theme."

The processional theme gathers momentum and changes character throughout. "In the Fugue, the processional theme at its height is called 'walk in the sun.'" The bells are an integral part of the processional character of the work, ringing out most clearly at the arrival of the procession, which concludes both the Passacaglia and the Fugue. At the end of the Passacaglia, the bell movement of the dancers is spirited, rapid, big, a *tempo* unison; the stage picture works as a whole and with great energy. In contrast, the Fugue ends with a heavy, deep-tolling, and expansive bell movement, amplified as the tolling is taken up by one dancer after another in a full-body tilt. "In this image of the bell," Payton-Newman states, "the whole body is tipping, and finding the thrust."

In spite of some representational imagery in Humphrey's work, Payton-Newman views the dance as an abstract formalist piece, one with a warm and vital human message. The dance satisfies both our desire for beauty, in the expressiveness of the movement, and our desire for clearly designed structure. It is thoughtfully conceived, and its abstract elements fully developed; it appeals to the intellect as well as the emotions. Regarding this, Payton-Newman concludes that "even though Humphrey's dance may be looked at as a bit old-fashioned from our present vantage point, it has, nevertheless, the kind of completeness in itself through its formal constructs and full-bodied movement, its forward momentum, its warmth and deep character, that continue to fulfill us. It is a wonderful dance to do and to watch, because it is a full-bodied dance."

Because of its clear architectural imagery, we are not left with a lot of questions about what it means. It captures and fixes our gaze; it is not easily forgotten or dismissed. It is a dance "of gracious ecstacy," says Payton-Newman.

SOKOLOW'S *DREAMS*

Anna Sokolow's *Dreams* (1961) has long been recognized as one of her major works and a masterpiece of dance drama.[5] Clive Barnes calls it "one of the most shattering and most impressive dances of the contemporary dance theatre."[6] I view it as one of the clearest statements of subjective existentialism in dance, expressing what Paul Tillich calls the existential "courage of despair in contemporary art."[7] The following interpretation of imagery in *Dreams* is derived from my impressions of the work, my study of Ray Cook's notation, and notes taken of directions to the dancers as the work developed in rehearsal during its 1981 reconstruction with Cook, Payton-Newman, and finally Sokolow herself. The work was performed to Bach's *Brandenburg Concerto* 1; Webern's *Six Pieces for Orchestra* 4, 5; and Teo Macero's *Exploration.*

"Miss Sokolow has said that this is not a dance, but only dancers could do it," Cook points out in his notation.[8] It is readily apparent that the work relates to the emotional values of the music, as dance often does, but that it stands outside of dance traditions that depend on musical rhythms. The rhythms are derived from the dancers' emotional rhythms as they work through the choreography to find its natural rhythm and their own in it. As in many of Sokolow's works, the dancer's problem in performing *Dreams* is akin to that of the Stanislavsky method actor in his emotional identification with an existential predicament. It is more important that the dancer find that feeling in himself that connects with the situation in the work than that he render a technically precise, dancerly performance. For this reason, Sokolow's works have been called dance drama. Martha Graham's works have also been termed dance drama, but her technical, highly stylized rendering of dramatic content sets her work apart from Sokolow's. Sokolow and Pina Bausch have much more in common, as they both give keen attention to dramatic gesture and avoid particular (role) identification with character.

Sokolow stresses use of dramatic timing. While musical cues structure *Dreams,* the dancer must find the momentum to arrive on the actor's beat within the cues. Here the dancer strives for the honest time in which a gesture lives, in its essence and through his being. Sokolow directs the performer toward the honest life span of the gesture, as he is capable of embodying and projecting it. Moreover, this is not raw self-expression; the performer must be able to repeat the movement – or perhaps the better term is *recreate* it – in performance. Sokolow's directions are specific to each performer, leading him toward the image she envisions and to his own unique possibilities to reveal it.

Dreams is a drama but not in the usual sense of the word. It has no script and few spoken lines. A short text from the beginning of the biblical Genesis is spoken by a performer leaning against the proscenium. The brief recitation comes suddenly out of nowhere, dreamlike, overlapping action onstage. The lines are not dramatically delivered; they are spoken more inwardly. If *Dreams* is not a drama in the usual sense, neither does it grow out of technically dictated dance movement. Exact positions, shapes, and rhythms are less important than fulfillment of the motivations inspiring the work. Cast in the realm of dreams, its agonistic images are created more through the director's art than choreographic crafting of distinct dance movement. Nevertheless, it uses movement as its expressive vehicle—movement motivated by pathos, pain, and nobility of spirit. In these terms, it is dance. It is dance about ugliness, struggle, survival, and heroism, ironically beautiful in its tense drama and sculptural qualities.

Sokolow's work is not about steps and certainly not about movement (or dancing) for its own sake. Every movement is motivated and attains its own reason in the full image. The imagery is clearly expressionistic, dramatic, symbolic, and telling, with specific motivations and commitments. Still it universalizes particulars. While time, place, and character are specific, the imagery usually yields them an unrestricted sense. *Dreams* is about Nazi death camps but more broadly about survival of the human spirit through adverse circumstances. It could be anytime, anywhere. Like Greek tragedy and Shiva's dance, it takes place in the human heart, invoking life against death.

Sokolow is a craftsman, but the essence of her work is not choreographic craft; it stems from her own dramatic intensity, her convictions, and her ability to imbue performers with the spirit of her beliefs. Regarding this, Cook states in his notated score, "I CAN SAY WITH HONESTY THAT NOBODY WORKS AS SHE DOES. Miss Sokolow can take a 'nobody,' a 'nothing' and yet when they appear on stage they look possessed. They become a different being. They go far beyond what they thought themselves capable, and are always BELIEVABLE IN THEIR PART."

Figure 11 communicates Sokolow's vivid dramatic intensity and her ability to impart the essence of character as she rehearses Henry Thomas and Bruce Agte (double cast) for their solo. "Look!" she directs them, stressing an undeviating line of vision in her stance and gesture, "you can't dismiss me . . . I am." Instantly transferring this image of resolve to the performers, she continues: "You are, you are . . . you are. . . . When we see your face, we know your name. *They* have given you a number, but *we* know your name."

Figure 12 captures the work's limpid dreamlike essence in the figure in white. One might imagine the agony of Anne Frank in this figure, yet Sokolow's method is to move beyond isolated characterization to get to the root of the human predicament. Sokolow envisions the figure as a transparency "seen through to the bone," an image she stressed in directing the work. The moment in the photograph occurs during the opening statement in the young woman's nightmare struggle with the cold emotionless Gestapo officers, who go about their duties routinely and impersonally. They are, in Sokolow's distilled image for them, "faceless," moving automatically, blankly, and unseeing.

The Anne figure feels her way carefully through the men, being knocked down by them as a thing in their way. Unheeding her, they move to their destination. She presses her face to a window, screams an unheard scream, then runs scrambling over walls and rooftops in an attempt to escape. Her run is not strictly choreographed; it is outlined openly so that she may find her own emotional pace in it. She is not directed to stumble, but within the framework of the frantic run, she might. The photograph shows the apex of the opening episode as the woman walks across the shoulders of the men who have now become the rooftops.

This image dissolves as the men separate from the group to stand alone. They might be people or places—people without concern, places without refuge. She runs to them for help, knocking on doors, beating the air, but no one is there, no one answers. Figure 13 catches an important aspect of this sequence in an image that Sokolow calls "face and no-face." Here the frightened woman is looking into a faceless, wall-like, impenetrable presence. The opening statement of the piece ends as she is reduced to desperation against an unyielding void of no-face, degraded to the status of a nonperson as she is made to feel invisible. More to the point, her face is alive with feeling, his is spiritually dead. The metaphorical image might be soul and no-soul, feeling and no-feeling, which Sokolow has also used. Evil is revealed in the loss of individual responsibility to an unthinking, unfeeling, anonymous mass.

In figure 14 we see a central image from the next section of the work. Here a man and woman try to protect their faces from recognition. The face is important once more as it is deliberately hidden and reluctantly shown, perhaps not simply to further a narrative but to remind us of the individual unrepeatable character etched in every face. In this duet, Sokolow stresses repetition of "my name is." The inviolable essence of each person becomes a transcendent metaphor throughout the work.

The couple in this duet are eventually detected. Looking up and out, and never where they are reaching, they do not know which way to turn. They cannot decide amidst the conflict and confusion. In the panic of the moment, the struggle is not only within each one but between them, even though they seek the same end. They cannot escape; no one does. But

Figure 11. Photo: June Burke.

Figure 12. Photo: June Burke.

Figure 13. Photo: June Burke.

Figure 14. Photo: June Burke.

as in the resolution of each section, there is no resignation. An image of struggle toward life in the midst of entrapment and certain death reappears throughout the work. Hope is cherished in the knowledge that, as Sokolow states, "They all die, but they are survivors. They can be killed, but they still won't go away."

The trio pictured in figure 15 develops an image of redemption and new life. The lifeless couple in a shattered heap on the ground are touched and spiritually lifted. The Christlike figure in the image first sinks down with them, then rises, reaching up. His eyes, although they are covered, are not unseeing; they are all-seeing. He erases the scene so that a larger vision may appear. This is the pivotal movement of the work, cohesive as an image that moves from horror to floating exaltation. Not necessarily a narrative or literal image, it symbolizes our dreamselves rising, passing through death, and being lifted to a plateau beyond human suffering. Bach's music, which enters here, supports this soothing image of relief, hope, and serenity.

Figure 16 captures the essence of *Dreams*'s next full image, a brief eerie image dramatizing the plight of victims of prostitution. Each young woman, unconvincing in the role she is forced to play, holds a flower,

Figure 15. Photo: June Burke.

Figure 16. Photo: June Burke.

symbolic of her tenderness and innocence despite the lie she lives. The women go through their sluttish gesturing without investing themselves in its reality. These women are ghostly figures, not what they seem—as the flowers indicate. Adding to their unreality, their faces are only hazily seen—their long hair is brought forward to cover their faces. As before, faces—what they hold and withhold—enter into the imagery.

In the next full image, the Anne figure from the first solo reappears still running wildly. When she finally collapses, a child enters and strokes her as if she were an injured animal. Finally, the child turns the woman's face to look into it, then she rises with her—as past, present, and future converge. The image speaks to our dreaming of ourselves at other ages. On the most immediate level, the gestural exchange between the characters creates an image of love and caring. But it is not one dimensional. The older and the younger eventually exchange places, pressing this image to another level. First the child comforts the woman, then the woman cares for the child. Figure 17 shows the dissolution of this image. Here the woman carries the limp and lifeless child (or perhaps her childhood self) into the darkness offstage.

Figure 18 shows the drummer's solo, seen here in a moment of wild

Figure 17. Photo: June Burke.

Figure 18. Photo: June Burke.

gesticulation. Behind this image, one senses a life story. Indeed there seems to be a short tragic story in each section of the dance, each developed through an overall image. These images can be interpreted from different vantage points, because the dance explores not only tragic situations but the human spirit released and realized through tragedy.

The young man drums to relieve the boredom of being locked in a cell. Drumming (with sticks he has found and an imaginary drum) is his means toward sanity. The drum, since it is not really there, can be anything, anywhere. The solo focuses our attention on the power of the imagination, as the drummer dances with a stool, drums the air, and finally tries to sing, though the words fail him. The stool changes throughout the image: it is a woman, his dancing partner, his beloved, and sometimes his drum. There is a lone figure in the background observing him quietly. Perhaps he is another cellmate—or the dreamer dreaming himself, as Cook notes in his score.

The lyric duet, occurring just before the closing statement, is shown in figure 19. This is a dance of meeting and parting, growing out of images of final embrace and remembrance. Payton-Newman describes this moment as one of "fragile flowering, as the lovers rise above the pathos

Figure 19. Photo: June Burke.

of their love to find the bond between them which can't be touched or destroyed."

The ending is pictured in figure 20, which restates the escape imagery of the first solo. All of the dancers are involved except the Anne figure and the child, who are conspicuously and symbolically absent. Shortly, images from other parts of the dance enter in and accumulate, until the vision threatens to disintegrate in frenzy. The maniacal dance extends finally to the walls, as the dancers throw and push themselves into the side arches of the stage. The movement is compelled by harrowing imagery of nausea, pain, and grief, communicated with a gripping physicality be-

Figure 20. Photo: June Burke.

yond a dancerly control. The group's final descent into the earth is marked by inward moans and shuddering. This imagery is abstracted from reality, sculpted in a tense and powerful shape as the group becomes welded together through a singular gesture. The gesture emerges from the group in a pointillist way, at separate but overlapping times — one arm clasped across and hiding the face, the other arm reaching.

The oppressive ending cannot be changed, but neither can the spirit be destroyed. The central visual image is dark and chilling but not hopelessly despairing. As is true in Sokolow's other works, existential courage supports even this darkest image. Despite the tormented descent, the arm reaches.

Because of its narrative influences, *Dreams* might be taken too literally. Payton-Newman explains the broader intent of the work:

> There are always three or four plausible solutions in developing the dramatic imagery Sokolow gives you. You then find the image in its largest framework. By letting all of the solutions ruminate, you find your own honesty in the work. *Dreams* is not just about the inhumanity of death camps; it is about all our past and future nightmares. Cer-

> tainly we can imagine with horror the feeling of being buried alive, which is part of the final image. We react to it; but the nightmare could be here and now as well as then.
>
> Sokolow never adorns her images—they are plain and clear. She goes to the root feeling of any image, and directs performers to a discovery of themselves in it—the most truthful part of themselves. No matter how experienced you are as a dancer, you find out more about yourself through working with her. The surprise is that you have the capacity to understand the truth of yourself in a gesture. You discover in working with her that the dance will take care of itself if you are truthful (fully there) in the gesture.

In viewing Sokolow's work as focused in subjective existentialism, I am reminded most of Soren Kierkegaard, who is at the foundation of existential despair and imposed solitude. He relates existentialism with subjectivity in his call for an ethics of spiritual inwardness and "honesty"—one of his most frequently used words and one of Sokolow's, also. Kierkegaard's whole life was lived in one unmistakable gesture.[9] This well might be said of Sokolow.

Falling Everyday Life: Farber's Ledge

Because dance has an aesthetic purpose, it allows us direct access to the experience of bodily freedom and signifies our power to move free of daily concerns. Yet it is precisely these daily concerns and commitments that we project imagistically into dance. Which is to say that we dance out of our experience of life as a whole. Viola Farber's works pose a special interest in this respect.

Farber's work, especially when it rides close to process and away from product, derives directly from everyday life. Yet there is never a lack of focus and structure, even in her process pieces. The other side of Farber, seen in works like *Private Revelations* and *Focus* (1979), is her polished choreography. It is difficult to pin down a style or a set of characteristics that describe her work, precisely because it ranges from process improvisational works to tightly structured, highly technical choreographies.

She organized her company in 1969. Her work was transitional, bridging late modern abstract formalism and postmodern dance. But it is neither one of these; it spans the gap in between. Its poetic essence is unmistakable and its metaphors absolutely open. They are not projected in some ethereal beyond but in the here and now. If viewed in terms of typical interpretations of grace (as flowing, light, open, or airy), her work falls short. It is too inclusive to fit such definitions. However, watching Farber's dances, one is aware of a graceful intersection of dance values with lived values and of a free play in this. At the same time, her focus is uncompromising and her works are multifocused as modern life is. Her work plays but is also disciplined; it never wanders.

Farber, who danced in Merce Cunningham's original company for twelve years, retains the technical concerns of the pure dance aesthetic of the late modern period. Her concern for technical challenge and clarity in movement derives from both modern dance and ballet, exacting high levels of skilled motion. The content of her work cannot be extrapolated from its form. There appears to be no dramatic intention beyond the performance of the movement, and the symbolism cannot be read aside from the whole. One takes her dance whole for what it is, or not at all. Some degree of experiment and surprise is apparent even in tightly choreographed pieces. Her aesthetic is tolerant and open, admitting all kinds of movement, from pedestrian to virtuoso. It does not say "no, we don't do that"; rather, the message "let's try that" is everywhere evident.

The movement images seem to be worked out — or danced out — as part of the dance, as the movement is worked on, not beforehand. Thus the images intone the fragility of present time — the irretrievable now — not worried recapitulations of the past or anxious tracings of the future. They are dance images in the abstract, focusing attention on the dancing moment as it unfolds in the now and on an uninhibited range of movement qualities.

Her dance is focused in the immanent defining condition of dance — the human body, which is always sensing and expressing something in movement. Like Cunningham, she discovers the intrinsic value in dance. Yet free of his concerns for shaping movement according to strictly followed chance procedures, she creates highly impressionistic allusive imagery. Her imagery is derived from the everyday, not the ideal, and focuses in the movement, trusting that the key to meaning is to be found within the movement itself.

Like Cunningham, she does not describe her motivations but leaves dancers free to discern the intent in the movement as it is formed. As Larry Clark, who danced in Farber's company for twelve years, explains: "Often Viola wouldn't tell you what the dance was about or where she had gotten her ideas for it until a year or so after it was finished. You had to find the image for yourself—each piece differed in this respect. There was not always a group consensus about the meaning of a work. She allowed us to have our own ideas about it, and the audience as well."[10]

However abstract, her dances are motivated. They stem from musical sensitivity, observations of people and their relationships, everyday events, and a keen response to nature. They also demonstrate a desire to reach other people. But as in the late modern dance in general, Farber's work does not compel a direct "this means that" association of meaning with movement. The works create a mood, a point of concentration, and a direct response to the dancing body—its intricacies and colorations of motion, its ability to reflect the ever-changing life within and around us. This is as true of her dance for herself, *Solo* (1978), as it is of her group works. *Solo* seems to take place within the person, with silence and intensity. Still it is abstract and open ended, maintaining a fresh unfixed relationship to the audience.

Much of her work might be described as abstract impressionism. To the extent that it lends itself to blurred rather than concise associations and open interpretations, this is true. Added to this, she incorporates the postmodern concern for the mundane and familiar occurrence, the life so plainly before us that it is often missed. Her work connects the high technical achievement of late modern dance and the postmodern pedestrian revaluation of the ordinary. Her theater dance cannot be performed by untrained dancers; yet technique might just as easily be set aside as used. Farber's incorporation of improvisation in the finished work (using it as an end rather than as a means toward an end) represents another point of departure from the technically oriented late modern dance.

The risk involved in improvised performance (or in structured improvisation, in which choices within a given structure are made by the dancers on the spot) contributes to the unpremeditated presentness in her imagery. This attitude toward the truth of the moment permeates her strict choreography as well. Farber, Cunningham, Nikolais, and Balanchine (each in a strikingly individual way) celebrate present time as they draw attention away from what dance might be about toward what dance is capable of revealing of present time, lived through the dancing body and experienced as the dance is experienced.

In *Ledge* (1980), which Farber choreographed to Jean-Pierre Drouet's music, we are drawn into the spatial, temporal, and tactile sensations that ground our perception of ledges. It is an abstract, impressionistic, movement poem concerning the brittle texture, steep inclines, and yawning cracks and crevices in our body's memory of ledges. It is about *edges*—the limits of ourselves. The dance presses limits to find out where they are and to know its own territory. It is not interested in means and middles. The movement is risky, as our sense of risk is increased on ledges. It explores the dangerous and painful edges of human motion, founding them in dance imagery. The movement ranges from precarious, slow-motion balances to violently thrown and caught motion. The ensemble of five dancers is often tangled together as it traverses the dangerous falling moment of the ledge. The sharp, clean edges of motion, which only trained dancers can lend, are necessary to create the image of sharp rock. Also apparent is the dancers' immediate being-in-the-moment, with some passages seemingly built through their improvised connections with one another—alive for only that moment, changing slightly at each performance. (See figure 21.)

Farber conceived of her choreography as "reporting." "My dances report what I see. They are my response to the way everything is mixed up together in this world—people and microbes and elephants and cassowary birds. Not only do we live in a mixed-up world of shapes and sizes, the ways in which we relate to each other are mixed up, as well. People laugh at funerals, and just the other day, on Seventh Avenue, two of the most sinister men I ever saw came up, and I was sure they were going to mug me. Instead, they wanted to know if I needed any help in crossing the icy street."[11]

As reports, however, her dances are not literal. *Turf* (1979) to Poulenc's *Organ Concerto* is a choreographic sports report, but she accepts that the audience may not recognize sports in it. Her reports on life situations are translated "into the imagery of dance."[12] She wanted dance to be "as fresh as life," dangerous and insecure. The danger she sought, moreover, is that which trained dancers enjoy as their mastery permits them to move beyond the ordinary with assurance.

Clark told me he enjoyed the freedom Farber allowed the dancers in

Figure 21. Photo: June Burke.

her work. "Working with Viola was exciting; you never knew what to expect next. That's why I stayed with her so long." Much of the sense of freedom he experienced in working with Farber came from the wide range of challenge in the work. "Viola is such a technician, she can be very precise," he said, "but sometimes she would throw caution to the wind in wild energy phrases." Farber had one foot in precise technical dancing and the other foot in experiment. Clark interprets her as "an important bridge to postmodern dance, breaking into a new mode close to the everyday life but maintaining an amazing sense of theatricality."

Farber also had a talent for using the individual qualities of her dancers. Clark says she developed his "energy and quickness," Andy Peck's "sensitivity," Karen Levy's "sensuousness," Anne Koren's "dramatic qualities," June Finche's "love of dancing," and Jumay Chu's "generosity."

Clark explains that Farber's images are not verbal; they come from her experience and her surroundings. "For me, her work was full of pictures, or snapshots. She took dance and made photos out of it. When we gave a lecture demonstration, she would often say, 'this is a lecture demonstration without the lecture!'"

Farber liked natural and environmental performing spaces; every tour included something outside, Clark observes. He remembers performing in basketball courts, day-care centers, town parks, outside patios, street fairs, and botanical gardens, as well as in or around city buildings. "I liked best the outdoor sneaker dances. One of my dances was on a motorcycle. I'd drive into the crowd, get off and dance, then drive away. That was it! Andy and June also had a great garbage can duet." He remembers dangling from ropes about twelve feet off the ground, strung from or between buildings and trees, then dropping and being caught by people below. He also performed in the glassed-in mall of the IDS building in Minneapolis and at Long Island's Sag Harbor.

In an Illinois town park, he used his climbing rope between two oak trees: "Viola had structured the work for the crowd to move with us as they followed the dance through the park. She constructed outdoor events to accommodate the physical requirements of the space, or for its function. One of the names we had for these works was 'dinosaur,' from her work *Dinosaur Parts* to Tudor's music. We always had rules to structure the event, and often used sections from our other works, using a duet here, a solo there, and maybe then a section of *Motorcycle Boat* at the end."

Farber's archetypes are challenge, change, and risk. Her works seem to say "every day is new," nothing will be repeated exactly the same way twice, so you had better keep your eyes open. Clark emphasizes that Farber liked the struggle, not just the perfect moment. She made her dances difficult to keep the dancers alert. "She created a language you couldn't master," says Clark. "It constantly changed; I never could fully accept her compliments. I knew there was always more to be accomplished. The work was demanding, but the process often contained considerable freedom also, calling upon both the technical proficiency and the creative and artistic abilities of the dancers. Viola especially liked working with raw energy and clumsiness, and loved watching the effort toward the end, as much as the end itself. *'I love to see people fall down,'* Viola liked to say."

Falling, we saw in chapter 9, is Heidegger's metaphor for *present time.* He describes the "ecstasy of time"—when past and future are realized in the present—as "the moment of vision." Being, which is "futural" in the process of "having been," can "take over its own thrownness and be in the *moment of vision* for 'its time.'"[13] We gain a similar vision of our ecstatic presence through Farber's work, of life, though "futural" and "having been," plainly in our everyday grasp, held there in our dance—ventured, flung and falling.

The Open Center

The open center is a symbol for a point in time and in psychic life when visible form and inner truth are perfectly integrated in right action. Right action in dance is centered: that is, it moves out of a still, calm center, open and responsive, having the dignity of full presence because it moves in consonance with intention. There is no separation of self and body, motion and intention. I have called this moment of opening "grace" and "becoming the dance." Grace moves out of a gravitational center; grace does not defy gravity but aligns with it. Grace is the unseen open center, the essence of freedom.

Since Isadora Duncan, modern dancers have understood the solar plexus as the center of the body and as the source of bodily lived freedom in dance, unseen but manifested, nevertheless, in our dancing, when we move in consonance with nature. Nina Wiener's *Wind Devil* (1983) and Garth

Fagan's *Oatka Trail* (1979) reflect this open and free essence of dancing. Each dance in its own way is a meditation on nature. Each also represents well the 1980s regeneration of the values of historic modern dance, with its concern to move out of an emotionally responsive, open center. I will consider imagery in both artists' work in this context.

WIENER'S *WIND DEVIL*

Wind Devil presents a subtle but important departure from postmodern dance, retaining the looseness and ease of postmodern devolved styles but gaining emotional tension in fluid expressive imagery and technical challenge, unlike minimalist or object-oriented postmodern work.

Wind Devil is an evening-length work in two parts. The overall imagery deals with a sense of place. The first part is imagined by Wiener to be "out-of-doors" in a wide and open place.[14] The second part, after the intermission, she says is "indoors." Although there is no set, there is an "intimate" use of space. It also explores such "internal environments" as "underwater," a small "Japanese house," and a "cave." The work originally did have a set, which changed radically from part 1 to part 2. Eventually the surroundings were left open to suggestion through the dance itself.

Wind Devil is most generally about environments, both internal and external. The first half evokes nature but without literal reminders—mainly through the elastic and wide-ranging emotional style of the movement and the music of Sergio Cervetti. It is seen by Wiener as "psychological," in spite of its evocation of nature. To this end, Wiener accounts for the dancers in her choreography. "Much of the outcome and the imagery in my dances depend on my perception of the dancers, and how they work with core phrases I give them."

Thomas Grunewald's steely solo, which Wiener refers to as "a man in the desert," is to me the most austere dance in the first part, weathered in both place and person (figure 22). Grunewald says Wiener spoke of Clint Eastwood in developing his performance persona for the solo. Wiener developed the movement in part from images of the slithery, cold, sensuousness of snakes and lizards. Marcia Trees's solo is warmer but equally enigmatic. It is based on the imagery of "conjuring arms," which Wiener thinks of as an "occult and compressed density."

A translucency pervades the first half, as solos, duets, and groups melt

Figure 22. Photo: Lois Greenfield.

one into the next, the wind blowing and shifting them, sometimes sighing gently through them, other times piercing through. The organic unfolding draws us swiftly into shifting currents and moods. The dancers feel "a healing" in this flow. Indeed they do not stop for any anxious, pretty, or even compelling pictures. The energies continuously change — they take us into their perpetual sweep. Thus the impression throughout is a long undulating fluid image. The photograph of Grunewald's solo catches just a split second of the pliant elasticity of this imagery. We are permitted to pass through our own tensions as we pass through the pulls and counterpulls of the whole. Likewise, there is a release in the final image of this section, when the dance melts away in the ghostlike disappearance of legs, leaving only arm and hand gestures floating down through the light as it fades.

Wiener's intent in the second half is to focus on internal environments. "It is about personalities"—but not in any literal sense. Her belief that "each person contains all emotions" motivates this half of the work. Each dance develops and completes an idea, feeling, or qualitative image. While in the first half, images rapidly dissolve into one another, like sands shifting, individual pieces in the last half have a crystalline clarity and completion. Perhaps this happens because Wiener conceived "bigger jumps between emotions" in the distinct pieces of this half. Nevertheless, all the dances belong together.

Waves of motion—darting, jumping, diving—open the second half. This imagery is derived from the feeling of watery environments and the dancers' portrayal of the characteristics of whales and porpoises. Wiener believes that evocations of unfamiliar "alien" environments bring sudden recognition of our hidden selves.

One of the most memorable images from this part occurs through an accumulation of momentum, reaching a high point in the duet between Marcia Trees and Heywood McGriff, Jr. (figure 23). Trees never touches the floor as she is held, twisted, turned, lifted, dropped, and caught by McGriff in a continuous stream of motion. There is no love story. Neither is there an intent to display technical virtuosity; yet the partnering is atypically skillful. The balancing, throwing, giving, and holding of energies, the psychic tension and the physical weight between the partners are the substance of the dance—mysterious, emotional, and dangerous. Wiener says she developed this duet from an image of Eve as the serpent, entwining Adam's body.

McGriff's solo transports us suddenly to a new but psychically familiar environment, an imagined cave. If we do not imagine a cave, we at least cannot miss that his amazingly tall body is filling a circumscribed and seemingly enclosed area. The delimited space defined by his dance becomes warm and exciting as he pitches, presses, and shapes himself into its every area. The dance extracts the last flavor from the motion, and takes pleasure in completely filling the space that encloses it.

In a quieter moment, a very tender duet between Erin Thompson and

Figure 23. Photo: Chris Callis.

McGriff grows naturally out of a solo by Mauri Cramer. The solo anticipates the duet then echos it in the background with an invisible partner. A group dance follows, which captures a childlike freedom, leaving us with a positive image of regenerative power. It is impossible not to feel good at the end of this dance. The dancers themselves describe it as "being reborn."

As a whole, *Wind Devil* evokes in me intimacy as well as distance. Esoteric magic and ritual is called up by the movement. The arm and hand gestures evoke the familiar while remaining abstract, unpredictable, and wondrously strange. The dance connects easily with the earth, using the floor rather than defying or ignoring it. Yet it is curiously light, evaporating at odd moments in a warm and fluid fog then reappearing with unexpected organically flowing passages. It seems to be a rite of passage from place to place, movement to movement, person to person, and within the self.

The work retains some postmodern innovations, especially as it moves easily at cross-purposes with traditional musical phrasing, not allowing for clear demarkation through predictable resolution of tension. Yet it is clearly expressive, deriving from an emotional intensity not common to conceptual postmodern dance but close to the original impetus of historic modern dance.

In the early part of Wiener's career, she was associated with the conceptual postmodern approach, which has to do with manipulating movement in an intellectually objective way. In later works, like *Wind Devil,* she draws from emotional life. She says that the key to this change was her discovery of a way of working with the upper body, and especially the arms, to bring out the emotional images she wants to project:

> I found that there were certain kinds of gesture, not necessarily literal, which set off emotions in the viewer. The arms and hands are very associative; they seem to speak. They have the most articulate and varied expressiveness of any of the body's possible movements. They are the freest in their capacity to take on many different shapes and qualities of movement. We most readily make associations through the gestures of the hands and arms. They produce an image or an association in the viewer beyond the mere fact of the movement.
>
> I discovered through translating arm and hand phrases to other parts of the body, or capturing the sensation and shape of an arm phrase with the entire body, that I could produce an intensity of emotion in dance without narrative. I'm more interested in producing a mood or a feeling. The intent in my mind is at first quite general; I often don't know what the full intent is until I have actually made the movement and come to terms with it in myself. I finally do have many specific images for myself and for the dancers, but I don't realize them completely until the dance is finished.

Figure 24. Photo: June Burke.

Regarding the communicative intent of such imagery, she says: "I think the audience picks up on the emotional quality and energies more than anything else. Some people might find definite images which they associate with the movement or the structure of the dance, others may just pick up on a feeling which is there."

FAGAN'S *OATKA TRAIL*

In its own way, Garth Fagan's work also contributes to the return of expressive imagery in modern dance.[15] His *Oatka Trail* seems to grow directly out of the yielding earth-feminine, the mythic archetype at the foundation of modern dance and important in the beginnings of postmodern dance. *Oatka Trail* celebrates the body's natural expressiveness but within a technical, virtuosic reach. It is responsive yet reserved and inward. Deriving its imagery in part from Native American regard for nature, it moves with earth, not against her; its mythical direction is descent. Even in the air moments, the dancers often relax the upward momentum by looking down (figure 24).

Oatka Trail is a work for three men. Fagan made it especially for the mature male dancers in his company, all of whom are over thirty years of age: Roger Smith, Jon Gourdine, and Steve Humphrey, who in 1984 won the first Bessie Award for dance performance. Fagan wanted to explore both the strength and virile grace of these dancers.

Oatka Trail is set against the powerfully dramatic and lush music of Dvorak's *Cello Concerto* (Second Movement). The dance seems understated, moving within or underneath the music rather than on top of it, using its silences as well as its sounds, taking on the casual air of a stroll through the woods. At the same time, it exacts an unusual dancerly control, one more common to ballet, as the trio catches and holds dangerously angled balances on one leg, often leaning on an easy incline then suddenly falling off balance, neutralizing resistance in a manner uncommon to ballet.

The work is more impressionistic than coolly abstract. There is compelling warmth in the fullness of the motion, as each dancer in a different way takes quiet pleasure in clearing paths through space; in stopping to embellish them with subtle hand gestures, lyrical flow of arms, and sculpted mass of body; and in taking up each other's movement motifs. But even as the dancers complement each other or move in unison, each remains alone with nature or, more, enveloped in her. This containment and soothing quietude is apparent in Smith's solo shown in figure 25.

In figure 26, Gourdine is pointing a clear direction in space, with Smith linked to him in a tautly stretched image. This image, which I think of as "the pathfinder," comes near the apex of the work, as movement themes collect and overlap. Just as the movement accumulates texture in the whole, it gradually disperses. At the end of the dance, each dancer takes a separate path, walking off at a natural pace with contained pride and self-possession.

Through Humphrey's dancing, we see most poignantly that *Oatka Trail* is about grace in nature. The strongest image of this appears in his solo at the beginning and reappears near the end. The image is caught at the point of its finish in figure 27, Humphrey's solo, from which the entire work seems to unfold. Humphrey enters with a run on a circular path, adding a leap along the way, which moves directly out of the run. His leap is not performed from a coiled preparation, it simply stretches out of the run, stepping up and over its space as the arms tense downward.

Figure 25. Photo: June Burke.

Figure 26. Photo: June Burke.

Figure 27. Photo: June Burke.

Humphrey stops the run behind the powerful center spot on stage, then settles into and unwinds around his own strong center.

He takes to the air first with a body tilt to the side, knees bent so that the legs form a tilted diamond shape in the air. As he lands, the arms immediately take over the focus of the movement. His muscular torso then circles around to the back, led by the arms, coming at last to a firmly planted symmetrical center, the reaching arms dissolving the lyrical line of motion with hand flutters. The symmetry is immediately renewed with arms extended to either side in a back arch, head disappearing then reappearing as Humphrey recovers center and passes through it. At the end of the image, his head descends between his arms, gently suspending them like wings lifted away from his body, just before enfolding.

Fagan's work derives from lyric and dramatic modern dance traditions, while maintaining a sensitivity to black culture. In its fusion of these elements, his work is strongly influenced by his Jamaican background and by two women, Martha Graham and Ivy Baxter, a Jamaican who pioneered aesthetic fusions of theater dance with African and Afro-Caribbean traditional dance. One of the first dances in Fagan's repertory, *Life Forms, Death Shapes* (1967), grows directly from Graham's influence.

Fagan is also open to postmodern experiments, as his unpredictable phrasing, inventions upon ordinary movement, and occasional incorporation of terse minimalism demonstrate. At the same time, he is critical of pretense in postmodern dance and believes that much of it never moved beyond experimentation. His work juxtaposes experiment with traditional values, clarity of form with expressive intensity. Fagan describes himself as a "die-hard modern dancer" who loves "weighted movement, passion, and inner landscapes," as well as the "speed" and precision of ballet.[16] While his dancers do take to the air, they are most true to the earth essence of modern dance and African dance. Fagan says, "I love to dance into the earth and of the earth—this is African."

Fagan's works display a tensile strength and vibrant grace even when they exploit intentional clumsiness and loss of control. In a section of Humphrey's solo in *Oatka Trail*, he plunges forward in a stumbling run, then staggers backward out of it, repeating this until his composure returns. This momentary image is abstracted from the real, but it is nevertheless motivated—its transient pathos is communicated.

UNCERTAIN GRACE

Through the work of Fagan, Wiener, Farber, and other modern dancers responsive to the earth polarity and the tolerant aesthetic of modern dance, we see that grace is a more encompassing value than classical ballet allows us to see. Western culture typically interprets grace according to Apollonian classical attributes, such as balance, flow, harmony, and a light and sometimes sentimental femininity. Romantic ballet associates grace with movement that seems to float above the earth.

With Martha Graham, for whom grace was a "relationship to the world," it came to be defined in existentially human terms. No longer a numen, grace became a phenomenon. In modern dance, it is attained through a reciprocity of freedom and discipline; through a melding of form and expression; through an awareness of the surrounding world; through an admittance of the natural rhythms of the seasons; and through an acceptance of life and death, the incarnate sensuous body, and the emotions. As such, it is also conceived in terms of one's relationship to others. In dance, the art so intimately of our lived and mythic body, we see the feminine and the masculine in new ways. A curved line and a right angle can both be graceful. In nature, they are.

Graham changed substantive concepts of grace in dance through her works and her words. "Grace in dancers is not just a decorative thing. Grace is your relationship to the world, your attitude to the people with whom and for whom you are dancing. Grace means your relationship to the stage and the space around you—the beauty your freedom, your discipline, your concentration and your complete awareness have brought you."[17]

The grace of earth contains the many shapes of nature. It is not the grace of strength, light, and intellect, alone, but also the grace of vulnerability, soul, and shadow. It appears symbolically in the heart of the mystic world mountain of heaven and earth, in the marriage of intellect and soul, and in dance that emanates from these complements. It is not egocentric and knowing; it admits "not-knowing," as dancer Daniel Nagrin describes the existential predicament. It is not passive; it is *receptive.* It grows from an open center that responds to others. It realizes what must finally guide our lives safely into the future: that we are continuous not only with the pleasant and harmonious but with everything that *is,* including the diabolical and destructive. It realizes that whatever we do to others and to nature, we do also to ourselves. There is no simple grace that is disconnected from our earth. As the dove flies above earth, so must it come to rest upon her.

Modern dance, in its existentially open aesthetic, founded a search for a grace in accord with nature, a grace imperiled in the West through its exploitation of the earth and its devaluation of the incarnate body and the uncontentious transport of the earth goddess, honoring embattled heroic gods instead. Modern dance has sounded out the dark yet diaphanous earth divinity—our female and inward subtle body, our body of flesh and tears, rich in nature as it is vulnerable and receptive by nature, as "uncertain" in its grace as Dionysus, the enigmatic earth dancer of the Greek godhead, whom Nietzsche addresses as "the concealed one" and "the ambiguous one," whose voice descends to the "netherworld of every soul":

> not having received grace . . . broken open,
> blown at and sounded out by a thawing wind,
> perhaps more unsure, tenderer, more fragile, more broken
> but full of hopes that as yet have no name,
> full of new will and currents, full of new dissatisfaction
> and undertows.[18]

Signature

We are seldom aware of our body. We seldom focus on it. Rather, it is simply lived. It is the ever-present yet most hidden condition of existence. This is the body given us beyond attentiveness. This is the body we take for granted, the body that eludes our attention, the body we are before we notice it, and the body we have when we reflect expressly upon it. Our perfectly centered and graceful presence, then, escapes our notice—it is hidden from us.

The thought that we can create our body and our selves, as we do indeed spin our world of action through choice, is tempered by the hidden presence of our body, the mystery our body keeps from us as it is experienced in the perishable moment, beyond reflective notice. So when we create ourselves in our dance and experience ourselves in the dance of others, we do these things within the mysterious tension that lies between the near and the remote presence of our body. Our body suspends us between mystery and revelation, action and receptivity, freedom and necessity, being and nonbeing.

As our body bears the tensions and schema of the world (of nature and of human existence), the world is thus inscribed in our dancing. Merleau-Ponty speaks of indirect language and the voices of silence, recognizing that we bear the schema of the world in ourselves.[19] This enables us to first constitute signs as signs, to make "that which is expressed dwell in them." When we direct our attention to the dancer as a sign, we look behind the poetic image or symbol to our immediate communion with the dancer; we focus on the immanent and inmost hidden body, our expressive elusive body of dance. We pay attention to a silent mystery underlying explicit aesthetic intention.

A sign points toward something, points it out in a more direct way than a symbol does, since a symbol stands for something outside of what it is. Seen as a sign, the dancer does not stand for anything outside of the dance or the vital presence of her dancing. She does not arise from the reflective "I think" but from the existential "I am." She is embodied in her dance and signs it with her being.

NOTES

INDEX

NOTES

PREFACE

1 Phenomenology derives from reflection, which occurs in many spheres of life, from reflection upon life's problems to reflection upon scientific problems. Phenomenology holds that philosophical knowledge must be general (not simply private) but also based upon direct experience. Theoretical knowledge begins from experience and returns to it for verification. Nathaniel Lawrence and Daniel O'Connor, eds., *Readings in Existential Phenomenology* (Englewood Cliffs, N.J.: Prentice-Hall, 1967), pp. 8–9.
2 Paul Weiss, *Sport: A Philosophic Inquiry* (Carbondale: Southern Illinois University Press, 1969), p. 16.
3 According to Wilson, a new and positive existentialism is represented in the work of many existential psychologists. He lists Medard Boss, Ludwig Binswanger, Erwin Straus, Vicktor Frankl, Igor Caruso, R. D. Laing, and Abraham Maslow, as well as the transactional psychologists and the "scientific philosopher" Michael Polanyi. Colin Wilson, *The New Existentialism* (London: Wildwood House, 1980), p. 148.
4 Havelock Ellis, *The Dance of Life* (New York: Grosset and Dunlap, 1923), p. 34.
5 Arnold Berleant, *The Aesthetic Field: A Phenomenology of Aesthetic Experience* (Springfield, Ill.: Charles C. Thomas, 1970). Mikel Dufrenne, *The Phenomenology of Aesthetic Experience*, trans. Edward S. Casey and others (Evanston, Ill.: Northwestern University Press, 1973).
6 Berleant, *Aesthetic Field*, p. 19.

INTRODUCTION

1 Sondra Horton Fraleigh, "Dance Creates Man," *Quest* 19 (June 1970): 65–72; and "Man Creates Dance," *Quest* 23 (January 1975): 20–27.
2 See Don Redlich, "Reflections on Reacher," *Dance Perspectives* 38 (Summer 1969): 24–27.
3 Marjery J. Turner, *New Dance: Approaches to Nonliteral Choreography* (Pittsburgh:

University of Pittsburgh Press, 1971) is concerned with Nikolais's work and contributions.

4 Lynne Anne Blom and L. Tarin Chaplin, *The Intimate Act of Choreography* (Pittsburgh: University of Pittsburgh Press, 1982), chap. 9, state why and how dance involves abstraction.

5 José Ortega y Gasset, *The Dehumanization of Art, and Other Writings on Art and Culture* (Garden City, N.Y.: Doubleday, 1956), p. 23.

6 Martha Graham, "A Modern Dancer's Primer for Action," in *Dance as a Theater Art*, ed. Selma Jean Cohen (New York: Harper and Row, 1974), pp. 136–41.

7 Horst's identification with existentialism and attraction to Nietzsche's works was confirmed by Janes Soares and Deborah Jowitt in Louis Horst: Principles and Legacies, a session at the Dance Critics Association Conference, New York City, June 1984.

8 This statement is made and illustrated in *When the Fire Dances Between the Two Poles*, a film on Mary Wigman by Allegra Snyder and Annette Macdonald, 1983.

9 For a comprehensive commentary on the theater of the absurd see Martin Esslin, *The Theater of the Absurd* (New York: Doubleday, 1961).

10 William Spanos states Nietzsche's importance to modern existentialism. "Since Nietzsche, philosophy, religion, and the arts (especially on the European continent, but increasingly in England and America) have reflected in one way or another the existential crisis of unaccommodated man. Whether atheistic or theistic, the philosophy and art of the twentieth century constitutes largely in an encounter with Nothingness and the effort to transcend the threat that it poses to man's existence as man. Thus what was the attitude of an occasional outsider is now that of a generation." William V. Spanos, ed., *A Casebook on Existentialism* (New York: Crowell, 1966), pp. 1–2.

11 Paul Tillich, *The Courage to Be* (New Haven: Yale University Press, 1952), pp. 123–24.

12 Arturo B. Fallico, *Art and Existentialism* (Englewood Cliffs, N.J.: Prentice-Hall, 1962), p. 5.

13 Sondra Horton Fraleigh, "Daniel Nagrin the Existentialist," 1976. Unpublished interview transcript.

14 Maxine Sheets, *The Phenomenology of Dance* (Madison: University of Wisconsin Press, 1966), p. 14.

15 This recalls William Butler Yeats's question, which comes at the end of his poem "Among School Children," How can we know the dancer from the dance? Selma Jean Cohen in *Next Week, Swan Lake: Reflections on Dance and Dancers* (Middletown, Conn.: Wesleyan University Press, 1982) states that dance writers have depended heavily on this line. I believe this is because Yeats's question contains its own answer and reveals a basic (phenomenological) truth.

16 Francis Sparshott, "On the Question: 'Why Do Philosophers Neglect the Dance?'" *Dance Research Journal* 15 (Fall 1982): 5–30.

17 David Michael Levin, "Philosophers and the Dance," in *What Is Dance?* ed. Marshall Cohen and Roger Copeland (New York: Oxford University Press, 1983), pp. 85–94.

18 Hilda Hein, "Performance as an Aesthetic Category," *Journal of Aesthetics and Art Criticism* 28 (Spring 1970).

19 Arnold Berleant, *The Aesthetic Field: A Phenomenology of Aesthetic Experience* (Springfield, Ill.: Charles C. Thomas, 1970).

20 Erick Hawkins, "The Body Is a Clear Place," *Focus on Dance* 5 (1969): 34–39.

21 Maxine Sheets-Johnstone, "Thinking in Movement," *Journal of Aesthetics and Art Criticism* 39 (Summer 1981): 399–407; Maxine Sheets-Johnstone, ed., *Illuminating Dance: Philosophical Explorations* (Lewisburg, Pa.: Bucknell University Press, 1984).

22 Ernestine Stodelle, *The Dance Technique of Doris Humphrey* (Princeton, N.J.: Princeton Book Co., 1978), p. 15.

23 *New York Times*, 16 April 1980.

24 John Martin, *Modern Dance* (New York: Dance Horizons, 1966), p. 20, says that modern dance is not a system but "a point of view." Likewise, Fallico, *Art and Existentialism*, p. 1, calls existentialism "a fundamental position from which to view human experience."

25 Mary Wigman is identified with German expressionism, and Martha Graham's early work is seen as expressionistic in style. Loie Fuller (1862–1928), with her visions of light, sound, and movement, and Isadora Duncan, with her desire to found a dance true to nature, are often considered precursors of the modern dance—the spirit behind its emergence as a theatrical concert form. The movement theories of Rudolph von Laban and the rhythmic experiments of Emile Jacques Dalcroze have also been credited in the development of modern dance.

26 Hawkins, "Body Is a Clear Place," p. 34.

27 Tillich, *Courage to Be*, pp. 113–55.

28 Huntington Cairns, introduction to *Collected Dialogues of Plato*, ed. Edith Hamilton and Huntington Cairns (Princeton, N.J.: Princeton University Press, 1961), pp. xviii–xix.

29 Tillich, *Courage to Be*, pp. 86–113.

30 Cohen, *Next Week, Swan Lake*, pp. 119–24.

31 Ibid., p. 129.

32 Friedrich Nietzsche, *Thus Spoke Zarathustra*, trans. Walter Kaufman (Viking, 1966), p. 15.

33 Doris Humphrey, *The Art of Making Dances* (New York: Grove, 1959), pp. 50–51.

34 Barbara Morgan, *Martha Graham: Sixteen Dances in Photographs* (Dobbs Ferry, N.Y.: Morgan and Morgan, 1941), p. 10.

35 Daniel Noel interprets the writings as postmodern because, even though we eventually see through Don Juan's tricks, our perfectly accessible interpretations do not satisfy us. If we are led to be "disillusioned with our modern disillusionments," we may accept "a mode of interpretation bordering on the paradoxical, the ineffable, the unknown." Daniel C. Noel, ed., *Seeing Castaneda: Reactions to the "Don Juan" Writings of Carlos Castaneda* (New York: Putnam's Sons, 1976), p. 25.

36 Martin Heidegger, *Being and Time*, trans. John Macquarrie and Edward Robinson (New York: Harper and Row, 1962), pp. 304–11.

37 Sondra Fraleigh, "The Relationship of Sokolow's Work to Existentialism," 1980. Unpublished interview transcript.

38 Emshwiller's dance films are explained with photographs and drawings in *Dance Perspectives* 30 (Summer 1967).

39 William Barrett, *Irrational Man: A Study in Existential Philosophy* (Garden City, N.Y.: Doubleday, 1958).

40 Mircea Eliade, *The Sacred and the Profane: The Nature of Religion,* trans. Willard Trask (New York: Harcourt, Brace Jovanovich, 1968).
41 Friedrich Nietzsche, *Joyful Wisdom,* section 125.
42 Spanos, *Casebook,* p. 6.
43 Johann Wolfgang von Goethe, *Faust,* part 2, act 5.
44 Jean-Paul Sartre, *Existentialism,* trans. Bernard Frechtman (New York: Philosophical Library, 1947), p. 27.
45 Ibid., p. 18.

1 DANCE AND THE LIVED BODY

1 Nathaniel Lawrence and Daniel O'Connor, eds., *Readings in Existential Phenomenology* (Englewood Cliffs, N.J.: Prentice-Hall, 1967), p. 1.
2 Colin Wilson, *The New Existentialism* (London: Wildwood House, 1980), p. 9.
3 Ibid., p. 29.
4 Hans Jonas, *The Phenomenon of Life: Toward a Philosophical Biology* (New York: Harper and Row, 1966), pp. 225–26.
5 Ibid., pp. 215–16.
6 Jean-Paul Sartre, *Existentialism,* trans. Bernard Frechtman (New York: Philosophical Library, 1947), p. 61.
7 Wilson, *New Existentialsim,* pp. 96–97.
8 Ibid., p. 153.
9 Ibid., pp. 176–80.
10 Arturo B. Fallico, *Art and Existentialism* (Englewood Cliffs, N.J.: Prentice-Hall, 1962), p. 7.
11 Wilson, *New Existentialism,* p. 99.
12 Ibid., pp. 99, 150.
13 Fallico, *Art and Existentialism,* p. 8.
14 Algis Mickunas and David Stewart, *Exploring Phenomenology: A Guide to the Field and Its Literature* (Chicago: American Literary Association, 1974), p. 26.
15 Richard Zaner (who does not account for all methods) summarizes the phenomenologist's basic approach. (1) *Intuitive:* seeking an original perceiving – not secondhand evidence but an original intuiting of phenomena. (2) *Explicative:* seeking to draw forward, or explicate, what is taken for granted (in the natural attitude of consciousness). This method is further "an original intuitive explicating or unfolding of mental life in respect of its structures." (3) *Descriptive:* seeking on the basis of the first and second methods, to describe (and to make descriptive judgments about) mental life – its structures and interrelations. (4) *Reflective:* using methods that reflect perceiving, since "the mode of giveness (*Gegebenheitsweise*) peculiar to mental phenomena is reflective giveness." (5) *Reductive:* using "a descriptive explication of mental life." Richard Zaner, *The Problem of Embodiment,* 2d ed. (The Hague: Martinus Nijhoff, 1971), p. 202.
16 John Dewey, *Art as Experience* (New York: Minton, Black, 1934), pp. 62–63.
17 See Herbert Spiegelberg, *The Phenomenological Movement: A Historical Introduction,* 2d ed., 2 vols. (The Hague: Martinus Nijhoff, 1971).

18 Mickunas and Stewart, p. 64.

19 Gabriel Marcel, *Metaphysical Journal*, trans. Bernard Wall (Chicago: Henry Regnery, 1952), p. 182.

20 Ibid., p. 4.

21 Zaner, *Problem of Embodiment*, p. viii.

22 Ibid., pp. 239–40.

23 Martha Graham, "A Modern Dancer's Primer for Action," in *Dance as a Theater Art*, ed. Selma Jean Cohen (New York: Harper and Row, 1974), p. 136–37.

24 Sandra Minton, *Modern Dance: Body and Mind* (Englewood, Colo.: Morton, 1984), p. 3.

25 Ibid., p. 111.

26 See Stuart Spicker's introduction to his collection of philosophies in rejection of Cartesian dualism: *The Philosophy of the Body*, ed. Stuart E. Spicker (Chicago: Quadrangle, 1970), pp. 9–11. Spicker also points out one of the ironies of the history of Western philosophy – that Descartes himself may not have been a Cartesian, since some of his penetrating insights into the nature of embodiment contradict the major dualistic thesis of his *Meditations*, which forms the basis of what has become known as Cartesian dualism. Some of Descartes's nondualistic insights are contained in part 5 of his *Discourse on Method* and in his letters to Princess Elizabeth of Bohemia (1616–1680), as for instance the view that "everybody always [has the awareness of the union of soul and body] in himself without doing philosophy."

27 Plato, *Laws* XII, #959, in *Collected Dialogues of Plato*, ed. Edith Hamilton and Huntington Cairns (Princeton, N.J.: Princeton University Press, 1961), p. 1503.

28 Paul Oscar Kristeller, "The Modern System of the Arts," in *Problems In Aesthetics*, 2d ed, ed. Morris Weitz (New York and London: Macmillan, 1970), pp. 115–16.

29 Plato, *Laws* VII, #791, p. 1363.

30 Aristotle differs from Plato, since in Plato's philosophy the real is unchanging and not subject to the whims of time. In Aristotle, a sense of the temporal is much stronger because of his powerful empirical curiosity about nature. For both of them, a pervasive rationality of the world permeates all levels – the divine, the natural, and the human – holding them in meaningful order. Aristotle's philosophy of the "material" interrelatedness of the body and soul places him surprisingly close to the nondualistic lived-body concept. He was concerned with articulating vital life principles. For Aristotle, art was a result of both the soul and hand of the artist and was seen as "patterned energy." For him, the soul was "not a precious spiritual essence, but a principle of life." Katherine E. Gilbert and Helmut Kuhn, *A History of Aesthetics* (Westport, Conn.: Greenwood, 1972), p. 62–64.

31 Huntington Cairns, introduction to *Collected Dialogues of Plato*, pp. xx–xxi.

32 Mickunas and Stewart, *Exploring Phenomenology*, pp. 96–97.

33 David Best, *Expression in Movement and the Arts* (London: Lepus Books, 1974), pp. 184–87.

34 Susanne K. Langer, *Mind: An Essay on Human Feeling*, vol. 1 (Baltimore: Johns Hopkins University Press, 1967), p. 29.

35 Best, *Expression in Movement*, pp. 113–32, 153–60, also identifies the problem of dual-

ism that arises from traditional expressionistic theories and from formalistic aesthetic theories.

36 Mabel Elsworth Todd, *The Thinking Body* (Brooklyn: Dance Horizons, 1959).

37 Maurice Merleau-Ponty, "The Relations of the Soul and the Body and the Problem of Perceptual Consciousness," in *The Structure of Behavior*, trans. Alden L. Fisher (Boston: Beacon, 1963), pp. 185–224, 246–49.

38 Ibid., p. 209.

39 Ibid., p. 210.

40 Jean-Paul Sartre, *Being and Nothingness*, 3d ed., trans. Hazel Barnes (New York: Citadel, 1965), p. 300.

41 Edward S. Casey summarizes the various positions taken regarding the continuity and/or the discontinuity of perception and imagination in *Imagining: A Phenomenological Study* (Bloomington: Indiana University Press, 1979), p. 130.

42 Erwin Straus, "Born to See, Bound to Behold: Reflections on the Function of Upright Posture in the Esthetic Attitude," in Spicker, *Philosophy of the Body*, pp. 334–59.

43 Jonas, *Phenomenon of Life*, p. 3.

44 Ibid., pp. 2–5.

45 Zaner explains this limitation in terms of "the body uncanny" in *The Problem of Embodiment*, pp. 47–66.

46 Ibid., p. 52.

47 Paul Ricoeur, *Freedom and Nature: The Voluntary and the Involuntary*, trans. Erazim V. Kohak (Chicago: Northwestern University Press, 1966), p. 328.

48 Ibid., p. 249.

2 DANCE AND SELF

1 Martha Graham, "A Modern Dancer's Primer for Action," in *Dance as a Theater Art*, ed. Selma Jean Cohen (New York: Harper and Row, 1974), pp. 136–37.

2 Arnold Berleant points out that aesthetic theory historically concentrates on explaining art through selected aspects that are partial and substitute (or surrogate) elucidations of it: art as expression, art as emotion, art as form, art as communication. He explains how expressionist, emotionalist, formalist, and communicative theories of art contribute to our understanding of art, but only in part. As a consequence, they misdirect our attention away from an understanding of the totality. Arnold Berleant, *The Aesthetic Field: A Phenomenology of Aesthetic Experience* (Springfield, Ill.: Charles C. Thomas, 1970), p. 29. The failure of expressionist theories to adequately explain dance art has been pointed out by Susanne Langer as she considered "the fallacy" of self-expression: Susanne K. Langer, *Philosophy in a New Key: A Study in the Symbolism of Reason, Rite, and Art*, 3d ed. (Cambridge: Harvard University Press, 1957), pp. 184–90; by David Best, *Expression in Movement and the Arts* (London: Lepus Books, 1974), pp. 153–60; and by Mary Sirridge and Adina Armelagos in "The Ins and Outs of Dance: Expression as an Aspect of Style," *Journal of Aesthetics and Art Criticism* 36 (Fall 1977): 13–24.

3 Heinrich von Kleist, *Über das Marionettentheater* (Wiesbaden: Insel Verlag, Insel-Bucherei

Nr. 481, 1954), pp. 5-13. English translation in *What Is Dance?* ed. Marshall Cohen and Roger Copeland (New York: Oxford University Press, 1983), pp. 178-84.

4 Soren Kierkegaard, *The Sickness unto Death*, trans. Walter Lourie (Garden City, N.J.: Doubleday, 1954), p. 146.

5 Although he utilizes Marcel's insights, Zaner takes up the embodied self not primarily as a metaphysical mystery, but as a phenomenon that appears *in context*. See Richard Zaner, *Context of Self: A Phenomenological Inquiry Using Medicine as a Clue* (Athens: Ohio University Press, 1981). He makes extensive use of Ricoeur's phenomenological philosophy. Marcel's existentialism underlies both Zaner's and Ricoeur's thought. Ricoeur states that "meditation" on Marcel's work lies at the basis of his philosophy of the will. He was influenced in particular by Marcel's "rediscovery of incarnation." Paul Ricoeur, *Freedom and Nature: The Voluntary and the Involuntary*, trans. Erazim V. Kohak (Chicago: Northwestern University Press, 1966), p. 15.

6 Zaner points out that opinions on the question What is self? have been astonishingly varied, including "affirmers of substance such as Augustine, Descartes, Locke, Leibnitz, or contemporaries such as Macmurry." He calls the early Sophists and skeptics, along with Hume, Sartre, and Gurwitch, "the firmly implanted deniers." He singles out those who argue that self is "wholly natural," and therefore "indistinguishable from brain-states, complex neurophysiology, or just plain matter," as the early atomists: Lucretius, Hobbes, LeMetrie, and modern identity theorists such as Armstrong. Zaner, *Context of Self*, pp. 111-12.

7 Christopher Lasch, *The Culture of Narcissism: American Life in an Age of Diminishing Expectations* (New York: Norton, 1978), pp. 71-99.

8 In Barbara Morgan, *Martha Graham: Sixteen Dances in Photographs*, (Dobbs Ferry, N.Y.: Morgan and Morgan, 1941), p. 10.

9 Ricoeur, *Freedom and Nature*, p. 59.

10 Ibid., pp. 63-64.

11 In Ricoeur's frame of reference, the willing of any project contains bodily action. "To say 'I will' means first 'I decide,' secondly 'I move my body,' thirdly, 'I consent.'" Ibid., p. 6.

12 Scott R. Kretchmar, "From Test to Contest: An Analysis of Two Kinds of Counterpoint in Sport," *Journal of the Philosophy of Sport* 2 (September 1975): 21-30.

13 Maurice Merleau-Ponty, *Signs*, trans. Richard C. McLeary (Chicago: Northwestern University Press, 1964), pp. 66-67.

14 Jean Battey Lewis, "Mary Wigman, Modern Dance Pioneer, Dies," *Washington Post*, 21 September 1973.

15 "Mary Wigman, Dance Innovator, Dies," *New York Times*, 20 September 1973.

16 Leo Tolstoy, *What Is Art*, trans. Aylmer Maude (Indianapolis: Bobbs-Merrill, 1960).

17 These impressions are gained from my study with Wigman, from her book, *The Language of Dance*, trans Walter Sorell (Middletown, Conn.: Wesleyan University Press, 1975), and the film of her work, *When the Fire Dances Between the Two Poles*, by Allegra Snyder and Annette Macdonald.

18 Gabriel Marcel, *Homo Viator*, trans. Emma Craufurd (Chicago: Henry Regnery, 1951), p. 15.

19 Richard Zaner, *The Problem of Embodiment,* 2d ed. (The Hague: Martinus Nijhoff, 1971), p. 10.

20 See her program notes for *Dance Da Da,* December 1979.

21 Calvin O. Schrag, "The Lived Body as a Phenomenological Datum," in *Sport and the Body,* ed. Ellen W. Gerber (Philadelphia: Lea and Febiger, 1972), p. 144.

22 This was pointed out by Albert Opoku (founder of the Ghana Dance Ensemble at the University of Ghana) in my African dance classes under him at SUNY Brockport, February through May 1982.

23 Maxine Sheets's principle thesis is that the phenomenological basis of dance is its created form. See *The Phenomenology of Dance* (Madison: University of Wisconsin Press, 1966).

24 See Arturo B. Fallico, *Art and Existentialism* (Englewood Cliffs, N.J.: Prentice-Hall, 1962), chaps. 3, 4.

25 Martin Buber, *I and Thou,* 2d ed., trans. Ronald Gregor Smith (New York: Charles Scribner's Sons, 1958).

26 Sartre's "I exist my body" is probably the most famous phenomenological statement to capture the nondualistic thesis of the lived-body concept. See Jean-Paul Sartre, *Being and Nothingness,* 3d ed., trans. Hazel Barnes (New York: Citadel, 1965), p. 327. See also Sartre, "The body is lived and not known," ibid., p. 300.

27 Gabriel Marcel, *Metaphysical Journal,* trans. Bernard Wall (Chicago: Henry Regnery, 1952), p. 303.

28 Buber, *I and Thou,* p. 9.

3 DANCE ITSELF

1 Paul W. Taylor, *Normative Discourse* (Englewood Cliffs, N.J.: Prentice-Hall, 1961), pp. 23–26.

2 James Joyce, *A Portrait of the Artist as a Young Man* (New York: Viking, 1944), p. 205.

3 George Beiswanger, "Doing and Viewing Dance: A Perspective for the Practice of Criticism," *Dance Perspectives* 55 (1973): 11.

4 Paul Ricoeur, *Freedom and Nature: The Voluntary and the Involuntary,* trans. Erazim V. Kohak (Chicago: Northwestern University Press, 1966), p. 217.

5 David Levin, "Balanchine's Formalism," *Dance Perspectives* 55 (1973): 34.

6 Ibid.

7 Gabriel Marcel, *Metaphysical Journal,* trans. Bernard Wall (Chicago: Henry Regnery, 1952), p. 274.

4 DANCE AND THE OTHER

1 Calvin O. Schrag, "The Lived Body as a Phenomenological Datum," in *Sport and the Body,* ed. Ellen W. Gerber (Philadelphia: Lea and Febiger, 1972), p. 146.

2 Jean-Paul Sartre, *Being and Nothingness,* 3d ed., trans. Hazel Barnes (New York: Citadel, 1965), p. 328.

3 Ibid., p. 327.
4 Ibid., p. 340.
5 Jean-Paul Sartre, *No Exit* (New York: Random House, 1955).
6 Gabriel Marcel, *Metaphysical Journal*, trans. Bernard Wall (Chicago: Henry Regnery, 1952).
7 Maurice Merleau-Ponty, *Phenomenology of Perception*, trans. Colin Smith (London: Routledge and Kegan Paul, 1962), ch. 6.
8 This statement is made and illustrated in *When the Fire Dances Between the Two Poles*, a film on Mary Wigman by Allegra Snyder and Annette Macdonald, 1983.
9 Sigmund Freud, *Beyond the Pleasure Principle*, trans. James Strachey (New York: Bantam, 1959), p. 109.
10 Marcel, *Metaphysical Journal*, p. 258.
11 Arnold Berleant, *The Aesthetic Field: A Phenomenology of Aesthetic Experience* (Springfield, Ill.: Charles C. Thomas, 1970), p. 52.
12 Roman Ingarten, "Aesthetic Experience and Aesthetic Object," in *Readings in Existential Phenomenology*, ed. Nathaniel Lawrence and Daniel O'Connor (Englewood Cliffs, N.J.: Prentice-Hall, 1967), pp. 308–23.
13 Arturo B. Fallico, *Art and Existentialism* (Englewood Cliffs, N.J.: Prentice-Hall, 1962), pp. 18–25.
14 Marcel, *Metaphysical Journal*, p. 257.
15 *The I Ching*, 3d ed., trans. Richard Wilhelm and Cary F. Baynes (Princeton, N.J.: Princeton University Press, 1967), pp. lv–lvi.
16 Ibid., p. 125.
17 Ibid., p. 59.
18 Jacques Seranno, *The Meaning of the Body* (Philadelphia: Westminster, 1966), pp. 91–92.
19 *Collected Dialogues of Plato*, ed. Edith Hamilton and Huntington Cairns (Princeton, N.J.: Princeton University Press, 1961), p. 222.
20 Merleau-Ponty, *Phenomenology of Perception*, p. 197.
21 Ibid., p. 236.
22 David Michael Levin, "On Heidegger: The Gathering Dance of Mortals," *Research in Phenomenology* 10 (1980): 268.

5 DANCE TENSION

1 Gabriel Marcel, *Metaphysical Journal*, trans. Bernard Wall (Chicago: Henry Regnery, 1952), p. 274.
2 Pierre Tielhard de Chardin, *The Phenomenon of Man*, trans. Bernard Wall (New York: Harper and Row, 1961), p. 43.
3 Katherine E. Gilbert and Helmut Kuhn, *A History of Aesthetics* (Westport, Conn.: Greenwood, 1972), p. 6.
4 Ibid., p. 4.
5 Ananda K. Coomaraswamy, *The Dance of Shiva* (New York: Noonday, 1957), p. 78.

6 Ibid., pp. 77–78.
7 Lincoln Kirstein, *Dance: A Short History of Classic Theatrical Dancing* (New York: Dance Horizons, 1969), pp. 13–14.
8 Ibid., pp. 14–17.
9 Valerie Preston-Dunlop, ed., *Dancing and Dance Theory* (London: Laban Centenary Publication, 1979), p. 133.
10 Doris Humphrey, *The Art of Making Dances* (New York: Grove, 1959), p. 72. It may be out of these early modern dancers' concerns with the sphere that modern dance has developed its curvilinear, three-dimensional sensitivity to movement in space, becoming more of a sculpted than a painterly art (Delsarte's spirals and curves probably also contributing). Likewise, modern dance rejects the traditional picture frame stage, first through the teachings of Laban and Humphrey and later through Cunningham's dispersal of movement, placing it in the space according to chance.
11 Plato, *Laws* X, #893–98, in *Collected Dialogues of Plato*, ed. Edith Hamilton and Huntington Cairns (Princeton, N.J.: Princeton University Press, 1961), pp. 1448–54.
12 Ibid., #898, pp. 1453–54.
13 *Timaeus* #47, in *Collected Dialogues*, pp. 1174–75.
14 Kirstein, *Dance*, p. 19.
15 Ibid., p. 1.
16 Ibid., p. 19.
17 Martin Heidegger, "The Origin of the Work of Art," in *Poetry, Language, Thought*, trans. Albert Hofstadter (New York: Harper and Row, 1971).
18 This complement, as I stated in chap. 4, is demonstrated in *The I Ching*. I take it up again in chaps. 10 and 11, in terms of mythic tension in dance. *The I Ching*, 3d ed., trans. Richard Wilhelm and Cary F. Baynes (Princeton, N.J.: Princeton University Press, 1967). Note also that sometimes the earth-heaven and female-male mythological principles are reversed, as in ancient Egypt's sky goddess, Nut, and earth god, Geb.
19 Heidegger, "The Thing," in Hofstadter, *Poetry, Language, Thought*, pp. 163–87.
20 David Michael Levin, "On Heidegger: The Gathering Dance of Mortals," *Research in Phenomenology* 10 (1980): 251–72.
21 C. K. Ogden, *Opposition: A Linguistic and Psychological Analysis* (Bloomington: Indiana University Press, 1967), pp. 90, 92. Ogden offers a critique of philosophy's explorations of the terms of opposition, from the cosmologists and Aristotle through Kant, Hegel, the logisticians, and the evolutionists.
22 Heidegger, "Origin of the Work of Art," p. 78.
23 Ibid., p. 76.
24 Ibid., p. 75.
25 Plato, *The Symposium*, trans. Walter Hamilton (London: Penguin, 1951), pp. 85, 205 b-c.
26 Heidegger, "Origin of the Work of Art," p. 76.
27 Ibid., pp. 75–76.
28 Ibid., p. 74.
29 Ibid.
30 Arturo B. Fallico, *Art and Existentialism* (Englewood Cliffs, N.J.: Prentice-Hall, 1962), pp. 18–25.

31 Jacques Seranno, *The Meaning of the Body* (Philadelphia: Westminster, 1966).
32 Nelson Goodman, *Ways of Worldmaking* (Indianapolis: Hackett, 1978), pp. 17–22.
33 Nelson Goodman, *Languages of Art: An Approach to a Theory of Symbols* (Indianapolis: Bobbs-Merrill, 1968), pp. 241–52.
34 Heidegger, "Origin of the Work of Art," pp. 63–64.
35 Ibid., pp. 48, 55, 63.
36 Paul Ricoeur, *Freedom and Nature: The Voluntary and the Involuntary*, trans. Erazim V. Kohak (Chicago: Northwestern University Press, 1966).
37 Ibid., pp. 321–22, 283.
38 Ibid., pp. 328–30.
39 That expression in dance is an aspect of style was first set forth by Mary Sirridge and Adina Armelagos in "The Ins and Outs of Dance: Expression as an Aspect of Style," *Journal of Aesthetics and Art Criticism* 36 (Fall 1977): 13–24. Here they explore the failure of expression theory to adequately explain dance art, especially as such theories reinforce a view that dance is self-expression. David Best also questions expression theory in terms of dance in *Expression in Movement and the Arts* (London: Lepus Books, 1974).
40 This view of style as integral to a work involving the *what* as well as the *how* is consistent with Nelson Goodman's more technical explanations of style as a metaphorical signature by which we may identify works as belonging to a person or a group or a period. Goodman, *Ways of Worldmaking*, pp. 34–40.
41 Heidegger, "Origin of the Work of Art," pp. 49–53.
42 Ibid., p. 55.

6 POINT COUNTERPOINT

1 Michael Kirby, "The Aesthetics of the Avant-Garde," in *Esthetics Contemporary*, ed. Richard Kostelanetz (Buffalo, N.Y.: Prometheus Books, 1978), p. 61.
2 Risieri Frondizi, *What Is Value? An Introduction to Axiology*, 2d ed., trans. Solomon Lipp (Lasalle, Ill.: Open Court, 1971).
3 *Complexification* is explained by Pierre Teilhard de Chardin in *The Phenomenon of Man*, trans. Bernard Wall (New York: Harper and Row, 1961), p. 48.
4 A value is considered important if it is necessary to the accomplishment of another value. We can perceive values as interrelated according to the feature of value importance. Paul W. Taylor, *Normative Discourse* (Englewood Cliffs, N.J.: Prentice-Hall, 1961), p. 321.
5 Heinrich von Kleist, *Über das Marionettentheater* (Wiesbaden: Insel Verlag, Insel-Bucherei Nr. 481, 1954). English translation in *What Is Dance?*, ed. Marshall Cohen and Roger Copeland (New York: Oxford University Press, 1983), pp. 178–84.
6 Henri Bergson, *Time and Free Will*, trans. F. L. Pogson (London: Allen and Unwin, 1910), pp. 11–13.
7 Drew A. Hyland, "The Stance of Play," *Journal of the Philosophy of Sport* 7 (Fall 1980): 87–99.
8 Eric Hawkins, "The Body Is a Clear Place," *Focus on Dance* 5 (1969): 34.

9 Paul Kuntz, "Limitation and Creativity," unpublished paper.
10 William Barrett, *Irrational Man: A Study in Existential Philosophy* (Garden City, N.Y.: Doubleday, 1958), p. 46.
11 For a study of the influence of Nietzsche, Kierkegaard, and later existential thought on modern psychology see Rollo May, Ernest Angel, and Henri F. Ellenberger, eds., *Existence: A New Dimension in Psychiatry and Psychology* (New York: Simon and Schuster, 1958).
12 The dance *The Peloponnesian War* was started in the spring of 1966 at New York State University College at Brockport, where Nagrin was artist in residence, and had its premier there in the fall of 1968. The diary he kept about the dance is published in "Dancers Notes," *Dance Perspectives* 38 (Summer 1969): 18–23.
13 Friedrich Nietzsche, *Thus Spoke Zarathustra*, trans. Walter Kaufmann (Viking, 1966), pp. 19–20.
14 Jennifer Dunning, "How to Dance Forever," *New York Times*, 7 May 1982.
15 *Making Dances: 7 Post-Modern Choreographers*, a film by Michael Blackwood.
16 Maurice Merleau-Ponty, *The Visible and the Invisible*, trans. Alphonso Lingis (Evanston, Ill.: Northwestern University Press, 1968).
17 Anna Kisselgoff, "Molissa Fenley Is Energy in Motion," Dance View, *New York Times*, 17 October 1982.
18 Sondra Fraleigh, "Interview with Elizabeth Streb," 1983. Unpublished interview transcript.
19 Remy Charlip, a member of Cunningham's original company, states that Cunningham stressed this point often and made his dances with the qualities of the individual dancer in mind. In *Galaxy* (1956), for instance, Cunningham conceived Viola Farber as water, Carolyn Brown as air, Marianne Simon as earth, and Remy Charlip as fire. This work was performed with Earle Brown's music *Four Systems* (1954) and explores the open-form musical concept utilized by Brown, in which parts might begin anywhere, end anywhere, or overlap. Any combination of the four solos is possible. These points were made by Charlip and Brown in Merce Cunningham and John Cage: The Forming of an Aesthetic, a session at the Dance Critics Association Conference, New York City, June 1984.
20 Martha Myers, "Invention in Dance: Alwin Nikolais." Videotape interview.

7 EXPRESSIONIST-FORMALIST TENSION

1 Plato, *Laws* VII, #795, in *Collected Dialogues of Plato*, ed. Edith Hamilton and Huntington Cairns (Princeton, N.J.: Princeton University Press, 1961), p. 1367.
2 The general tone of Plato's philosophy of dance is decidedly formalist, in agreement with the intellectual thrust of Greek art. Edith Hamilton states the overriding concern Greek art had with balancing emotion and intellect, rendering it on the whole, "an intellectual art." See her preface to *Ion*, in ibid., p. 215.
3 Selma Jean Cohen, *Next Week, Swan Lake: Reflections on Dance and Dancers* (Middletown, Conn.: Wesleyan University Press, 1982), p. 87.
4 Ibid., pp. 87–88.
5 Nelson Goodman, *Ways of Worldmaking* (Indianapolis: Hackett, 1978), pp. 57–63.

6 Katherine Everett Gilbert, "Mind and Medium in the Modern Dance," in *What Is Dance?*, ed. Marshall Cohen and Roger Copeland (New York: Oxford University Press, 1983), pp. 298–99.

7 Friedrich Nietzsche, *The Birth of Tragedy*, trans. Francis Golffing (New York: Doubleday, 1956).

8 Susanne K. Langer, *Mind: An Essay on Human Feeling*, vol. 1 (Baltimore: Johns Hopkins University Press, 1967).

9 Louis Arnaud Reid, *Meaning in the Arts* (London: Allen and Unwin, 1969), pp. 66–68.

10 Nelson Goodman, *Languages of Art: An Approach to a Theory of Symbols* (Indianapolis: Bobbs-Merrill, 1968), p. 5.

11 Ibid., pp. 46–53.

12 Goodman, *Ways of Worldmaking*, pp. 57–66.

13 Reid, *Meaning in the Arts*, pp. 75–89.

14 Ibid., p. 61.

15 Ibid., p. 81.

16 Jacques Seranno, *The Meaning of the Body* (Philadelphia: Westminster, 1966); Martin Heidegger, "The Origin of the Work of Art," in *Poetry, Language, Thought*, trans. Albert Hofstadter (New York: Harper and Row, 1971).

17 Langer, *Mind*, p. 115.

18 Ibid., p. 127.

19 Yvonne Rainer, *Work 1961–73* (New York: New York University Press, 1974), p. 51.

20 Sally Banes, *Terpsichore in Sneakers: Post Modern Dance* (Boston: Houghton Mifflin, 1980), pp. 49, 51.

21 Ibid., p. 54.

22 Richard Griffith and Erwin Strauss, eds., *Aisthesis and Aesthetics* (Pittsburgh: Duquesne University Press, 1970), p. 174.

23 Maxine Sheets, *The Phenomenology of Dance* (Madison: University of Wisconsin Press, 1966), p. 150.

24 Several postmodern dancers speak for themselves in Michael Blackwood's film, *Making Dances: 7 Post Modern Choreographers.*

25 Banes, *Terpsichore in Sneakers*, p. 50.

26 Laszlo Moholy-Nagy, "The Function of Art," in *Esthetics Contemporary*, ed. Richard Kostelanetz (Buffalo, N.Y.: Prometheus Books, 1978), pp. 71–73.

27 Maurice Nathanson, "The Fabric of Expression," in Griffith and Strauss, *Aisthesis and Aesthetics*, pp. 155–70.

28 Banes, *Terpsichore in Sneakers*, p. 50.

29 Rainer, *Work*, pp. 275–76.

30 Anna Kisselgoff, "Notes on Post-Modernism," Dance View, *New York Times*, 25 October 1981.

31 Anna Kisselgoff, "A New Expressionism Is Emerging in Dance," Dance View, *New York Times*, 13 March 1983.

32 Jack Anderson, "The Move to Dance Drama," *New York Times*, 25 October 1982.

33 Kisselgoff, "Notes on Post-Modernism."

34 Ibid.

35 Noel Carroll, "Post-Modern Dance and Expression," in *Philosophical Essays on Dance: With Responses from Choreographers, Critics and Dancers*, ed. Gordon Fancher and Gerald Myers (Brooklyn: Dance Horizons, 1981), p. 12.

36 Steve Reich, "Notes on Music and Dance," in Cohen and Copeland, *What Is Dance?*, p. 336.

37 In Marianne Goldberg, "Transformative Aspects of Meredith Monk's Education of the Girlchild," *Women and Performance: A Journal of Feminist Theory* 1 (Spring/Summer 1983): 19.

38 Anna Kisselgoff, "How Emotion Is Being Dealt with in '80's Dances," Dance View, *New York Times*, 11 November 1984.

39 Ananda K. Coomaraswamy, *The Dance of Shiva* (New York: Noonday, 1957), p. 73.

40 Jonathan Culler states that "deconstruction has been variously presented as a philosophical position or intellectual strategy, and a mode of reading." *On Deconstruction: Theory and Criticism after Structuralism* (Ithaca, N.Y.: Cornell University Press, 1982), p. 85. Jacques Derrida, in *Positions*, trans. Alan Bass (Chicago: University of Chicago Press, 1981), describes intellectual strategy as an attempt to deconstruct a position and to reverse a hierarchy. Culler adds that feminist criticism is a good example of deconstruction, as it attempts to reverse an established hierarchy.

41 Walter de Maria, "Meaningless Work," in Kostelanetz, *Esthetics Contemporary*, pp. 242–43.

42 See Carolyn Brown's chapter in *Merce Cunningham*, ed. James Klosty (New York: Dutton, 1975). Marianne Simon and Remy Charlip also state that Cunningham stresses "doing the movement correctly." "We formed our own scenarios," says Charlip. These statements were made in Merce Cunningham and John Cage: The Forming of an Aesthetic, a session at the Dance Critics Association Conference, New York City, June 1984.

43 Roger Copeland, "Merce Cunningham and the Politics of Perception," in Cohen and Copeland, *What Is Dance?*

44 Marshall McLuhan, *Understanding Media: The Extensions of Man* (New York: McGraw, 1964).

45 Copeland, "Merce Cunningham."

46 Philip Kapleau, ed., *The Three Pillars of Zen* (Boston: Beacon, 1967), pp. 64–65.

47 Ibid., p. 64.

48 Ibid.

49 Klosty, *Merce Cunningham*, p. 24.

50 Plato, *Laws* X, #893–98, pp. 1448–54.

8 MYTHIC POLARITY

1 Mary Wigman, "My Teacher Laban," in *What Is Dance?*, ed. Marshall Cohen and Roger Copeland (New York: Oxford University Press, 1983), pp. 302–05.

2 Elizabeth Kendall, *Where She Danced* (New York: Knopf, 1979), p. 58.

3 Ibid., p. 13.

4 Ibid., pp. 8–19.

5 Barry Laine, "Whose Wave Is This Anyway?" *Dance Magazine* 57 (October 1983): 58–67.
6 Roger Copeland, "Why Women Dominate Modern Dance," *New York Times*, 18 April 1982.
7 Jennifer Dunning, *New York Times*, 2 September 1984.
8 The association of the male with heaven and the female with earth is sometimes reversed in myth, as in the Egyptian sky goddess, Nut, and earth god, Geb.
9 Joseph Campbell, *The Hero with a Thousand Faces* (Princeton, N.J.: Princeton University Press, 1949), p. 171.
10 Joseph Campbell, *The Masks of God: Primitive Mythology* (New York: Viking, 1959), p. 472.
11 Friedrich Nietzsche, *The Birth of Tragedy* with *The Geneology of Morals*, trans. Francis Golffing (New York: Doubleday, 1956), p. 19.
12 Ibid., p. 97.
13 Ibid., pp. 40–57.
14 Edward C. Whitmont, *Return of the Goddess* (New York: Crossroad, 1982), p. 142.
15 David Michael Levin, "Philosophers and the Dance," in Cohen and Copeland, *What Is Dance?*, pp. 85–94.
16 Friedrich Nietzsche, *Beyond Good and Evil*, trans. Walter Kaufmann (New York: Random House, 1966), part 9, #295.
17 Marija Gimbutas, *The Goddesses and Gods of Old Europe* (Berkeley and Los Angeles: University of California Press, 1982), pp. 236–38.
18 Charlene Spretnak, *Lost Goddesses of Early Greece* (Boston: Beacon, 1984).
19 Whitmont, *Return of the Goddess*, p. 120.
20 Ernestine Stodelle, *The Dance Technique of Doris Humphrey* (Princeton, N.J.: Princeton Book Co., 1978), pp. 260–61.
21 See Starhawk, *The Spiral Dance: A Rebirth of the Ancient Religion of the Great Goddess* (San Francisco: Harper and Row, 1979).
22 See Loie Fuller, *Fifteen Years of a Dancer's Life* (Boston: Small, Maynard, 1913), chap. 3.
23 Robert Pierce, "Kei Takei's Moving Earth," *Dance Scope* 9 (Spring/Summer 1975): 18–27.
24 Deborah Hay, *Moving Through the Universe in Bare Feet: Ten Circle Dances for Everybody* (Chicago: Swallow, 1974), p. 5.
25 Yvonne Rainer, *Work 1961–73* (New York: New York University Press, 1974), p. 51.
26 Merlin Stone, *Ancient Mirrors of Womanhood* (Boston: Beacon, 1984), p. 236.
27 Ibid., pp. 222–23.
28 Joseph L. Henderson and Maud Oakes, *The Wisdom of the Serpent: The Myths of Death, Rebirth, and Resurrection* (New York: George Braziller, 1963), pp. 11–13.
29 Sylvia B. Perera, *Descent to the Goddess* (Toronto: Inner City Books, 1981), pp. 24–25.
30 Carl Jung, as quoted by Joseph Campbell in his foreword to *Man and Transformation: Papers from the Eranos Yearbooks*, ed. Joseph Campbell (Princeton, N.J.: Princeton University Press, 1980), p. xiii.
31 Daisetz T. Suzuki, "The Awakening of a New Consciousness in Zen," in ibid., pp. 196–97.
32 Ibid., p. 181.

33 Ananda K. Coomaraswamy, *The Dance of Shiva* (New York: Noonday, 1957), pp. 10–11.
34 Joseph Campbell, Transformation of Myth Through Time, seminar in Realms of the Creative Spirit series, New York City, 1981.
35 In Joseph Campbell, *Masks of God*, p. 372.
36 Simone de Beauvior, *The Second Sex*, trans. H. M. Parshley (New York: Knopf, 1961), p. 5.
37 Campbell, *Hero with a Thousand Faces*, p. 171.
38 Henderson and Oakes, *Wisdom of the Serpent*, pp. 23–24.
39 Arthur Amiotte, "The Road to the Center," *Parabola* 9 (August 1984): 48.
40 Campbell, *Hero with a Thousand Faces*, pp. 170–71.
41 Ibid., pp. 149–72.
42 Rainer Maria Rilke, *Duino Elegies and the Sonnets to Orpheus*, trans. A. Poulin, Jr. (Boston: Houghton Mifflin, 1975).
43 Paul Ricoeur, *Freedom and Nature: The Voluntary and the Involuntary*, trans. Erazim V. Kohak (Chicago: Northwestern University Press, 1966), p. 227.
44 Henderson and Oakes, *Wisdom of the Serpent*, p. 29.
45 Joseph Campbell, *The Mythic Image* (Princeton, N.J.: Princeton University Press, 1974), p. 77.
46 Ibid., p. 167.

9 ACTS OF LIGHT

1 The title of a dance by Martha Graham (1981).
2 Gilbert Ryle, *The Concept of Mind* (London: Hutchinson, 1963), p. 12.
3 Ibid., pp. 29–33.
4 Ibid., p. 43.
5 See Michael Murray, ed., *Heidegger and Modern Philosophy: Critical Essays* (New Haven, Conn.: Yale University Press, 1978).
6 Martin Heidegger, *Being and Time*, trans. John Macquarrie and Edward Robinson (New York: Harper and Row, 1962), #16–17.
7 Ibid., #181.
8 Ibid., #176.
9 Ibid., #436.
10 Ibid., #437.
11 Ibid., #179. Karsten Harris examines more fully Heidegger's view on questions of transcendence in "Fundamental Ontology and the Search for Man's Place," in Murray, *Heidegger and Modern Philosophy*.
12 Wittgenstein's view is included in a commentary by Murray in "On Heidegger on Being and Dread," *Heidegger and Modern Philosophy*.
13 Martin Heidegger, *Poetry, Language, Thought*, trans. Albert Hofstadter (New York: Harper and Row, 1971), pp. 163–86.
14 "Thrownness is neither a 'fact that is finished' nor a fact that is settled," Heidegger, *Being and Time*, #179.
15 Heidegger, *Poetry, Language, Thought*, pp. 101–02.

16 Ibid., p. 101.

17 Murray, *Heidegger and Modern Philosophy.* p. 282.

18 Ibid., pp. 271–91.

19 Henri Bergson, *Introduction to Metaphysics,* trans. Mabelle L. Andison (New York: Philosophical Library, 1961), pp. 1–8.

20 Ibid., pp. 81–82.

21 Ibid., pp. 6–7.

22 Gary Zukav, *The Dancing Wu Li Masters* (New York: Bantam, 1980), p. 263.

23 See Martin Heidegger, *On the Way to Language,* trans. Peter Hertz (New York: Harper and Row, 1971). Ronald Bruzina explains the metaphorical-metaphysical link in "Heidegger on the Metaphor and Philosophy," in Murray, *Heidegger and Modern Philosophy.*

24 Robert Frost, "Education by Poetry: A Meditative Monologue," in *Robert Frost: Poetry and Prose,* ed. Edward Connery Lathen and Lawrence Thompson (New York: Holt Rinehart and Winston, 1972), p. 334.

25 Havelock Ellis, *The Dance of Life* (New York: Grosset and Dunlap, 1923).

26 Heidegger, *Poetry, Language, Thought,* p. 192.

27 Ellis, *Dance of Life.*

28 Heidegger, *Being and Time,* #346–47.

29 James Klosty, ed., *Merce Cunningham* (New York: Dutton, 1985), p. 33.

10 MOVING TIME-SPACE

1 Gaston Bachelard, *The Poetics of Space,* trans. Maria Jolas (Boston: Beacon, 1969).

2 Henri Bergson, *Introduction to Metaphysics,* trans. Mabelle L. Andison. (New York: Philosophical Library, 1961).

3 Ibid., p. 48.

4 Ibid., pp. 48–49.

5 Ibid., p. 49.

6 Deborah Jowitt, *Dance Beat: Selected Views and Reviews 1967–1976* (New York: Marcel Dekker, 1977), p. 53.

7 Bachelard, *Poetics of Space,* p. xxxii.

8 Ibid., p. xxx.

9 Martin Heidegger, *Being and Time,* trans. John Macquarrie and Edward Robinson (New York: Harper and Row, 1962) pp. 401–03.

10 William Barrett, *Irrational Man: A Study in Existential Philosophy* (Garden City, N.Y.: Doubleday, 1958).

11 Paul Tillich, *The Courage to Be* (New Haven: Yale University Press, 1952).

12 Anna Kisselgoff, "Dance: A 'Bluebeard' by Pina Bausch Troupe," *New York Times,* 13 June 1984.

11 MEASURE AND RELATIONSHIP

1 Paul Ricoeur, *Time and Narrative,* vol. 1, trans. Kathleen McLaughlin and David Pellaur (Chicago: University of Chicago Press, 1984), p. xi.

2 Soren Kierkegaard, *The Concept of Dread*, trans. Walter Lowrie (London: Oxford University Press, 1944), p. 12.

3 Sondra Fraleigh, "Conversation with Josephine Endicott," September 1985. Unpublished interview transcript.

4 Mircea Eliade, *The Sacred and the Profane: The Nature of Religion*, trans. Willard Trask (New York: Harcourt, Brace Jovanovich, 1968); and *The Myth of the Eternal Return*, trans. Willard Trask (Princeton, N.J.: Princeton University Press, 1954).

5 For degrees and kinds of oppositions, see C. K. Ogden, *Opposition* (Bloomington: Indiana University Press, 1967).

12 DANCE IMAGES

1 Colton made this statement in Musical Choreographers/Musical Dancers, a session at the Dance Critics Association Conference, New York City, June 1984.

2 Reconstruction of Humphrey's *Passacaglia and Fugue in C Minor* in 1979 was by Susannah Payton-Newman (State University of New York, College at Brockport).

3 All quotations from Payton-Newman are based on my interview with her at Brockport, New York, in 1985.

4 Doris Humphrey, *The Art of Making Dances* (New York: Grove, 1959), pp. 49–59.

5 Notation for Sokolow's *Dreams* was done by Ray Cook in 1974. Reconstruction in 1981 was by Ray Cook and Susannah Payton-Newman, with final direction by Anna Sokolow (State University of New York, College at Brockport).

6 Clive Barnes, as quoted by Ray Cook in his notated score of *Dreams.*

7 Paul Tillich, *The Courage to Be* (New Haven: Yale University Press, 1952).

8 Ray Cook, "Notation of *Dreams*, Introductory Material and Production Information" (New York: Dance Notation Bureau Library).

9 Georg Lukacs, *Soul and Form*, trans. Anna Bostock (Cambridge, Mass.: MIT Press, 1974), pp. 28–41.

10 Sondra Fraleigh, interview with Larry Clark, 1984. Unpublished transcript. Subsequent references to Clark are also from this interview.

11 Jack Anderson, "Choreography Conceived as 'Report,'" *New York Times*, 26 February 1978.

12 Ibid.

13 Martin Heidegger, *Being and Time*, trans. John Macquarrie and Edward Robinson (New York: Harper and Row, 1962), p. 437.

14 Commentary in this section is based on my impressions of imagery in *Wind Devil;* my interview with Nina Wiener about her work: my conversations with Thomas Grunewald; and my observation of his teaching of phrases from *Wind Devil* in a master class at the New York State College and University Dance Festival, Brockport, New York, April 1983.

15 Commentary on *Oatka Trail* is based on my impressions of the dance and my conversations with Garth Fagan.

16 Comments in this paragraph are from a videotaped interview by Carvin Eison, Roches-

ter, New York, 1984. See also Fagan's commentary on the black aesthetic in a videotaped interview with Sondra Horton Fraleigh, Brockport, New York, 1981.

17 Merle Armitage, *Martha Graham* (New York: Dance Horizons, 1966), p. 101.

18 Friedrich Nietzsche, *Beyond Good and Evil*, trans. Walter Kaufmann (New York: Random House, 1966), part 9, "What is Noble," #195.

19 Maurice Merleau-Ponty, *Signs*, trans. Richard C. McLeary (Chicago: Northwestern University Press, 1964), pp. 66–67.

INDEX